GW01158453

ORDNANCE SURVEY LEI

NORTH YORK MOORS

▲ Cottages at Thornton Dale

Produced jointly by the Publishing Division of
The Automobile Association and the Ordnance Survey

Consultant for the North York Moors National Park: Ian Sampson, Information Officer

Editorial contributors: Dr R Brown (The Wildlife of the Moors); John McDonnell (Christianity on the Moors); Rebecca Snelling (Fact File); Joan and Bill Spence (The Coast, Heather Moorland and the Dales, Railways on the Moors and the Gazetteer short features); Alan Staniforth (Walks); Derek Statham (Man and the Landscape); Peter N Walker (A to Z Gazetteer); Geoffrey N Wright (Gazetteer revisions for new edition).

Original photography: Rick Newton and Steve Gregory

Typeset by Avonset, Midsomer Norton, Bath
Colour separation by Mullis Morgan Ltd., London
Printed and bound by William Clowes Limited, Beccles and London

Maps extracted from the Ordnance Survey's 1:63 360 Tourist Series, 1:25 000 Pathfinder Series and 1:250 000 Routemaster Series with the permission of Her Majesty's Stationery Office. Crown copyright.

Additions to the maps by the Cartographic Department of The Automobile Association and the Ordnance Survey.

Produced by the Publishing Division of The Automobile Association.

Distributed in the United Kingdom by the Ordnance Survey, Southampton, and the Publishing Division of The Automobile Association, Fanum House, Basingstoke, Hampshire RG21 2EA.

First edition 1987
Revised edition 1992

A CIP catalogue record of this book is available from the British Library.

AA ISBN 0 7495 0385 8 (hardback)
AA ISBN 0 7495 0375 0 (softback)
OS ISBN 0 319 00289 6 (hardback)
OS ISBN 0 319 00280 2 (softback)

Published by The Automobile Association and the Ordnance Survey.

Introduction: Stonegate Mill Farmhouse, near Lealholm

Contents

▲ Littlebeck

Introduction

Wide uninterrupted expanses of heather moorland, secluded farming dales and a dramatic coastline are just a few of the ingredients that make up the North York Moors. Discover the ruins of great abbeys, a stretch of road built by the Romans and the places Captain James Cook knew as a boy. This book takes the visitor to stone-built market towns, traditional seaside resorts and romantic fishing villages redolent of smuggling and whaling tales. It contains tours and walks enabling exploration of the countryside, explains the legacies of the past and highlights the attractions that can be enjoyed today. Written by people who live in the North York Moors, and backed by the AA's expertise and the Ordnance Survey's mapping, this guide is as useful to those who return to the area year after year as it is to the first-time visitor.

Man and the Landscape

Walking across Glaisdale Moor in the heart of the North York Moors provides an experience of wilderness and solitude rarely found in the Britain of the 20th century. With only the haunting cry of the curlew, the harsh call of the grouse and the occasional bleating of sheep to break the peace, one's overwhelming impression is of a natural environment untouched by the hand of man. Nothing could be further from the truth. The upland moorland is a man-made landscape just like the familiar farming landscape of the lowlands.

A few miles to the south around Keldy is another man-made landscape of much more recent origin, the coniferous forest. Planted mainly during the inter-war period, these huge expanses of conifers have replaced belts of moorland and farmland along the southern fringe of the North York Moors. Dull and monotonous some of the more recent woodlands undoubtedly are, with their straight lines of pine or larch, but as the forests mature and more selective felling and replanting is carried out, a much more varied and attractive landscape results – so much so that these forest areas are fast becoming one of the main recreation zones of the Moors. The forest drive around Dalby, one of the first areas to be planted, attracts many visitors with its secluded car parks, picnic areas and viewpoints. Forest walks and trails are laid out for the rambler, often conveniently beginning and finishing at car parks. The remote

Glaisdale Moor above Great Fryup Dale. Inset: Cropton Forest. A 5½-mile forest drive starts at Levisham and has fine views of Newtondale

railway halt in Newtondale is also a starting point for forest walks.

Unlike the 20th-century forest, the farmlands of the National Parks are steeped in history. There are two main types. One is the sheep and dairy farming country of the main valleys, or dales as they are known in Yorkshire, which presents a well-tended farming landscape of stone walls, hedges, copses, small fields and neat stone-built farmhouses. Particularly unspoilt dales are Bransdale and Farndale.

The second type of farming landscape is found on the plateau surfaces of the Tabular Hills on the southern edge of the Park and along the coastal plain. Here are mixed farms with a varying proportion of arable land growing corn and root crops, interspersed with pasture grazed by cattle and sheep. The coastal plain is covered with a thick deposit of boulder clay laid down during the last Ice Age and this gives rise to more fertile soils than the sandstones and gritstones farther inland which were not covered with ice. As a result there is a farming belt around the moorland core, and only at Ravenscar above Robin Hood's Bay do the moors sweep down to the sea.

Man's first appearance

To begin the story of man's influence on the natural environment, we need to go back to the period when man first appeared in the area, shortly after the last Ice Age over 10,000 years ago. Although it has been known for some time now that man began to inhabit the area very early in this period hunting animals and gathering wild fruits and berries, only recently has it come to light that he appears to have learned how to manipulate the environment for his benefit. He realised that by burning, and thus opening up the lightly wooded canopy on the higher hills, the large animals on which he depended for food would be encouraged to breed and multiply. This deliberate burning marked the beginning of a long, but increasingly intensive, management of the land which continues today with modern technology.

Early farmers

Perhaps the greatest change in the prehistoric landscape of the Moors however, occurred around 3,000BC when agriculture was first practised. It is not known how it was brought to the area or by which people, but it spread rapidly on the

Hambleton Hills in the west of the area and on the fertile soils of the Tabular Hills between Helmsley and Scarborough in the south of the National Park. Later, in the Bronze Age around 2,000BC, it spread onto the higher plateaux of the Moors where the remaining woodland was cleared away. Apart from a few scattered remains of pottery and primitive tools, these early farmers left little to remind us of their long years of toil. However, their burial places, or tumuli, are found everywhere on the moors, often on the highest points. There are over 3,000 of them, ranging from slight bumps to mounds up to 20ft high and 100ft in diameter. Good examples can be seen on the main moorland divide, now followed by the route of the famous Lyke Wake Walk. Loose Howe on Glaisdale Moor, Shunner Howe on Rosedale Moor and Wheeldale Howe on Wheeldale Moor mark the site of Bronze Age tumuli. 'Howe' is an Old Norse word meaning a grave mound. The chiefs and leading members of Bronze Age tribes were cremated and their remains placed in urns which were buried under the barrows. In some cases, such as the Bridestones on the ridge between Bilsdale and Tripsdale, the burials were also marked by stone circles. In other places the howes and stones lie in long lines – right across Fylingdales from the Bridestones to Maw Rigg above Langdale, for example. Some well-marked settlement sites can also be traced, with cemeteries of barrows, hollow cattle-tracks, hut sites and the remains of small fields.

Most of the North York Moors was settled during this time and many of today's parish boundaries probably follow the dividing lines between Bronze Age clans. The communities were self-sufficient and their territories planned to contain water courses, pasture and woodland. What is particularly significant, however, is that the cultivation and grazing on the plateau surfaces of the area rapidly exhausted the thin, infertile soils. This made them acidic, encouraging the heath and moorland so familiar today.

The Bronze Age gave way to the Iron Age around 500BC when the climate took a turn for the worse. Despite this, recent results from advanced research techniques show that the population increased and livestock and arable farming were the dominant land uses. By this time, the tribes were larger and organised well enough to carry out warfare. Some evidence for this comes from the construction of massive parallel dykes, presumably defence works, at various sites around the edges of the moorland area. The most well known are the Scamridge and Levisham Dykes in the Tabular Hills and the Cleave Dykes in the Hambleton Hills.

The Roman occupation

The Romans left few physical reminders of their occupation which was probably limited to military control. There is a well-preserved 1¼-mile stretch of road on the edge of Wheeldale Moor, called Wade's Causeway (see page 43) and other Roman remains include a fort at Lease Rigg near Grosmont and coastal signal stations at several places along the coast which warned of raids by Saxon invaders. Perhaps the most exciting Roman remains, however, are the military camps at Cawthorn near Pickering. The camps are now owned by the National Park Authority and will shortly be opened up for inspection and study by the public.

Remains of a Roman coastal signal station on the Castle Headland near Scarborough. Other signal station sites are Kettleness, Saltburn and Ravenscar

Invasion and settlement

The settlement of the area by Teutonic invaders after the collapse of the Roman Empire produced the pattern of villages and countryside we inherit today. Angles and Saxons were followed by Vikings and eventually by Normans after 1066. Most place-names in the Moors are of Anglian or Norse derivation. Villages ending in 'ham' or 'ton' are Anglo-Saxon in origin, those ending in 'by' or 'dale' are Norse. Many names of landscape features have a Norse 'hardening' such as rigg instead of ridge, or beck instead of stream or brook. It is not known in detail how the area fared during the upheavals of invasion and settlement but certainly the population seems to have declined from the high point of the Roman occupation, and did not recover until the Middle Ages.

The Middle Ages

During the Middle Ages the rural economy was carefully geared to the natural resources available. Each parish was largely self-sufficient but, inevitably in an upland area, there were marked differences between the fertile lands on the limestone of the Tabular Hills and the acid moorlands farther north. Bartering for corn and livestock was commonplace and some livestock were driven long distances to markets in the south.

The farming of the area was transformed in the 13th and 14th centuries by the monastic sheep farmers who improved the wild and barren land, first for sheep and later for arable or dairy produce. These skilful husbandmen became large and wealthy landowners operating from their strikingly beautiful abbeys at Rievaulx, Byland and Guisborough. With the dissolution of the abbeys in the 16th century, an era of high farming was brought to a close.

There was little in the way of agricultural innovation until the 18th century but, nevertheless, many new farms were established in the 17th century when enclosure of common land occurred. Reclamation of the moorland edge also intensified as the population increased. During the late 17th century a number of farmhouses were built on the newly enclosed land using local stone.

The improvements in agricultural techniques in the 18th century, especially the introduction of root crops such as turnips and mangolds, led to an intensification of farming which continued into the mid-19th century as the population increased with the growth of industry. Enclosure of the former open fields of medieval times was completed and much common grazing was also enclosed, especially during the Napoleonic Wars in the 19th century.

Left: many of the houses in the former fishing village of Runswick Bay retain the traditional red-pantiled roofs of the area. Other unspoilt coastal villages are Staithes and Robin Hood's Bay
Above: an old alum quarry opposite Carlton Bank

Mining and quarrying

The Moors possess a great wealth of mineral resources which have been mined since prehistoric times, but the introduction of the railway to this isolated area in the early 19th century heralded a new industrial boom.

Of particular importance was iron ore, mined in the Cleveland Hills, Eskdale and Rosedale. Vast quantities of ore were extracted. There was an iron-smelting works at Grosmont, a smelting works and ore-export harbour at Port Mulgrave, as well as several smaller treatment plants and mineral railways, especially in Rosedale. The landscape at this time must have been a discordant mixture of moorland farming and heavy industry with expanding mining towns and villages in parts of Rosedale and the Esk Valley.

Other minerals mined include alum, used to 'fix' the coloured dyes in cloth and in paper making (see also page 24) and jet, a fossil carbon deposit much admired in Victorian England for its ornamental qualities (see page 26). The brown sandstones on the moorland above Whitby provided building stone for many famous buildings including the Houses of Parliament and Covent Garden but the quarries have now closed. Limestone is still quarried today but at one time the lime obtained by burning the stone was used as a fertiliser. Nearly every village and often individual farms had their own kilns, many of which can still be seen. Coal from deposits on the moors – albeit of poor quality – was used as fuel for the kilns and the open pit scars remain as evidence of this activity.

At one time the only volcanic rock found in the Moors was valuable for road construction. This rock, 'whinstone' as it is locally called, was formed from the hot lava which occupied a crack in the northern part of the moors stretching east from Great Ayton towards the coast at Ravenscar. Recent projects involve the mining of potash at Boulby and natural gas drilling at several places.

Villages

The villages of the Moors represent one of its greatest scenic assets. Their buildings are in local stone, a soft honey-coloured limestone around Helmsley merging to a grey limestone farther east and a rugged brown sandstone throughout the rest of the area. The red pantile is the traditional roofing material and the vernacular style is simple with clean-cut, robust lines. Some villages are completely unspoilt by modern additions but during the mining era of the 19th century different styles and materials, such as red brick and terracotta, were introduced in some areas.

The challenge of the 20th century

The creation of the National Park in 1952 does not mean that the area is publicly owned, but that the landscape is managed for its natural beauty and the enjoyment it gives to visitors. These objectives have to be married with the social and economic needs of the local population. The policies and projects of the National Park Authority are geared to these aims and of particular importance are the various grant aid schemes for such matters as tree planting, moorland management and maintenance of old buildings. As the need for primary food products from the area decreases in an era of surpluses, so the demand for an attractive outdoor environment for recreation increases. Thus in the 20th century the Moors are taking on another function in addition to the ancient activities of agriculture, forestry and mining.

Christianity on the Moors

In 657 King Oswy gave his daughter, Hilda, land to found a monastery after he was successful in battle against a pagan king: Whitby Abbey was the result

The windswept hulk of Whitby Abbey perched on its cliff above the harbour is an enduring reminder of the great monastic tradition in north-east Yorkshire. Yet the first stone of the building we see was laid less than 800 years ago. Almost 600 years earlier still the site had held the double monastery (for men and women) of 'Streoneshalch', ruled over by Abbess Hilda, kin of the Northumbrian royal house. The monastery numbered among its brethren the humble oxherd Caedmon who, with a little help from on high, achieved renown as England's first religious poet. The 8th-century historian, Bede, tells his story: 'It sometimes happened at a feast that all the guests in turn would be invited to sing; when he saw the harp coming his way, he would get up and go back to the stables. On one such occasion he settled down to sleep. Suddenly in a dream he saw a man standing beside him who called him by name. "Caedmon," he said, "sing me a song." "I don't know how to sing," he replied. "It is because I cannot sing that I left the feast." The man then

said: "But you shall sing to me." "What should I sing about?" "Sing about the Creation of all things." And Caedmon immediately began to sing verses in praise of God the Creator that he had never heard before.' A 20ft-high sandstone cross near St Mary's Church on the cliff-top commemorates the story of Caedmon. On one side of the cross, erected in 1898, are the lines of his 'Song of Creation'.

Not only Whitby but the whole area is full of reminders of the Anglo-Saxon period of Christianity in England. There are parish churches dedicated to saints like Oswald, Hilda, and Gregory, quite a number of which preserve in their fabric fragments of pre-Norman stonework, notably re-used churchyard crosses. Bede and others have recorded the work of men like the brother saints Cedd and Chadd who established a monastery at Lastingham contemporary with St Hilda's foundation at Whitby. Despite the short-lived mission by the Roman-trained Paulinus who came from Kent to Northumbria in the early 7th century and baptised both the future St Hilda and her great-uncle King Edwin, the predominant Christianising influence came from St Columba's 6th-century foundation on Iona. Besides the controversies over the dating of Easter and the style of monastic tonsures (shaved heads), there were marked differences of missionary practice between the followers of St Augustine from Rome and the Celtic monks. The latter established their monasteries as focal preaching centres, from which members of the community (often ranked as 'bishops' but subordinate to an abbot) travelled out to preach the Word at stone crosses. These were set up as rallying points and often later became the site for the parish church. To this system is due, at least in part, the peculiar and durable tendency of churches like St Gregory's Minster at Kirkdale to be situated not in a settlement but at the strategic centre of an area of scattered hamlets. However, the clash between the Roman and Celtic factions in England was finally resolved at the Synod of Whitby in AD663, in favour of the Augustinians. Henceforward the date of Easter was standardised.

Devastation

Between them the Celtic and Roman missions Christianised most of pagan Yorkshire. But this 7th-century flowering of Christianity was soon to face new threats from other, fiercer pagans. The first assault by marauding Danes involved the sacking of St Cuthbert's sanctuary on Lindisfarne in Northumberland in 793. Two generations later came Yorkshire's turn. The monasteries of 'Streoneshalch' and 'Laestingau' (Lastingham) were ravaged by 870, and it was on subsequent occupation by Danish settlers that 'Streoneshalch' was renamed 'Witebi'. Danish invasions from the sea were followed by Irish-Norse settlers from across the Pennines in the following century, and a Norse kingdom was established at York. Christianity was securely rooted however. Despite the horror-stories associated with the Vikings the

Below: the ruins of Byland Abbey. Founded by the Cistercians in 1177, it was stripped of its treasures when Henry VIII dissolved the monasteries
Right: the Norman crypt of St Mary's, Lastingham

Danes were eventually converted when the whole Danelaw – the area of Danish settlement and rule in Eastern England – was absorbed into the English kingdom by the end of the 10th century.

Worse was yet to come however for north-east Yorkshire. The Norman Conquest brought in its train, in 1069, the appalling harrying of the North by William I. Domesday Book, compiled a few years later, shows parish after parish as laid waste and worthless. It was exceptional to find, as at Old Byland, a church recorded as still standing, and with a priest to serve it. Whitby was one of the very few centres to escape, largely, no doubt, because of its inaccessibility by land, but perhaps also because a new Benedictine community was even then erecting a successor to St Hilda's monastery. Its reprieve was brief, for 10 years later an attack by Danes drove the monks out. Some went to Hackness and Lastingham, but eventually returned in the following century to build the present abbey at Whitby, others went to York where they founded the separate house of St Mary's Abbey. For over half a century the few lay communities on and around the Moors had a struggle to survive and re-establish, and the clergy also had problems restoring its organisation.

Recovery: the age of the monasteries

Help for those in social, economic and spiritual straits arrived in the mid 12th century. Many Norman lords, unable to develop their new estates for lack of manpower, handed over portions of them to religious orders. These portions were often the remotest and least promising areas of an estate, and sometimes the new owners were monks invited from Normandy. In particular, new

Above and left: the most complete and beautiful survival of a medieval abbey in England, Cistercian Rievaulx has attracted admiring visitors for centuries. Of particular note are the 13th-century chancel and refectory – the main room of the south range

offshoots of the Benedictine tradition like the Cistercians, vigorous and intent on separating themselves from the world and its temptations, welcomed such grants, though in the interests of self-sufficiency they also made sure of getting benefits like mineral rights and fisheries. In 1131 Walter L'Espec, Lord of Helmsley, gave some land at Rievaulx to the Cistercians for the site of a new monastery which became the largest and finest Cistercian house in England. These orders were respected, and in a position to recruit willing hands. Within a generation great tracts of moorland and dale, especially in the western part of the Moors, were being successfully developed by the new abbeys at Byland and Rievaulx.

The Cistercians had one innovative feature which fitted them uniquely for large-scale reclamation of waste-land. Beside the core of priest-monks common to all communities following the Rule of St Benedict, whose presence was required in choir seven times a day and who could therefore spend little time working with their hands outside the cloister, the Cistercians developed a second tier of 'lay-brethren' or *conversi*, the 'bearded ones'. Often skilled farmers, masons or miners, these illiterate men were not ordained but joined the order in considerable numbers and wrought a remarkable transformation in the landscape. Rievaulx under the third abbot, St Aelred, for example, grew to a community of 650 men; 150 of them choir-monks, the other 500 laybrothers and abbey servants. Because the religious observances required of the *conversi* were much less time-consuming, it was even possible to establish groups of them at considerable distances from the

mother-house, from where they returned only for the major feasts. Thus most of Bilsdale, a few miles north of Rievaulx, was organised into a closely integrated set of 'granges' (farms) which ran huge flocks of sheep. At one time these contained over 14,000 sheep, the wool being sold to cloth merchants from Flanders, France and Italy. Iron was also mined and stone quarried for the abbey's new buildings. Further east, in the marshes below Pickering, other *conversi* teams drained the land (some channels are still called ' Friar's Ditch') and created more pasture with rich hay-meadows. Rievaulx even had a sea-fishing 'grange' at Teesmouth and a stud-farm in Upper Teesdale. Paradoxically, the Cistercian impulse to flee the world and tame the wilderness led to the creation of a major 'agribusiness' which put the Order, in areas like the Moors and the Cumbrian fells, among the foremost entrepreneurs of the age.

The success of the Cistercians encouraged older-established orders like the Augustinians of Kirkham and Guisborough, and the Benedictines of York and Whitby, to follow suit and develop large upland tracts for stock-farming and mineral extraction. Smaller religious houses also appeared in the heart of the Moors, like the Premonstratensian Priory of Grosmont, and small, often ill-endowed convents of nuns, as at Baysdale, Arden and Rosedale (this latter was a priory, not an abbey despite the modern name of the village). A late addition (c1400) to the roll of major monasteries was Mount Grace Priory. The most complete survival of a Carthusian house, with its pattern of 'hermit-cells', Mount Grace fully deserves a visit.

The Cistercians played little direct part in the cure of lay souls, since their rule forbade the acquisition of parish churches. The older orders, however, led the way in re-establishing parish organisations. From the 12th century onwards a majority of churches in the area were built, or rebuilt from whatever remnants the Harrying of the North had left. Lay lords of the manor followed suit, as on the estate of Pickering belonging to the royal Duchy of Lancaster.

The heyday of the *conversi* lasted less time than is generally realised. Well before the end of the 13th century their numbers dwindled, and then economic recession followed by the Black Death brought an end to the monasteries' period of growth. Their granges were generally broken up into family-sized farms and leased to a new class of independent husbandmen. Even the Cistercians joined the older orders in living off their rents instead of taking an active part in developing their estates. Nevertheless, in addition to the imposing ruins of the abbeys themselves the numbers of 'grange' and 'cote' farm-names on and around the moors are a memorial to monastic enterprise.

After the Reformation

The dissolution of the monasteries under Henry VIII brought about less disruption or indeed bloodshed in north-east Yorkshire than in some parts of the North, though moorsmen did march to join the Pilgrimage of Grace, the 1536 northern rebellion against Henry VIII. Although the abandoned monastic buildings inevitably decayed to the ruins we see today (Rievaulx was not only stripped of its treasures after its closure, but part of its fabric was used to provide building material for cottages in the village) the Reformation took a long time to achieve a final impact here, especially in areas protected by Catholic-inclined landowners like the Meynells and the Earls of Rutland. Indeed, Catholicism never entirely died out in some remote corners of the Moors. One of the last priests to die for his faith was Nicholas Postgate. Executed in York in 1679 at the age of 83, he was a native of Egton and had spent half a century serving the Catholics of the lower Esk Valley. His main base was at Ugthorpe, where the Old Hall contained a priest's hole.

Inexorably, though, deprived of its clergy, the old faith dwindled. Often its role was taken over not by the established church but by Nonconformists. Sir Thomas Hoby of Hackness was one Puritan squire who actively promoted Calvinist doctrines. Following the tour of Yorkshire by their founder, George Fox, in 1651 the Quakers established a vigorous presence in the area. The 18th-century Meeting House at Laskill, a stone's throw, as it happens, from the Rievaulx Abbey Woolhouse site, is one of the various relics of the Friends' great days.

Presbyterians, Congregationalists and eventually Methodists also came to play an important part in the area. A century after Fox, both John and Charles Wesley paid missionary visits to this part of Yorkshire. Rare is the moorland dale without at least one chapel in it, though some are now turned to more worldly uses. Castleton in Esk Dale, which grew from a handful of cottages at the end of the 18th century to a miniature market town by 1850, had acquired by then an iron-built Anglican church, a Quaker meeting house, and Wesleyan and Primitive Methodist chapels. There were increasingly clear social differences between those who adhered to the established church, mostly gentry and estate employees, and Nonconformists, who tended to be independent farmers and tradesmen. Even in Victorian times one senses bafflement and incomprehension, to say nothing of snobbery, in the Church of England's view of Nonconformists. One vicar complained at the 'wild sort of Methodists' who inhabited the fringe of his parish and who celebrated Good Friday with 'regular jollification, a fruit banquet, a series of races, and a concert'.

Two Victorian vicars

By Victoria's day the Church of England clergy had rediscovered a degree of fervour for converting others to their faith and there were a number of distinguished parsons in the area. Canon J C Atkinson of Danby, best known as a medieval scholar, also took his parish work seriously, and wrote that enchanting classic *Forty Years in a Moorland Parish* (recently abridged and published in paperback as *Countryman on the Moors*). On his arrival in Danby his churchwarden took him to inspect the church. Atkinson was startled to note that the man did not remove his hat on entering, and even more dismayed to see that the ragged green baize covering the altar was smothered in stale crumbs. His guide saw nothing odd in this: 'Why, it is the Sunday School teachers, they must get their meat somewhere, and they gets it here.' Essex-born gentleman though he was, Atkinson soon won the confidence of his flock by his obvious interest in their way of life and sympathy with their problems.

A different sort of parson was dominating Helmsley at about the same time. Vicar Gray had been known to use his fists to effect on a recalcitrant parishioner. A man of overflowing energy and generosity, he campaigned vigorously against lack of sanitation, unreasonable hours for apprentices, and the tight-lacing of stays, to mention but a few pet causes. He also indulged in often public arguments with his patron and lord of the manor, as well as with Methodists and Roman Catholics. Perhaps his most bitter attacks were against a 'Mr Burge', who was in fact Prior of the Benedictine monastery at Ampleforth.

Ampleforth – a modern monastic community

The monks had established themselves at Ampleforth in 1802, when the English community of St Lawrence, resident in France since the 17th century, was driven out by the French Revolution. With its famous Roman Catholic boys' school already developing, the Abbey was even then becoming an influential element in the district. It seems fitting to end this brief review of Christianity in north-east Yorkshire at the place where the Rule of St Benedict is once again kept by a monastic community, as it had been in the days of St Aelred and St Wilfrid.

The Quaker Meeting House at Laskill, completed in 1734, had a regular attendance of 20. Meetings were originally held in licensed private houses and between 1689 and 1708 there were eight of these in Bilsdale

Heather Moorland and the Dales

The North York Moors National Park covers an area of 553 square miles, 40 per cent of which is now open moorland. This is the largest expanse of heather moorland in England, a breaktaking sea of purple when it is blooming in all its glory during July, August and early September. In winter the moor takes on a dark and desolate air, well-deserving its old romantic title of 'Blackamore'. It seems hardly surprising that William the Conqueror and his retinue should have got lost in a blizzard up on the moors when he was inspecting his new kingdom after the Battle of Hastings.

The first tinges of colour appear in July when the ling (Scotch heather) with its tiny triangular leaves, begins to flower. There are two other types of heather to be found on these heights, the bell

Wheeldale Moor, the location of Wade's Causeway — a well-preserved stretch of Roman road
Inset: Young Ralph Cross, near the head of Rosedale

heather, which is a deeper purple, and the cross-leaved heath bearing large rose-pink flowers. Someone has calculated that three million flowers are produced by every square mile of moorland each year. During autumn the purple of the heather is edged with the rusty browns of the bracken, intermingled with green patches of bilberry.

The extensive moorland of the Park contrasts with intermittent dales. Some, such as Rye Dale and Riccal Dale, contain dappled-green oak and ash woods. Their warm south-facing slopes have areas of scrub, and sweet-smelling grassland is wedged between farmland and dark, shady conifer plantations. Farndale and Rosedale in the south, and the shorter valleys such as Danby, Fryup and Glaisdale in the north are a tapestry of small fields, rivers, hedges and woods.

Sheep farming on the moors

Heather, a hardy plant able to subsist on the poor

soil of the moors, is vital to the economic cycle related to sheep farming and the sport of red grouse shooting. The moors are still an essential part of farming in the area, although they once supported considerably more sheep than the 50,000 that are there today. Moorland grazing rights are valuable to farmers in the dales who keep their sheep on the moors for most of the year, bringing them to the lower ground as lambing time approaches. Though there were once many more sheep sales than there are now, they are still an important part of the farming life and attract buyers from a wide area. Critical eyes assess the sheep gathered in their pens before they come under the auctioneer's hammer at Goathland, Blakey, Rosedale, Castleton and Danby.

The most common sheep on the moors is the Swaledale, a hardy breed, easily recognisable by its black face, white muzzle and grey speckled legs. The ram's horns are massive and curly, whereas the ewe's, whose horn is valued by walking-stick makers, consists of a single curve. The Swaledale was introduced to the North York Moors in the 1920s and eventually took over from the Scottish Blackface as the most popular breed on the heights, although some Scottish Blackface are still kept on the moors. These do not have the white nose, they are broader in the back, and their wool is longer than the Swaledale's.

Sheep are said to be 'heafed' to the moor,

This view from Chimney Bank Top, Rosedale, is worth the climb up a 1-in-3 gradient from Rosedale Abbey

indicating that each flock knows its own territory. This knowledge is apparently passed down to the lambs by their mothers, but intermingling is inevitable as there are no fences on the moors. In order to avoid disputes of ownership the sheep are marked in various ways. A splash of colour near the shoulder or on the loin makes identification

easy from a distance, but ear notching, initials branded on the horns, and ear tags are also used.

These moorland sheep are extremely hardy as they have to withstand severe conditions on the wild, bleak heights. One of the greatest threats to their lives however is not the weather but the motor car. Sheep do not have much road sense and the motorist needs to be aware of them grazing by the roadside and drive with care. Losing an animal is costly to the farmer.

Grouse on the moors
The red grouse, dark reddish-brown in colour and about the size of a small chicken, is the 'moor bird', its low flight over the heather characterised by a whirring of wings followed by a glide. Its distinctive call may be described as 'go-bak, bak-bak-bak'. During the grouse shooting season, 12 August to 10 December, sportsmen stand in the shooting butts which are built of stone and topped with heather or bilberries so that they merge with the surrounding ground, while beaters work in a line across the moor, driving the birds to flight in the direction of the guns.

Controlled burning
The grouse is dependent on heather, needing the young, green shoots for food and older heather for nesting. With this in mind gamekeepers and farmers manage the moor by maintaining a patchwork of old and new heather. Controlled burning burns off the top, woody stems of the heather, encouraging the growth of new stems. A six-year rotation of areas burned, known as 'swizzens' or 'swiddens', ensures a continued supply of new growth. The burning is carefully carried out when the peat is damp, between 1 November and 31 March. At this time of year the fire will not penetrate the peat to smoulder for weeks or months and damage the heather roots.

A special licence is needed to burn the heather at other times of the year because of the permanent damage that can be caused. Wheeldale Moor and Glaisdale Moor still bear the scars of accidental fires which smouldered for months after the hot summer of 1976. Altogether four per cent of the heather moorland was destroyed. These areas may be covered by moss, lichen or rough grass by the year 2000, but before then it is more likely that wind and rain will have eroded the scarred areas

Top: red grouse on nest. The female scrapes out a hollow in the ground and lines it with grass or heather. Four to nine eggs are laid in April or May, and these have to be protected from the hooded crow. Above: a shooting butt

leaving a rocky, dusty desert.

If controlled burning did not take place the surrounding bracken would encroach more and more on the old, ailing heather, eventually taking over completely. Not only would the grouse disappear but a valuable source of late nectar for bees would go too. Hives are taken up to the moors by local beekeepers when the heather begins to flower and heather honey can be bought locally.

Routes across the moors
Trackways from many ages cross the moor, the oldest being the Roman road on Wheeldale Moor, known locally as Wade's Causeway (see page 43). There are also a considerable number of tracks from the days when packhorses and ponies were the only means of transport over the moors. These routes were often paved with flag-stones called 'trods' to allow the packhorses dry passage over the boggy moor. One very ancient route is the Hambleton Drove Road. This was used between the 17th and 19th centuries by Scottish drovers bringing their cattle south for sale at markets and fairs. A booklet on the road is available from the North York Moors National Park Authority. A good starting point from which to follow part of the route is Sheepwash, where the trackway crosses the beck. From here, where there are a number of car parks in an attractive moorland setting, the route passes the Chequers Inn on Osmotherley Moor before climbing 1,257ft Black Hambleton, with good views over the Vale of York. The route then splits, one way going southwards to York, the

A moorland track — part of the Hambleton section of an ancient drove road which ran from the south of England to Scotland. Inset: a Swaledale ewe

other turning eastwards to Malton.

The 93-mile Cleveland Way, the second long-distance footpath to be established by the Countryside Commission, was opened in 1969. This route, between Helmsley and Filey, is signposted and waymarked with the acorn symbol. It follows three-quarters of the perimeter of the National Park, encompassing the Hambleton Hills, the Cleveland Hills and the coast from Saltburn down to Scarborough, and takes 10 days to a fortnight to complete. In 1975 a 50-mile 'missing link' walk was devised between Crook Ness on the coast north of Scarborough and Helmsley.

The tough, 40-mile Lyke Wake Walk from Osmotherley to Ravenscar is a well-known walk across the moorland. The object of the walk is that it should be completed in under 24 hours, a feat which has been accomplished by over 80,000 people since the walk was established by Bill Cowley in 1955. Those who complete it can join the Lyke Wake Club, although you need to be reasonably fit and take sensible safety precautions before embarking on the entire walk. It has been necessary in recent years to dissuade large parties because of erosion along the path. 'Lyke' means corpse and 'wake' means the watching over of a corpse. The name of the walk is taken from the ancient 'Cleveland Lyke Wake Dirge' which suggests that after death the soul would make a journey over the moors.

Another long-distance walk is the 37-mile White Rose Walk linking the landmarks of Roseberry Topping and the White Horse at Kilburn. There is also the 54-mile North York Moors Crosses Walk which takes in 13 of the moorland crosses and starts and finishes at Goathland. An official walk of the route is held in July.

Stone crosses

The North York Moors contain hundreds of standing stones and crosses, probably Britain's largest assembly, and certainly unique in such a compact area. They include parish boundary markers, way markers, religious crosses and memorials and vary in shape from complete crosses to mere stumps. Some are of great antiquity and craftsmanship while others are rough blocks.

Over 30 of the moorland crosses have been given names. One of the most distinctive and best known is Ralph's Cross, or Young Ralph, used by the North York Moors National Park as its emblem. This 9ft-tall, slender stone cross stands prominently beside the road which crosses Blakey Rigg between Hutton-le-Hole and Castleton, near the crossroads to Westerdale and Rosedale on a site which affords marvellous views across the moors and into several dales. Its age is not known, but it is thought to be an 18th-century replica of an original highway marker. For centuries, it has been customary for travellers to place coins on the top, for the benefit of those less fortunate than themselves. This custom almost destroyed Young Ralph. In 1961, the slender stem broke as a man tried to recover some coins. The cross was carefully repaired, but in October 1984 vandals smashed the cross and it had to be repaired once again.

This medieval cross is Old Ralph, not to be confused with Young Ralph, a taller cross 200yds away. From Old Ralph there is a view of the sea

Old Ralph, only 5ft high, stands on the moor almost hidden by heather about 200 yards to the south-west of Young Ralph and along the road to Rosedale is Fat Betty, formally known as the White Cross. This has a separate round headstone sitting on top of the main 'body'. These are now cemented together because of vandalism, but coins also used to be left here under the top stone for poor travellers. The Margery Stone, sometimes called Old Margery, is also nearby and serves as a marker for the Lyke Wake Walk. A legend seeks to account for the presence of these stones. Ralph, an aged servant at a nunnery in Rosedale, escorted Sister Elizabeth to the moors to meet Sister Margery from Baysdale. The fog descended and they were lost, but had the sense to sit and wait until it cleared. Thus the rendezvous was eventually accomplished. Old Ralph is said to have marked the occasion by erecting these stones.

Lilla Cross on Fylingdales Moor may be the oldest Christian monument in the north of England. It is named after Lilla, a faithful servant who lost his life in AD626 saving King Edwin from an assassin's dagger. The cross is also a marker, standing near the crossroads of two ancient moorland roads.

The dales

The wide tracts of harsh moorland are cut by pastoral valleys where villages and isolated farms brighten the landscape with their red pantile roofs. The peace of many of these secluded dales has changed little since St Aeldred, the 12th-century third Abbot of Rievaulx, spoke of the tranquillity of Rye Dale: 'Everywhere peace, everywhere serenity and a marvellous freedom from the tumult of the world.' Roads use the pattern of moor and dale by following the riggs (ridges) between these features. The rigg roads give extensive views of heather moorland for often the valleys cannot be seen and the heather seems to stretch to the horizon without interruption.

Bilsdale, with easy access at both ends of the dale, carries a road from Helmsley to Teesside. There are only two tiny villages in the dale, Chop Gate and Fangdale Beck. This is one of the farming dales which was cultivated by the Cistercian monks of Rievaulx. Today there are about 1,300 farms throughout the North York Moors and in the dales they are primarily livestock concerns where sheep and cattle are reared. However, now that transportation of produce is easier, some of the farms are concentrating on dairy farming, as the milk tankers frequently seen on the roads testify. If the livestock farmer does not have enough land available for producing winter feed, the young animals are sold to be fattened or cross-bred on farms in lower areas.

Newtondale carries the North York Moors Railway but no motor road. This 12-mile long dale contrasts with the other dales, being formed when Ice Age lakes in Esk Dale and Wheeldale overflowed. The water rushed south towards Pickering, carving out a twisting, steep-sided valley as it did so. Sheer cliffs overlook nature holding sway far below.

On the north side of the Park, Westerdale, Danby Dale, Great Fryup Dale and Glaisdale are smaller than those to the south. These dales run into Esk Dale which runs west to east carrying the River Esk to the sea at Whitby. North of the Esk Valley the land rises to more expanses of moorland before dropping down towards the flatter land of Teesside beyond the borders of the Park. To the west the moors roll to the Hambleton Hills, where much moorland has been reclaimed for rich farmland. They end at the western escarpment with magnificent, often awe-inspiring views westwards across the Vale of York to the Pennines 20 miles away at such points as Roulston Scar, Sutton Bank and Whitestone Cliff. To the north are tree-studded hills and Lake Gormire, to the south Hood Hill.

Rising gently from the Vale of Pickering the land flattens to form a table-like top about 3 miles wide and about 25 miles long from east to west, giving it the name Tabular Hills. The northern side of the table ends suddenly and leaves a bold escarpment with a number of cliff-like promontories pointing northwards. One of the results of this is that the traveller, whether on foot, in the saddle or in a car comes across delightful surprise views which will make him stop and take in the breathtaking scenic panorama.

Lovely Little Fryup Dale is one of the numerous tributary dales of the Esk Valley. Walk 7 descends from the moors to pass along the dale to Danby

The Wildlife of the Moors

The unique, isolated upland block of the North York Moors is in many ways the meeting place for the north to south and east to west variation in our countryside and its wildlife. The combined influence of geology, weathering processes – including glaciation – and human management over thousands of years has given rise to a landscape which contains many interesting and unusual plant and animal communities. If you are patient you may be rewarded with the exciting sight of a merlin pursuing a meadow pipit, or a badger returning to its sett; a pine marten or a red squirrel; a rare bat, butterfly or orchid.

Moorland

The beautiful purples of the flowering heathers in August and September are an eye-catching sight and, occupying over 40 per cent of the National Park, moorland is a major wildlife and landscape resource. Man had managed it to create ideal conditions for the red grouse which is a permanent resident of the moor, totally dependent on the ling or common heather for its life cycle, and by encouraging more birds to breed for shooting man has also favoured visiting species. Waders such as the golden plover, curlew, the familiar lapwing, snipe and redshank overwinter at the coast, but breed on the open moor as do colonies of black-headed gulls. Britain's smallest bird of prey, the merlin, breeds in the older, woody banks of heather. Little bigger than a mistle-thrush, this rare member of the falcon family has been a symbol of the 'Watch over the National Parks' campaign. Meadow pipits and skylarks also nest in these old heather areas and the blue streak of a merlin pursuing a pipit as it rises vertically into the air from cover is not an uncommon sight. While most birds are summer visitors, the snow bunting comes south from Scandinavia to the relatively mild moors in winter.

In their turn the birds are all directly or indirectly dependent on the insect and other invertebrate life found on the wetter parts of the moors. Surface-living beetles, spiders and harvestmen swarm in great numbers in the spring, but their food source is a mystery. The beautiful emperor moth caterpillar is obvious on the heather, as is the northern eggar moth. The tipulid flies, or daddy-longlegs, larvae hatch from the peat in spring and are vital food sources to the pipits, curlews and visiting starlings, jackdaws and crows when they have young to feed. Red grouse chicks must have insect food in the first 10 days of their lives and even merlins make use of the larger moths for their chicks. This is why the wet and boggy areas are so vital to the overall ecology of the generally dry moors. In the floor of the deep, sinuous channel of Newtondale, thought to have been shaped by glacial meltwater, lies Fen Bog. This unique bog is a 40-acre nature reserve, but in places the peat is up to 59ft deep, and it is very dangerous to walk on its surface.

At the other extreme are the 'dry litter' areas on well-drained slopes. The soils here are peaty from a build-up of heather, leaves, sedges and mosses. They are covered in bracken, which poses an ever-increasing threat to the rest of the moor where it has started to invade the heather, pushing its underground rhizomes (root-like stems) forward by as much as 33ft a year. In the 'litter' lives the sheep tick, which feeds on the blood of mammals and birds and may seriously weaken or kill them through stress or disease.

Scavenging foxes, hares, common and pygmy shrews are found on the heather moor. On the bracken edges live the fast-flying whinchats, wheatears and brightly-coloured pheasants. Wood mice and bank voles are found feeding on the

Grey heron in flight. There are only about 4,000 pairs in the British Isles but there are several heronries in the North York Moors. Herons feed on fish, water-voles, beetles, frogs, moles and rats, ranging more than 12 miles in their search

bilberry at certain times of year on the drier slopes. Although rarely seen, these small mammals are important food sources for the birds of prey and the adder, which is often seen basking in the sun on old stone walls – also a favourite haunt for common lizards. The adder, with its zig-zag markings, is a timid creature which will not bite readily but should be left alone if found.

Short-eared owls breed and hunt over several moors and are sometimes seen gliding silently over the land in the day. Hen harriers, buzzards and rough-legged buzzards can sometimes be sighted flying over the moor seeking larger bird and mammal prey, while the magnificent peregrine occasionally passes through. Although ling is the dominant species of heather, other types are found too. These include the bell heather on dry banks, along with the very common bilberry, and cross-leaved heath on the wetter, peaty soils. This is one of the early flowering species. Cotton grass dominates the wetter blanket peat with its white carpets of flowers in the late spring, but the first green shoots are grazed heavily by sheep and hares. In the valley bogs insectivorous plants, such as the sundew and common butterwort, trap tiny flies to obtain the nitrogen they need for growth. The yellow spikes of the bog asphodel are frequently seen along with the rushes, but the bog bean is a much rarer find. Along stream sides the heathers are complemented by the fragrant bog myrtle and occasional juniper bushes, prized for making beer and gin respectively.

Woodland

Although deciduous woodland covers only five per cent of the land, much of it has been there a long time and some pre-dates the Norman Conquest. There is much variety in terms of tree species and ground flora but the two different types of underlying soil produce distinctive vegetation.

On the acid soils of the moorland fringes the main trees are sessile oak, birch, mountain ash, alder and Scots pine. The ground flora is poor on dry soils and is often stunted by heavy grazing from sheltering sheep. Wavy hair grass and bracken are widespread but on wetter soil species such as bluebells, and opposite- and alternate-leaved golden saxifrage indicate that the area has been wooded for a long time. These woods provide cover for many animals and birds, including short-eared, long-eared and tawny owls, the great-spotted and 'yaffling' green woodpeckers.

On basic and neutral soils more varied and extensive woods are found. These are often dominated by pedunculate, or lowland, oak and ash, with wych elm, field maple, alder by water and sometimes small-leaved lime. The shrub layer contains willow, hawthorn and honeysuckle. Hazel, often coppiced in the past, produces a valuable nut supply for birds and mammals. The Rye Valley contains large areas of such woods where the ground is covered with carpets of grasses, wild garlic, dog's mercury, ground ivy, wood anemone, wood sorrel, primrose and bluebell, to name but a few. The flora is particularly rich where sunlight breaks through the leafy canopy of the trees.

The networks of well-worn paths under the tall vegetation are not man-made, but long-established badger routes linking setts, latrines and feeding places. Of the 400 badger setts in the North York Moors over 250 are in woodland and another 80 in conifer plantations. Woodmice, grey squirrels

and bank voles are common. Recently, the presence of the shy common, or hazel, dormouse has been confirmed. Stripped honeysuckle bark and neatly nibbled hazel nuts are often the only clues to this secretive creature's whereabouts. Over 50 species of bird have been recorded from the woods. These include woodpecker, tree creeper, wren, spotted and pied flycatcher, woodcock, reed and willow warbler, blackcap and woodcock. A common sign of the presence of thrushes are the snail shells left scattered around stones used as 'anvils'. In spring several traditional heronries are occupied by breeding birds. Groups of the great grey birds build their huge twig nests together in a few trees. The same pair often add to the same nest over the years, and noisy squabbles between neighbouring birds are common. Their favourite trees for nesting are old pines, but plantations of other tree species are also used.

Relict wood pasture, or parkland, is a unique feature at Duncombe Park, near Helmsley, as the variety of trees found here is more characteristic of ancient southern parkland. Ancient small-leaved lime and oak stand in grassland once grazed by cattle and deer and many types of rare beetle live under the bark on living and fallen wood.

Plantations

Although the coniferous plantations are largely the product of intensive planting by the Forestry Commission in the last 60 years, they have many similarities with the forests of northern Europe in terms of wildlife. In mature plantations the large blocks of spruce, fir, larch and pine have needle-covered floors, with few plants in their dark interiors, although wood ants are at home – as the large conical nests of needles show.

Cone-producing trees are a valuable source of food to birds and mammals. Squirrels, woodmice and woodpeckers strip the scales from pine and spruce cones in a distinctive way to reach the seeds inside. The little green crossbill uses its scissor-like bill to split the cone scales neatly. Areas of young plantation provide very important nesting and roosting sites for the nightjar.

There may still be a few pine martens left in some remote areas and the red squirrel, which had disappeared in the 1960s, has been recorded from forests in the south-west corner of the National Park, although it can be easily confused with a dark form of the grey squirrel from a distance. Roe deer had almost become extinct in England in the early part of this century, but man-made forests with their wide rides and clearings have encouraged an increase in the population. Fallow deer, either the dappled-brown or black form, may be seen crossing roads at dusk in the Hambleton area. Often it is only the rear end of a deer which is seen as the otherwise camouflaged animal retreats among the trees. The 'scut' or tail, is white in the roe deer and black-and-white in the larger fallow deer.

The variety of mammal and bird life on the edge of the forests resembles that of the broadleaved woodlands. Blue-winged jays, 'thieving' magpies, tiny goldcrests and firecrests, badgers, foxes and stoats are all found here.

The great crested grebe, nearly exterminated during the last century because its feathers were in demand for women's hats, breeds on Scaling Dam Reservoir. Their floating nests are anchored to reeds. Inset left: bell heather Inset right: Duke of Burgundy fritillary, the only European member of a family of tropical butterflies

A man-made environment

The wildlife found in the farming areas, in and around towns and villages, and along roadsides is broadly similar to that found in other parts of the country. However, the wetter meadows are home for some unusual butterflies such as the Duke of Burgundy and dark green fritillaries, the green and white letter hairstreaks and brown argus, and in some areas of scrub the rare fly, bee and greater butterfly orchids may be found. Barn owls are still common, compared with other parts of the country, and they are often seen gliding like silent ghosts at dusk. Their survival is partly due to the availability of food and suitable nesting sites in old barns and buildings. Buildings and old woodlands, along with a rich insect life, have also helped to maintain a healthy bat population. The moors area is a northern stronghold for bats and both the pipistrelle and brown long-eared bats are common. Their survival is helped by the existence of a series of limestone fissures, known as 'windypits', which are used as winter hibernating locations. The whiskered bat, Daubenton's bat, Natterer's bat and the brown long-eared bat have all been recorded in these caves. Signs of use by the very rare lesser horseshoe bat have also been found.

Marshes, rivers and reservoirs

Perhaps the best examples of freshwater marshes in the North York Moors are the banks of the River Dove in Farndale which are covered in yellow carpets of wild daffodils in the spring. There are still some fens in the Dalby Forest, and Ashberry Pasture is an interesting marsh, although modern drainage is drastically reducing this habitat type.

Freshwater lakes are scarce in the area, Scaling Dam reservoir being the largest. This is an overwintering and breeding site for birds such as the great crested grebe, with its prominent neck ruffs, little grebe, teal, wigeon, gadwell, tufted duck, pochard, goldeneye, Canada goose, mute swan and Bewick's swan. Fish-eating ospreys are occasionally seen hunting over small areas of water and trout ponds, which are also a favourite with herons as they pass through in spring and autumn.

There are long stretches of gently-meandering and fast-running unpolluted rivers and streams. The banks of many are wooded with alder, ash and willow. Unfortunately Dutch elm disease has taken its toll of the elm as the bare skeletons show. There

Unlike many other species, the whiskered bat is solitary. It is 3½ins long with a wingspan of 9ins

are populations of the bumbling water vole and the tiny black-and-white water shrew. The unpopular Canadian mink was introduced to Britain in 1929 and is present on most rivers in the area, taking fish and water fowl. There is even a small population of the now very rare and mischievous otter. The brilliant blue of a darting kingfisher is an exciting sight and the flicking tail of the dipper is sometimes to be seen on faster-flowing stretches of water. Small numbers of sand martins excavate nests in sandy banks on the Rivers Esk and Rye.

The coast

Much of the coast is designated as 'Heritage Coast' and long lengths of it are protected as Sites of Special Scientific Interest. On the cliffs maritime turf areas of sea pink and scurvy grass mix with farmland, small woods and old quarries. Hunt Cliff near Saltburn has colonies of fulmar, kittiwake, herring gull, cormorant and even house martin. Rarer visitors, such as Adouin's gull and red kite, have been seen passing through. Both the grey, or Atlantic, and common seal, are occasionally seen.

Enjoying the wildlife of the Moors

Much may be seen by driving the moorland roads, by walking short stretches of the 1,125 miles of public rights of way, by waiting quietly in the many rides of the Forestry Commission plantations or by following nature trails, such as that at Sutton Bank. The National Park contains over 20 Sites of Special Scientific Interest and there is a National Nature Reserve at Forge Valley and a Local Nature Reserve at Farndale. Eight nature reserves are managed by the Yorkshire Wildlife Trust and a permit to visit these may be obtained from 10 Toft Green, York YO1 1JT. Telephone (0904) 59570.

It is important to remember that many birds and mammals nest on the ground, especially on the open moor, so be ready to move away quickly if you come on them by accident. Leave wild flowers for others to enjoy and try to avoid damaging plants. It has taken hundreds, if not thousands, of years for the present variety of wildlife to develop and it is constantly under pressure. When looking at the wildlife adopt the approach of leaving only footprints and taking only photographs.

The Coast

Soaring cliffs, quiet bays, attractive beaches and picturesque villages combine in an endless variety of scenery to form the coastline of the North York Moors National Park. The word 'moors' does not readily conjure up a coastline, yet this boundary to the Park is as dramatic as the heather uplands, with the busy seaside towns of Whitby and Scarborough providing a contrast to the solitude and peace of the moorland.

To encourage the conservation of lengths of Britain's unspoilt coast, the Countryside Commission has designated certain sections, worthy of special protection, as Heritage Coasts. The coastline of the Park comes within the North Yorkshire and Cleveland Heritage Coast which stretches for 35 miles from Saltburn-by-the-Sea to Scalby Ness, Scarborough.

There is no better way to explore this coast than to use part of the Cleveland Way. A section of this 93-mile long-distance waymarked walk winds its way within sight and sound of the sea between Saltburn and Filey. There is no motor road which follows close to the shore so the motorist has to make short detours inland before exploring the next road leading down to the coast.

Boulby Cliffs

About a mile within the boundary of the Park, on its northern extremity, are Boulby Cliffs – at 666ft the highest point on England's east coast and England's second highest coastal cliff. Needless to say the cliff top commands a fine prospect of the coast and countryside.

The village of Staithes at the mouth of Roxby Beck. It is still the fifth lobster port in the country

Close by, deserted quarries and their adjacent tips recall the days when the chemical alum was obtained for the textile and leather industries, as well as for the manufacture of parchment and candles. Over 20 quarries were worked extensively for nearly 300 years but in the mid-19th century, overproduction and the high costs of a lengthy and complicated process of obtaining alum from shale started a decline in the industry. Closure was hastened by the development of a process which obtained alum by treating colliery waste with sulphuric acid and the last mine closed in 1871. In 1973, however, mining came back to Boulby with the opening of the first potash mine in Britain near Staithes.

Fishing villages
Until the arrival of the railway the handful of attractive fishing villages which huddle under the cliffs for protection against the onslaught of the sea were almost cut off from the rest of the world and consequently evolved their own character and traditions. Here the stalwart womenfolk cured the fish, repaired nets, collected bait and baited the lines and sold the fish brought back by their menfolk. The traditional haul was herring, but over-fishing in the North Sea has reduced stock considerably. Today the catch along the Yorkshire coast is mostly crabs, lobsters and white fish such as cod, plaice and haddock.

In the early 19th century cobles sailed out of the fishing harbours daily. Not exclusive to Yorkshire, this strong, sturdy, open boat is designed to cope with the harsh North Sea. Heavy in relation to size, it is flat-bottomed, a design which allows it to be launched from a beach. The boat was first introduced by the Vikings and its basic design remains unchanged, although inboard engines have replaced sails and oars. Dear to the heart of many fishermen, even though it needs skill in handling, the coble (pronounced 'cobble') is often painted in bright colours, with certain ones predominating in particular areas.

In Victorian days Staithes women would own several of these distinctive bonnets: white was for daily use

Women wearing Staithes bonnets were once a familiar sight in the village but even today this distinctive headwear can be seen. Made from nine pieces cut from a yard of material, the bonnets were designed to prevent water trickling down the fisher-wife's neck when she carried baskets of fish on her head. Different coloured bonnets were worn for differing occasions. Ganseys were worn by all the fishermen and the designs on these jumpers were a means of identification should a man be lost at sea.

Folklore and legends
In common with other remote places with close-knit, self-contained communities the coastal villages were riddled with folklore and superstition. Boats were burned after a sea tragedy and cats were sacrificed as the cobles returned from fishing trips to ensure a safe landing. To ward off bad weather, children would dance around fires on the cliff top as they sang, 'Souther, wind, souther; Blow father home to mother'.

The association of Robin Hood's Bay with the outlaw of that name are dubious, but romance is in this coast. According to one story, Sir Gurth of Ravenscar, a Saxon earl, sought Robin's aid when no Norman would help to repel raiding Norse pirates. Robin and his men successfully attacked when the pirates beached their vessel in the bay. Their victory saved the countryside from the ravages of the Norsemen. Another story is that whenever Robin was sorely pressed by his hunters in Sherwood Forest he would flee north to this quiet bay which served as a perfect retreat. He kept a fleet of boats in constant readiness, and used them to escape to sea until his pursuers had gone. One version maintains that he disguised himself as a fisherman. The ancient burial mounds behind the village known as Robin Hood's Butts were once thought to be a training ground for the outlaw.

Legends have also grown up around St Hilda, founder of Whitby Abbey, who was highly regarded by all those who knew her. One tale relates how she rid the area of snakes by cutting off their heads and turning them into stone. Support for this legend is seen in the coiled, snake-like stones found on the shore and cliffs. Those with less romantic ideas will tell us that these are fossilised ammonites, an extinct genus of shellfish belonging to the family of Cephalopoda. These multiplied here in great numbers in the early Lower Jurassic Period, 100 to 130 million years ago, when the area was under the sea. An extensive collection of the ammonites can be seen in the Whitby Museum.

Smuggling
Just as exciting as these legends, but soundly based on fact, are the tales of smugglers associated with much of this coastline. The houses huddle so close together up the cliff face at Robin Hood's Bay that it is said that contraband, mainly tobacco and spirits such as brandy, could be passed from one to another without appearing above ground. Some of the houses had secret rooms in which the smugglers could hide, and these still exist today. Another special feature of the houses is the landing windows through which coffins could be more easily removed than down the steep stairs.

Captain James Cook
James Cook, one of the greatest circumnavigators of the world, was born at Marton in Cleveland in

Scraping whalebone at Whitby in 1813, when the town was one of Britain's foremost whaling ports
Inset: William Scoresby Senior. A leading Whitby skipper, he earned today's equivalent of £70,000 a year

1728 – the son of a day labourer who rose to become the bailiff at a farm near Great Ayton, now on the edge of the National Park. Here Cook went to school before his apprenticeship with William Sanderson, a grocer and draper, in Staithes. This shop on the seafront where, as a boy of 17 Cook first smelled the sea and listened to mariners' tales, no longer exists having been washed away by the sea. However, Cook's Cottage incorporates some parts which were salvaged and bears a plaque unveiled in 1978 by His Royal Highness The Prince of Wales to mark the opening of the Cook Heritage Trail. This links places associated with Captain Cook: Marton; Great Ayton; Marske; Staithes and Whitby.

Before long Cook took the road to Whitby where he was apprenticed to John Walker, a Whitby shipowner and the house in Grape Lane where he lived with his master still stands today. Cook make his first voyage in 1747 on a collier (coalship), signed on as a seaman in 1750 and two years later became mate. He was offered command of a collier in 1755, but turned it down to join the Royal Navy. His navigational abilities were soon recognised and his work in helping to chart the St Lawrence River in Canada enabled General Wolfe's army to capture Quebec in 1759. Promotion came and with it command of an expedition to the Pacific (1768-1771) in the *Endeavour*, a Whitby-built ship. During the voyage he accurately charted the coasts of both Australia and New Zealand. Two more expeditions followed in the *Resolution* accompanied by the *Adventure* (1772-1775) and the *Discovery* (1776-1780), all Whitby-built ships. The first expedition, to find a new 'Southern Continent' in the South Pacific Ocean was unsuccessful, although Cook sailed the equivalent of three times the equatorial circumference of the earth. Cook never returned from his next expedition, which was to discover a new trading route to the East Indies around the top of North America. Tragically he was killed by natives of the Sandwich Islands (now known as Hawaii) in 1779.

Whaling

Close by Whitby Harbour a whale's jawbone commemorates the days when Whitby was a great whaling port, sending 58 ships on a total of 557 whaling voyages to the Arctic between 1753 and 1835. Two well-known whaling captains from this period were the Scoresbys, both William, father and son. Local men would often accompany them on their voyages lasting six months or more.

The whaling ships hunted the Greenland whale in the Arctic to bring back blubber which was turned into oil for lighting, and whalebone – a thin horny substance from the whale's mouth – to make ladies' stays and hoops for dresses and sieves. The town's tryworks, brick constructions holding large metal pans in which the blubber from the whales was boiled to extract its oil, disappeared long ago.

The great days of fishing and whaling have gone but much of the atmosphere from that era remains in the old town. Modern harbour developments include a marina, which caters for sailing, and facilities enabling ships with timber and paper from Europe to use the port.

Lifeboats

The cliffs of this coast have been the graveyard of many ships, especially in the days when hundreds of colliers shipped coal from the Durham coalfield to London. There have been many daring deeds by lifeboatmen along this coast, but none more remarkable than that on 19 January 1881 when a vicious north-easterly gale with driving snow and hail lashed the Yorkshire coast and a ship was wrecked in Robin Hood's Bay, six miles south of Whitby. There was no chance of rowing the lifeboat through the open sea from Whitby so the men decided to take their boat overland, which meant a 500ft climb onto the wind-lashed moors, a battle with drifting snow, then a perilous descent into Robin Hood's Bay. Eighteen horses pulled the boat and 200 helpers cut through the drifts while villagers from Robin Hood's Bay made their way to meet them. Such was the effort that just two hours after receiving the call the boat was launched and although the lifeboat suffered severe damage in

A Yorkshire lifeboat goes to the rescue in 1860. The last rowing lifeboat was used at Whitby from 1947 to 1957

the treacherous seas, the rescuers managed to save the crew of six from the stricken vessel.

Whitby lifeboat crews have won more RNLI gold medals for gallantry than any other in Britain and Whitby has one of the best lifeboat museums in the country.

Whitby jet
Cook, the Scoresbys and other great seamen are recorded in the Pannett Park Museum at Whitby. Another aspect of the town's history traced in the museum is that of the jet industry. Jet, a glossy

Elaborate jet necklaces dating back to prehistoric times have been found in the Whitby area, but it was not until about 1850 that the industry boomed. There are now only one or two jet workers in the town

black fossilised wood, has been carved and polished to make jewellery since the Bronze Age. Nowhere else in England does it occur in such quantity or with such quality as at Whitby. It rose in popularity when Queen Victoria introduced it as a mark of mourning for Prince Albert and was obtained locally by combing the beaches or digging mines into the cliff faces. Between 1870 and 1872 over 1,000 men and boys were employed in extracting and carving the jet, but the trade declined after the import of jet from the Continent. Though there has been some revival of interest in recent times, and pieces of jet can be found on the beach, today there is only one shop engaged in producing jet jewellery.

Two creative geniuses
Frank Meadow Sutcliffe, who was born in Leeds in 1853, came to live in Whitby when he was about 17. He recorded the town and its people in photographs which have become recognised as masterpieces in atmospheric re-creation. The writer Bram Stoker stayed at Whitby in the late 1890s while writing his novel *Dracula* and the book was clearly influenced by local features. After being shipwrecked off Whitby, Count Dracula takes the form of a large dog and seeks refuge in the grave of a suicide victim in the graveyard of St Mary's Church. From here he wanders forth at night.

The idea may have come from an actual grave bearing a skull and crossbones, and anyone can immerse themselves in the atmosphere of the book by coming up here on a stormy moonlit night.

A cautionary note
This can be a dangerous coast, especially when it is enveloped by a clinging, cold, damp fog, known locally as a roak, or sea-fret. The holidaymaker must take care, particularly in the more rocky and secluded places. They are not all suitable for bathing and even walking under the cliffs can be dangerous for, apart from falling rock, there is the possibility of being cut off by the tide which must be watched carefully. It is all too easy to be caught unawares when one's attention is held by rock pools teeming with life, or when watching the fascinating range of sea birds.

The times of high tides can be obtained from local coastguards and details are also available in small booklets available from fishing tackle shops, although weather conditions may affect the times.

Railways on the Moors

The success of the Stockton and Darlington Railway, which was opened in 1825, caught the interest of business people in Whitby. With the decline of the traditional industries of whaling, shipbuilding and allied trades and the nearby alum mines proving less prosperous, the town needed to look elsewhere for an income. Development was hindered by the lack of good communication inland and the railway was seen as a lifeline.

Whitby to Pickering

It was thought that a line in the direction of Pickering would help to develop the timber, sandstone and limestone industries in the hinterland and thereby benefit Whitby as the exporting port: such a line was proposed in 1826. At a meeting in 1831 it was decided to ask George Stephenson, the engineer of the Stockton and Darlington Railway, to report on the possibilities of constructing a route from Whitby to Pickering. His report was favourable and, on 6 May 1833, an Act of Parliament authorised a local company to promote a railway between Whitby and Pickering.

A Moorsrail train climbs to Goathland. Right: interesting features on the route of the North Yorkshire Moors Railway. The longest privately-operated railway in the country, it runs for 18 miles

The first sod was cut on 10 September 1833 and on 8 June 1835 a regular service between Whitby and Grosmont was started. In the first three months it carried 6,000 passengers, the third passenger line to be opened in Yorkshire. When the complete line was formally opened on 26 May 1836 it was the fruition of foresight and some wonderful feats of engineering. Trees, and heather bound in sheepskins, were used to create a firm base for the track in boggy areas and the highest point on the railway, 500ft, had to be surmounted by creating a 1-in-15 incline from Beck Hole to Goathland Bank Top. For the first 11 years of its existence the passenger coaches and the goods wagons were pulled by horses along the 24-mile track except up this incline. Here the coaches were hauled up by a rope using a self-balancing system of water-filled tanks. Later this was replaced by a steam-winding system.

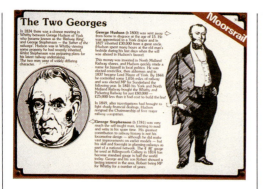

The Two Georges

Both George Stephenson and George Hudson were associated with the Whitby to Pickering line

George Hudson, the Railway King, had shown great interest in this railway almost from the start and he had certainly met Stephenson in Whitby. When the Whitby to Pickering company got into financial difficulties, Hudson's York and North Midland Railway bought the line in 1845. Hudson, concerned that the line was isolated, linked it to his York to Scarborough line by building a branch line from Rillington to Pickering which opened in 1845. Hudson then set about converting the Whitby to Pickering line to steam and the first locomotive pulled into Whitby in 1847. However, the incline still presented a danger and negotiating it was very time-consuming. The problem was eventually overcome by blasting a line along the Eller Beck Valley between Beck Hole and Goathland and the new section was opened on 1 July 1865.

The Whitby to Pickering line was now part of the growing trunk railway system and with it came greater prosperity. Now it was easier to transport raw materials both within and out of the area as well as giving even wider distribution to goods imported through Whitby. With passengers able to come from farther afield Whitby was also able to promote itself as a holiday resort.

The Esk Valley and coast lines

In 1865 the Whitby to Pickering line was connected to the railway running through the Esk Valley to Middlesbrough. Travelling by train direct to Scarborough from Pickering became possible in 1882 and three years later the coast line between Scarborough and Whitby was opened. At Whitby it joined the Whitby to Loftus line, which had been opened in 1883, and there linked with lines to Saltburn and Middlesbrough. So by the end of the century the North York Moors was served by a network of railways of which the Whitby to Pickering line was an integral part.

In 1872 the abandoned incline route between Beck Hole and Goathland was used by a Leeds firm to test an engine it was building for use in Brazil's coffee belt. The line also came into use again when, in 1908, an autocar service was operated especially for tourists during the summer. This proved popular but closed with the outbreak of World War I and was never reopened.

Between the two wars all the North York Moors lines were popular as they were among the most scenic routes in the country. The coast line ran for most of its length within sight of the sea.

Closures

Alas this line did not survive the enforced closures in the decades after World War II. British Rail, as the system had become after nationalisation, was already bringing in cuts and closures to facilitate economies and the Beeching Report in 1963 caused the axe to fall more sharply.

In 1950 the Pickering to Scarborough line closed, followed by the Pickering to York line via Kirkbymoorside in 1953. The beautiful coast line between Whitby and Loftus was also closed in 1958 and the Beeching Report proposed the closure of all lines serving the National Park. The furore was tremendous, especially from the people of Whitby who saw this plan as a move which would set the town back 100 years. However a compromise was struck and the line from Whitby to Middlesbrough along the Esk Valley was left open, although in 1965 the line from Whitby to Scarborough was closed, as was the Grosmont to Pickering section of the Whitby to Pickering line.

Restoration of the Grosmont to Pickering line

The much-loved scenic routes had gone. But as the Esk Valley line had had champions so there were those who sprang to the defence of the Grosmont

Cottage on the original 1836 1-in-15 incline between Beck Hole and Goathland on the Whitby to Pickering line. Below: disaster at the foot of the gradient which was too steep for either horse or locomotive

Moorsrail near its 550ft summit at Ellerbeck. Farther south is the entrance to remote Newtondale

to Pickering line. Alas, there could be no salvation for the railway along the coast. The undertaking to save this was formidable. It seemed this was so too with the Grosmont to Pickering line at first and even the small body of enthusiasts must have been daunted when attempts by several local councils to re-open and subsidise the route collapsed.

However, in 1967 the North Yorkshire Moors Railway Preservation Society was formed and after negotiations with British Rail it purchased the line from Grosmont to Eller Beck. Renovation work began on 2 February 1969 an engine operated on the line – the first for almost four years.

Talks were also going on behind the scenes. People were beginning to see the potential of restoring the complete railway and carrying passengers. After all, this was a route of exceptional scenic beauty where cliffs soared in some parts to

A 9,000-strong preservation society formed in 1967 saved the Whitby to Pickering line. Here a young volunteer tackles the first stage of restoration work on an old van housed at Goathland

400ft. The dale had no motor road, and its position made it an attraction not only to local people but to day visitors and tourists as well. The North York Moors National Park Committee and the English Tourist Board showed interest and were prepared to help with grants.

The outcome of this was the formation in 1971 of the North York Moors Historical Railway Trust Ltd and the purchasing of the remainder of the line to Pickering. After a great deal of hard work the first public services operated by the Trust began on 22 April 1973 and the line was formally opened by the Duchess of Kent on 1 May.

The scheme was now more than just a line operated by and for railway enthusiasts. It had become an immense tourist attraction and part of a transport system linked with the existing British Rail line through the Esk Valley to Whitby and Middlesbrough. Accordingly, new strategies of operation and promotion came into play.

Moorsrail

The success of the North York Moors Railway, or Moorsrail as it is affectionately known, is evident: over 300,000 passenger journeys are undertaken each year. Both steam and diesel engines operate on the line and engines can be seen being repaired at the Grosmont loco shed. This train journey will fascinate anyone visiting the Park or nearby areas. Undoubtedly, apart from the steam trains themselves, a main attraction is the scenery and there is plenty of information available to help you enjoy it. Walks are marked and there are leaflets which explain the routes. The Historical Railway Trail booklet describes the railway route from Grosmont to Goathland and a return walk follows a section of the original track along the old incline.

The Esk Valley Line today

There are similar delights to be enjoyed along the Esk Valley where most of the tiny stations display a poster showing maps of walks – either circular or to the next station. The railway provides an excellent means of exploring this valley and the picturesque villages of Kildale, Commondale, Castleton, Danby, Lealholm, Glaisdale, Egton Bridge, Grosmont, Sleights and Ruswarp. From Danby station it is a mile to the Moors Centre and Information Centre, run by the National Park Authority, at Danby Lodge. This is an ideal place for an introduction to the Moors for there is an exhibition area and talks with slides and films as well as 13 acres of grounds.

A line to Rosedale

When valuable ironstone was discovered in Rosedale there arose the problem of transportation to Teesside. At first it was moved by road to the railway at Pickering and the Ingleby Mining Company opened a private line in 1858. This ran from their mine near Burton Howe, close to Greenhow Bank (an escarpment on the edge of the Cleveland Hills) to Ingleby where it connected with a new line which gave it access to Stockton. However the mining companies in Rosedale wanted something more direct and they negotiated with the North Eastern Railway to construct a line direct to Rosedale. An Act of Parliament in 1859 authorised the North Eastern to carry out such a project and the private line was incorporated into the new scheme. The incline on this line only ran as far as the Ingleby mines and it now had to continue to the top of the moor at a height of 1,370ft. The maximum gradient was 1-in-5 and wagons were hauled up by steel ropes.

The track kept to the moor top, following the contours in sweeping curves around the head of Farndale. At Blakey Junction it reached the road between Hutton-le-Hole and Castleton where a parapet of the original bridge over the railway can still be seen, though the bridge itself has been filled in. The track of the old line is clearly visible. From the Junction a line ran along the west side of Rosedale to Bank Top, close to the road from Rosedale to Hutton-le-Hole with its notorious 1-in-3 gradient. The completed line was officially opened on 27 March 1861 and on 18 August 1865 a branch line from Blakey Junction, built to serve mines on the east side of Rosedale, came into operation.

In its heyday the railway moved an average of 1,200 tons of iron ore per day and brought goods back on the return journey. This was a boom time for the dale, but life was hard for the miners,

End of the day at Grosmont. The train journey from here to Pickering takes just over an hour

Five bands played at Pickering station when it was opened in 1836. In the heyday of the railways stations vied with one another to be the best kept on the line

especially in winter. The weather could be severe on the moorland heights where the line reached a height of 1,370ft above sea-level. Heavy snowfalls often closed the line and in the winter of 1916/17 the line was closed for five weeks with drifts 30ft deep.

Production of ironstone in Rosedale gradually declined until the mines were shut down in 1926, although the railway remained in use during the dismantling and was not finally closed until 13 June 1929. Most of the railway and mining buildings have since disappeared but some rows of cottages remain and, although the railway track has marked the landscape for ever, it provides an ideal route for exploring the North York Moors.

Gazetteer

▲ Cottages at Lythe

Each entry in this Gazetteer has the atlas
page number on which the place can be
found and its National Grid reference
included under the heading. An
explanation of how to use the National
Grid is given on page 78.

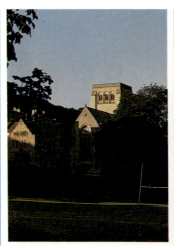

▲ Ampleforth Abbey and College

AMPLEFORTH
MAP REF: 95SE5878

Known for its modern Benedictine Abbey and College, Ampleforth was once called Ampreforde, meaning the ford of the sorrel. The main street stretches almost a mile and contains two fine inns, shops, a post office and two churches. Clearly-marked footpaths lead between yellow limestone cottages with red pantile roofs and brick chimney stacks. The village market used to be held outside the White Swan, and the Ampleforth Sword Dance, once part of a folk-play, has recently been revived here (there is no green).

St Hilda's Church, whose registers go back to 1690, has a Norman font and a 12th-century doorway, as well as a carving of the signs of the zodiac. The nearby Catholic Church of Our Lady and St Benedict contains some early work of the Kilburn woodcarver, Robert Thompson.

In 1802 three Benedictine monks fleeing from France settled here. They started their abbey and monastery a mile from the village while earning a living by teaching. Ampleforth College is now England's premier Roman Catholic public school – the present Cardinal Archbishop of Westminster, Basil Hume OSB, is a former Abbot. The Abbey Church is open to the public and parties may be guided around the buildings by contacting the Abbot.

St Benet's Chapel in the crypt contains the high altar stone from Byland Abbey, and the abbey also contains fine oak carvings by 'Mousey' Thompson. Orchestral concerts are regularly held and the public may join a club and enjoy the facilities of the College's sports centre, opened in 1975.

There are magnificent views from Ampleforth Beacon on the road to Helmsley. Nearby Studford Ring is probably the finest enclosure-type earthwork in the area. Fifty-four yards in diameter, it is thought to date from the Bronze Age but its purpose is unknown.

ROBERT 'MOUSEY' THOMPSON

All over the world a mouse carved from oak seems to crawl up table legs, run along chair arms, sit on ash trays, play on book-ends, or prowl on bowls and cheese boards – identifying the work made in the workshops of Robert Thompson's Craftsmen Limited at Kilburn, a tiny village nestling beneath the south-west corner of the Hambleton Hills.

The business was started by Robert Thompson who was born in Kilburn in the Old Hall in 1876, son of the village carpenter and wheelwright. On leaving school he went to Cleckheaton to be apprenticed to a firm of engineers, but he was homesick for Kilburn and at the age of 20

◄ Kilburn craftsmen continue the work of Robert Thompson

APPLETON-LE-MOORS
MAP REF: 91SE7387

This textbook example of a linear or 'street' village is breezily situated on the limestone uplands above the valley of the River Seven, a few miles north-west of Pickering. Most of its houses and farms date from the 17th and 18th centuries, their frontages preserving an ancient property line in a village plan similar to that shown in medieval documents. Some historians believe it to date from the 12th century.

The present road through the village would formerly have been much narrower, and the verges wider. Back lanes survive behind long, narrow tofts extending about 100yds. Stone houses, cottages, farms and barns, most with pantiled roofs, give character to the village, and one building on the east side of the street has three carved heads which are supposed to represent a clergyman, a doctor and a lawyer.

▼ Limestone cottages with pantiled roofs at Appleton-le-Moors

persuaded his father to let him return and join him as a carpenter.

Young Thompson had seen the wonderful 15th-century oak carvings in Ripon Cathedral and they inspired in him a desire to emulate the art of the great medieval craftsmen. In his spare time he studied wood, experimented with tools and gradually taught himself to carve.

A turning point in his life came when he met Father Paul Nevill, a monk of nearby Ampleforth Abbey. Father Paul was also the parish priest of Ampleforth village and he wanted someone to make an oak cross for his churchyard. Thompson was recommended to him and on seeing the carver's work Father Paul recognised his talent. After the cross orders followed for a refectory table and a chair for Ampleforth College and these – two of Thompson's earliest commissioned works – are still in use.

Gradually, as Thompson's reputation spread, orders started to come in from far and wide and to cope with the demand he trained other men to work alongside him. On one occasion Thompson and one of his carvers were working on a cornice for a screen and the man happened to use the phrase 'poor as a church mouse'. Thompson carved a mouse there and then, and it struck him that the mouse would make an appropriate trade mark – signifying industry in quiet places – and it has been used as such ever since. This idea of a signature was not a new one: Grinling Gibbons – 17th-century sculptor and woodcarver – chose a pod of peas.

To start with the mice, always carved as part of the piece and never detracting from the finished object, were depicted with their front legs showing but after a while the form varied. Apart from the mouse, another characteristic of much of the work is the wavy surface formed by the use of an adze – a traditional wood-working tool resembling an axe with an arched blade set at a right angle to the handle. This finish enhances the grain of the wood.

Robert Thompson died in 1955 at the age of 79 but his work is carried on today by his two grandsons; his old home is used as the showroom. The workshop, which employs 36 people, is usually surrounded by stacks of sawn oak being left to season naturally.

The tiny local pub is Birch Hall Inn whose sign was painted by Algernon Newton, a member of the Royal Academy. Framed in oak, his 'canvas' is sheet metal and his work is protected by glass. Depicting Eller Beck, this is believed to be one of the few inn signs in Yorkshire painted by a member of the Royal Academy.

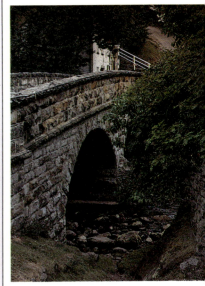

▲ The swift flowing waters of the Murk Esk at Beck Hole

The quiet hamlet of Beck Hole resting deep within its sheltered, green moorland valley ▼

BECK HOLE
MAP REF: 86NZ8202

Deep in a moorland valley, Beck Hole lies about a mile from Goathland and is accessible by car only via very steep, narrow moorland roads. However, the journey is worthwhile, for the scenery is dramatic and the hamlet is fascinating. Trains from the North York Moors Railway steam past and there are some lovely walks through woodland and across the windswept moors.

Moorland streams converge here to form the short Murk Esk; one of the streams, the Eller Beck, cascades over Thomason Foss into a deep pool just above Beck Hole and the Murk Esk, its waters often a rich brown colour from the surrounding peat, flows rapidly over a rugged landscape until it joins the River Esk at Grosmont.

It is difficult to believe that between 1858 and 1864, some 200 men worked in the iron-ore mines. But the mines were closed and the area's peace is now undisturbed.

Here quoits is still played. The game continues in many moorland villages but Beck Hole was the focus of the game's revival when, in 1984, BBC television featured the village in a clash between two local teams.

▲ A broad sweep of Bilsdale seen from the Forestry Commission picnic area and car park high up on Newgate Bank. Extensive views open up in all directions

BILSDALE
MAP REF: 89SE5796

The B1257 from Helmsley to Stokesley sweeps through Bilsdale, a broad valley of scattered farms, hamlets and isolated cottages. Five miles north of Helmsley the Forestry Commission's Newgate Bank car park and picnic area gives panoramic views. Beyond it the road descends to the valley floor on its way to Bilsdale's only village, Chop Gate.

Locally, Chop Gate is pronounced Chop Yat, 'yat' being a dialect word for gate. Chop may come from 'kaup', the Scandinavian for pedlar or chapman. Beyond Chop Gate, the road climbs to the summit of Clay Bank which, with parking and picnic facilities, affords splendid vistas.

William the Conqueror is said to have marched through Bilsdale after his awful Harrying of the North; it was snowing heavily and he got lost. As he shouted for his army, his language was so frightening that the locals still refer to 'cussing like Willy Norman'.

Legends of witch hares being hunted continued into this century, and the Bilsdale Fox Hounds are probably one of the oldest packs in England. The 17th-century Duke of Buckingham hunted with them, but the local hunting celebrity was Bobby Dawson. He died in 1902 aged 86 after a lifetime of hunting. He could outwit a fox and was reputed to have been at every kill. To the right of the door of

the modern Sun Inn in Bilsdale is Bobby's tombstone; the vicar banned it from the churchyard because of its hunting theme.

Nearby is Spout House, the former Sun Inn. This lovely thatched cruck house ceased to be an inn in 1914 and fell into disrepair. Its restoration was authorised by the National Park Committee and it was opened to the public in May 1982. It was in this old pub that Bobby Dawson told his hunting yarns, hence the presence of his memorial.

The landlord of the Sun Inn, which has its own cricket team, has been a William Ainsley for 200 years. The eldest son is always called William and by tradition becomes landlord.

BRANSDALE
MAP REF: 89SE6297

A minor road leads northwards from the eastern edge of Helmsley (signposted Carlton) and runs for 7 miles to the heart of the moors at the head of Bransdale, one of the remotest and most beautiful valleys in the area. The road loops round the sheltered valley head, climbs to the moorland ridge separating Bransdale from its eastern neighbour, Farndale, before swinging south-eastwards to Gillamoor and Kirkbymoorside.

With no way out at the head of the valley, Bransdale is one of the least-visited and most unspoilt dales. Early 19th-century farms, with their

associated buildings grouped cosily around, dot the valley sides. Their hedged or walled fields pattern the valley bottom, and some plantations reach up towards the moors. It is hard to realise that, about 200 years ago, 400 people lived in Bransdale.

The National Trust owns nearly 2,000 acres of land, including a number of farms at the valley head, and have recently restored Bransdale Mill, which had been rebuilt by William Strickland in 1812–42. Reached only by footpaths it nestles by Hodge Beck, and, though not open, illustrates perfectly a typical early 19th-century group.

THE BRIDE STONES
MAP REF: 89SE5797

There are several collections of stones known as 'the Bride Stones' on the North York Moors. Some are huge natural pieces of rock shaped into strange forms by the wind and weather and others appear to have been positioned by man, either as complementary to burial mounds or perhaps in connection with pagan fertility rites.

One group of about 40 stones is located on Nab Ridge, on Nab End Moor in Bilsdale. These may have formed the retaining wall of a burial chamber whose earth cover has disappeared.

High Bride Stones lie beside the road which climbs out of Grosmont and joins the A169 above Sleights. These stones are the remains of two

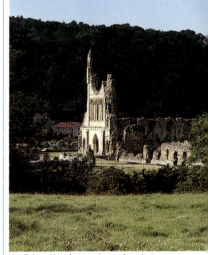

◄ A group of Bride Stones can be found on an 873-acre National Trust site on Grimes Moor, within the Dalby Forest

circles, each some 30ft or 40ft in diameter, and in each circle only three stones still stand. The circles could be associated with some standing stones nearby. Low Bride Stones can be found beside the same road, closer to Grosmont.

On the western edge of Dalby Forest on Grime Moor, just above a stream called Dovedale Griff, there is another group of stones. These huge outcrops of rock, taller than a person, have been fashioned by the elements into some curious shapes. They are now in the care of the National Trust and can be easily reached by a pleasant walk.

Bride Stones must not be confused with the Wainstones, the largest group

One of the Bride Stones, a strange Jurassic rock which 260 million years ago stood at the bottom of the sea ▼

of rocks in the National Park, which are on the escarpment above Carlton in Cleveland. These are popular with rock-climbers and their name, perhaps meaning 'the stones of lamentation', may come from the Saxon 'wanian' meaning 'to howl'; the wind does create strange noises among these rocks. Alternatively, the name may be a derivation of whinstone, a volcanic rock known locally as blueflint or bluestone. Many ancient graves are made from this and at one time it was used for road building.

BROMPTON
MAP REF: 93SE9487

This quiet village on the A170 near Scarborough has a special place in aviation history. In 1853, some 50 years before the Wright Brothers flew their aircraft at Kitty Hawk, North Carolina, Brompton's squire Sir George Cayley devised a craft which carried a man in the air.

Cayley's machine was a glider and it flew 50yds across Brompton Dale while carrying his coachman. The coachman shouted to Sir George when the flight ended, 'I wish to give my notice. I was hired to drive, not to fly.' Cayley had flown a glider as early as 1804, and the first known flight by a full-sized scientifically-designed aircraft, albeit

without an engine, took place in 1809.

The Cayley family has lived here since Stuart times, and among Sir George's other schemes was the impressive Sea Cut which prevented the River Derwent flooding around Pickering and Malton (see Forge Valley).

Brompton's history is interesting. The castle, now gone, used to be the residence of the Kings of Northumbria and the village was probably the birthplace of John de Brompton, Abbot of Jervaulx Abbey and chronicler of events from the arrival of St Augustine to the time of Richard I.

There was a church at Brompton when Domesday Book was compiled. The present building dates from the 14th century and it was here, on 4 October 1802, that poet William Wordsworth married local girl Mary Hutchinson from Gallows Hill Farm.

There is an enjoyable drive through Sawdon to the Wykeham Forest trail with its viewpoint and picnic site.

▲ Byland Abbey's dramatic west front; just a hint of what once existed

BYLAND ABBEY
MAP REF: 95SE5478

Below the wooded southern flanks of the hills south-west of Helmsley are the impressive ruins of Byland Abbey, dominated by the remarkable west front of the church with its distinctive 26ft diameter window. Cistercian monks moved here in 1177 from an earlier site near Rievaulx, and the plan of their monastery is exceptionally complete, larger in ground area than either of the more famous Fountains and Rievaulx abbeys. A rare survival at Byland is the lay-brothers' 'lane' in the west range, which excluded them from the cloister, thus keeping them apart from the monks.

The gatehouse to the whole abbey precinct, including a 13th-century arch, lies to the west of the main road.

CARLTON IN CLEVELAND

MAP REF: 82NZ5004

In spite of its name, Carlton is in North Yorkshire, a few miles from Stokesley. The road from the village to Chop Gate at the head of Bilsdale climbs to almost 1,000ft during the ascent of moor-topped Carlton Bank on the northern edge of the Cleveland Hills. From here there are fine views across Cleveland. The Cleveland Way crosses the summit and the Wainstones, weathered rocks loved by climbers, are nearby. Carlton Bank has a gliding club and at one time had a motor cycle scrambling course.

Sheltering beneath the north-west corner of the moors, Carlton's past links with alum mining are reflected in the name of the stream which flows prettily through the village, Alum Beck. Alum shale is unique to the North York Moors and was extensively mined here between 1600 and 1880 for use in the tanning and cloth industries.

The church has a chequered history. When vicar George Sangar arrived last century the church was derelict so he worked day and night to build a new one. He not only raised the cash but also did all the labouring. The church was completed in 1881 but sadly a fire destroyed it shortly afterwards. Sangar was charged with setting fire to it for some strange reason, but he was acquitted.

Another curious church, St Botolph's, now occupies the site. Its tower is half in and half out of the nave and there is a quaint two-in-one arch which opens both to the nave and the ringers' gallery.

Well-known vicar Canon John Kyle, who died in 1943, ran three farms and rode with the local hunt.

After weddings at nearby Faceby church, the groom and best man still throw pennies for the children. It was also at Faceby in 1634 that Anthony Lazenby established 'for all time' a dole of 12 loaves. These loaves, gifts for the poor, are purchased with money collected from four farms.

CASTLETON

MAP REF: 84NZ6808

The sturdy dark stone houses with roofs of pink pantiles or blue slates are typical of a moorland village and present a picture of durability and reliability. At one time the largest village in Esk Dale, Castleton used to be a centre of industry with a market and busy railway station. Today it is a peaceful place, as a weavers' mill stands empty, the market ended a few years ago and one well-known inn, The Robin Hood and Little John, recently closed. Its sign said, 'Kind gentlemen, and yeomen good, Call in and drink with Robin Hood; If Robin be not at home, Step in and drink with Little John.'

Once the site of a wooden Norman castle with three moats, Castleton overlooks the River Esk. Information about fishing between April and September can be obtained from the post office. There are picturesque views from the road leading over Castleton Rigg to the isolated Lion Inn on Blakey Moor and into Hutton-le-Hole. Another road with good views climbs out of Castleton northwards towards Lockwood Beck reservoir. Lockwood Beck operates a 'Trust the Fisherman' scheme for permits (late March to October) and boats may be hired. The reservoir offers opportunities for bird-watching and nature study too, but no water sports are allowed.

Castleton's surroundings are rich in archaeological remains, especially evidence of the Bronze Age people.

Freebrough Hill, beside the A171, has a curious conical shape and may be named after Freya, the goddess of fertility. The hill, a natural feature with a sandstone cap, was possibly the site of an ancient Anglian court.

A magnificent view from Castleton Rigg showing Danby Dale stretching away in the background ▼

CAWTHORN CAMPS
MAP REF: 91SE7789

North of the A170 as it heads through Wrelton and Middleton into Pickering is the tiny hamlet of Cawthorne. It can be approached on very minor roads, through Cropton or Wrelton, or even from Pickering and Newton-on-Rawcliffe.

On a 500ft escarpment overlooking Cropton Forest are the Roman Cawthorn Camps (the hamlet is spelt with an 'e', the moor and camps are not). Excavated in the 1920s but subsequently blanketed by afforestation, the site was bought in 1983 by the National Park Committee in order to protect its archaeological and wildlife interest, and to explain its significance to visitors. The 103-acre site has now been largely cleared of trees and scrub, and from a newly-created car park, where there is an excellent information board, a waymarked route, suitable for disabled visitors, leads for about 600yds to the main site, where a rougher track skirts the perimeter of two of the four camps.

These four Roman camps were established around AD100 during two separate occupations. One of the camps had a system of turf buildings with streets in between and a Bronze Age round barrow had been enlarged to create a platform for the commander to survey his troops.

Excavations have also revealed a few Roman artefacts such as chariot wheels, seats and pottery. An incense stone in Lastingham church probably came from here.

It is believed these were not permanent bases, but temporary camps for soldiers on the march. They straddle the route of the Roman road which ran north from Malton towards the North Yorkshire coast and are possibly the only remains of this type in the world.

steeply down to the Vale of Stokesley. They sweep round in a splendid arc, from the impressive peak of Roseberry Topping in the north, by Ayton Moor, Kildale Moor, Battersby Moor and Greenhow Moor to the highest point, 1,490ft, on Urra Moor. Then westwards, across the B1257, to Hasty Moor, Cringle Moor, Carlton Bank and Live Moor, the hills gradually lose height as they swing southwards towards Osmotherley and the Hambleton Hills.

▲ Dark, impressive and brooding, a narrow glimpse of the Cleveland Hills, rising to the north of the North York Moors National Park

CLEVELAND HILLS
MAP REF: 88SE4997

The name Cleveland comes from the Norse *Klifland*, meaning 'land of cliffs', and geographically the term includes the northern and north-western edges of the North York Moors, as well as the fertile plain which extends between them and the Tees. Until 1974 this whole area was part of the North Riding of Yorkshire, but local government boundary changes resulted in the creation of the new county of Cleveland, embracing this north-eastern part of the old North Riding together with the large slice of south-east Durham. A small area of the North York Moors National Park comes within the county of Cleveland.

The Cleveland Hills themselves form a distinctive range of shapely hills, with their northern scarp dropping

Some of the villages at their feet carry the 'Cleveland' suffix in their names, and the area has also given its name to a sturdy breed of horse, the Cleveland Bay, as well as to a popular long-distance footpath, the Cleveland Way, whose most dramatic inland section carries it purposefully across the proud crests of these hills.

Bronze Age tumuli and cairns point to a long history of settlement on and behind the hills. In the 17th century alum was discovered and worked near Guisborough and above Carlton, while jet was extensively mined last century, especially in Scugdale, above Swainby. More recently afforestation has clothed the lower slopes of the hills, mainly near Guisborough, Kildale and Ingleby Greenhow, but the uplands themselves still retain their clean profile, so familiar in the view from industrial Teesside a few miles to the north.

COMMONDALE

MAP REF: 84NZ6610

Until recently Commondale was not a particularly pretty village as it endured almost a century of prosperous industrial activity after the railway opened on 2 October 1865.

A Mr Pratt established a thriving brickworks which also produced tiles, pottery, chimneys and drains. This brought prosperity to Commondale, and the works continued through two world wars. Some local cottages contain bricks bearing the name 'Pratt', and the sewage systems of many towns were created at Commondale. After the brickworks closed in the 1950s, Commondale looked derelict for a while. However, it has now rid itself of its industrial image and with the Sleddale Beck meandering through, and set in a deep, broad valley in the hills, it attracts visitors because of its delightful moorland setting.

Known as Colmondale in medieval times, it was the meeting place of travellers because several moorland tracks converged here, including the Monks' Causeway which led from Whitby to Gisborough Priory.

▲ Newburgh Priory, dissolved in 1529, became the property of Anthony Bellasis, Henry VIII's chaplain

A LITERARY GENIUS

'I am happy as a prince at Coxwold and wish you could see how in princely manner I live. . . . I sit down alone to venison, fish and wild fowl or a couple of fowls or ducks, with curds and strawberries and cream and all the plenty which a rich valley under the Hamilton Hills can produce; with a clean cloth on my table and a bottle of wine on my right hand, and I drink your health.

I have a hundred hens and chickens about my yard and not a parishioner catches a hare or a rabbit or a trout but he brings it as an offering to me. I am in high spirits; care never enters this cottage.'

So wrote 18th-century novelist Laurence Sterne when he was vicar of Coxwold living at Shandy Hall. The house, which stands at the west end of the village a short distance from the church, was built as a cottage around the middle of the 15th century and renamed and rebuilt by Sterne. However, after his death it fell into disrepair until the Laurence Sterne Trust took it over in the 1960s and opened it as a museum of the life and work of this eccentric figure.

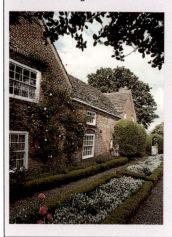

◀ Shandy Hall, former home of Coxwold vicar and novelist Laurence Sterne

Sterne was born in Clonmel, southern Ireland, in 1713 and spent his first years there. He was the son of a soldier who, although coming from a well-to-do family had no inheritance and had run away to join the army.

When he was 10 years old, young Laurence was sent to school at Hipperholme, near Halifax, where he gained a good education. After his father's death in Jamaica in 1731 his mother, still in Ireland, seemed to want to have nothing to do with him. However, his education was continued by favour of a generous cousin who was squire of Elvington in East Yorkshire. At the age of 20 Sterne went to Jesus College, Cambridge, where his great-grandfather, who had been Archbishop of York, had once been a Master. It was here that his life-long battle with tuberculosis began.

After taking holy orders Sterne was ordained in the Church of England and, with the help of another uncle (this one Precentor of York Minster) he became vicar of Sutton-on-Forest – a few miles north of York – rising sometime later to be a Canon of York Minster. But Laurence was drawn to the social whirl of 18th-century York, with its balls, cock fights, gambling and races and because of disagreements with his uncle over this his chances of progressing in the church were marred. In 1741 he married Elizabeth Lumley, a sweetheart of two years standing, but the marriage was not a happy one and his wife, always unstable, eventually suffered a nervous breakdown. They had one daughter, Lydia. Three years after his marriage Sterne became vicar of the neighbouring village of Stillington. He loved riding and shooting and a story relates how, on his way to take a service at Stillington, he saw a covey of partridges so returned to Sutton for his gun and left the congregation waiting.

Amateur painter and musician, Sterne had also always been something of a writer but it was not until 1759 when he began *The Life and Opinions of Tristram Shandy* that his genius emerged. The first two volumes were published and at the same time he acquired the Living of Coxwold. The novel was an immediate success and Sterne received high acclaim from all quarters: Sir Joshua Reynolds painted his portrait and he was invited to Windsor Palace.

Prosperity followed. Sterne loved the social whirl and travelled a great deal to London and the Continent, although always returned to Coxwold to write – usually leaving his family behind in France. He had completed volumes three to nine of *Tristram Shandy* by 1766 and wrote *A Sentimental Journey Through France and Italy*, but while in London for its publication in 1768 he contracted influenza which turned to pleurisy and he died on 18 March.

Sterne was buried in the parish of St George's Church, Hanover Square and the story goes that body-snatchers stole the body and sold is for medical dissection but someone recognised Sterne and his corpse was returned to the grave. When the burial ground was sold in 1969 for development the Laurence Sterne Trust received permission to remove Sterne's remains to Coxwold. They now lie outside the south wall of the nave, where his original tombstone stands, in the village this extraordinary man loved so much.

The villagers wanted a memorial (which would endure for ever) to their men lost in World War I and demanded an edifice of Commondale stone crafted by a Commondale stonemason. The name panels were made by Edward Overy from finest Commondale earthenware and a time-capsule is buried underneath.

▲ The existing Newburgh Priory dates predominantly from the 18th century

COXWOLD

MAP REF: 95SE5377

Rich in interesting buildings, Coxwold is small, compact and highly attractive. The most southerly village in the National Park, its wide, well-tended green verges, and its range of beautiful stone buildings present a charming rural scene.

At one end of the village stands the literary shrine of Shandy Hall; it was here that the modern English novel was born. It was the home of Laurence Sterne (1713-68), one-time vicar of Coxwold and author of *The Life and Opinions of Tristram Shandy, Gentleman* and *Sentimental Journey*.

Filled with Sterne's books and manuscripts, including the largest collection of first editions of Sterne's works, 15th- to 17th-century Shandy Hall draws literary pilgrims from all over the world.

At the other end of Coxwold stands Newburgh Priory, founded in 1145 as an Augustinian Friary and now a beautiful country home. It is said that the body of Oliver Cromwell is entombed here, having been brought here by his daughter Mary, wife of Thomas, the 2nd Viscount Fauconberg of Newburgh. The house, tomb and grounds containing a splendid water garden are open to the public.

Other sights in the village include Coxwold's impressive parish church; Colville Hall; the Fauconberg Arms; an old grammar school dating from 1603; almshouses built during Charles II's reign and a modern pottery where purchases can be made. Many of Coxwold's houses and cottages were rebuilt in the second half of last century by Sir George Wombwell, lord of the manor, and display his crest, monogram and the date.

CROPTON

MAP REF: 91SE7689

This tiny moorland community lies on the National Park boundary north-west of Pickering. On the edge of the village is the site of its ancient castle with views along Rosedale. Just beyond, where the road leads to Cawthorne, is a vantage point with extensive views across the moors and Cropton Forest. Today there is little evidence of the castle's existence and around AD1200 the site contained a half-timbered manor house; the earthworks and mounds are still known as 'T'Hall Garths'.

Cropton's modern church is built on the site of the castle chapel. There is a striking yew-lined approach to it, and outside is a piece of an old cross. Years ago a drinking cup was placed on this cross for the benefit of travellers and a verse ran, 'On Cropton cross there is a cup, and in that cup there is a sup.'

The wide main street is flanked with attractive stone moorland houses and contains what appears to be a disused animal pound, although it has no entrance. This used to contain the village water supply, pumped from the River Seven below. While on the subject of drink, an unusual feature of the village pub, The New Inn, is that it now makes its own beer.

There are walks and drives in Cropton Forest, with a 150-pitch Forestry Commission caravan and camping site set deep among the trees at Spiers House.

◄ Cropton Forest

▲ Canon Atkinson described Danby Dale as 'the loveliest it has ever been my lot to behold'.
Inset: scything in the dale

DANBY
MAP REF: 84NZ7008

A wealth of information about the North York Moors and the National Park Committee's work is available at the Moors Centre, Danby. There are refreshments too, with a picnic area in delightful surroundings.

Danby, sometimes known as Danby in Cleveland to distinguish it from other places of the same name, is a pleasant village deep in the valley of the River Esk. In strict moorland terms, Danby should perhaps be known as Danby End, the term 'end' indicating the mouth of a dale. The closed portion of a dale is called the dale head. Danby was immortalised by Canon J C Atkinson (1814-1900), vicar of Danby, in his book *Forty Years in a Moorland Parish*.

Rugged moorland sheep exploit the shade at Danby village ▼

Canon Atkinson is buried beside St Hilda's Church in Danby Dale, almost 2 miles from the village.

Higher into this rugged dale is Botton Hall. Since 1955, it has housed a community of mentally and physically handicapped people who maintain themselves and their own 'village' by making high-quality goods. These are on sale from shops at Botton Hall. The 'village' has its own post office, workshops, shops, social centre and coffee bar and help is provided by volunteer staff. The emphasis is on self-sufficiency and the project is one of several established in Britain and overseas by the Camphill Village Trust.

Downstream from Danby is Duck Bridge, an ancient and narrow pack-horse bridge which spans the Esk. Probably built around 1386, it was reconstructed by George Duck of Danby Lodge in 1726. It carries a minor road which leads to Danby Castle, which was the seat of the Latimers, and Catherine Parr, a wife of Henry VIII, once lived here. The castle is not open to the public although a nice letter to the farmer at the farmhouse, Danby Castle, might open its doors to groups such as school parties. One of its rooms is still used by the ancient Danby Court Leet and Baron which administers rights of way and parking on common land (see page 56–7).

EBBERSTON
MAP REF: 92SE8982

Ebberston and neighbouring Allerston are pretty villages on the A170 between Pickering and Scarborough. A local royal mystery involves Bloody Field and Alfred's Cave on the nearby moors. Legend says that in the 7th century, King Aldfrith of Northumbria fought his father, King Oswy, at the Battle of Ebberston. Aldfrith was stabbed and sheltered in a cave, since known as Alfred's or Aldfrith's Cave. Some accounts suggest that Aldfrith survived, others that he died.

The battle may have occurred on the moors above Ebberston and Allerston among the extensive and remarkable early earthworks called Scamridge Dykes. Now with a viewpoint and picnic site, this series of mounds and ditches is a prehistoric settlement of indeterminate age. In the last century 14 skeletons dating from about 1,000BC and an early communal thatched dwelling were discovered.

Ebberston church and Ebberston Hall are out of the village in a wooded dale on the opposite side of the A170. The church, built into a hillside, has Norman portions, while the Hall, built in 1718 and described as a Palladian villa, is of interest. Designed by Colen Campbell, it is open to the public.

▼ The Dining Room, Ebberston Hall

EGTON BRIDGE
MAP REF: 85NZ8005

Beautifully positioned on the River Esk in a steep-sided valley, Egton Bridge is one of Yorkshire's prettiest villages. Legend says that William the Conqueror's blacksmith left him at York to settle here.

This is one of England's most famous Roman Catholic parishes, known as 'the village missed by the Reformation'. It is the birthplace of Father Nicholas Postgate, 'Martyr of the Moors', who kept the faith alive when Roman Catholics were persecuted. He was executed in York, aged 82, for baptising a child into the Catholic faith in 1679.

The massive Catholic church of St Hedda dominates the village. Built in 1866, its great roof is ribbed and painted blue with golden stars and there is Belgian terracotta work on the altar. Halfway up the hill towards Egton is the Mass House where Postgate conducted secret Masses and St Hedda's Church contains relics of his ministry. One of the village pubs is called The Postgate.

▲ A scene from the life of Jesus, in Egton Bridge's Roman Catholic church

The Egton Bridge Old Gooseberry Society, formed in 1800, holds a show of giant gooseberries each year on the first Tuesday of August. The world record for the heaviest gooseberry is held by a berry shown here in 1982.

Egton, from 'Egetune' meaning town of oaks, stands on the hill above. Its Horse and Agricultural Society arranges Egton Show in August, one of the largest in the region.

There are some fine walks in the area, particularly through Arncliffe Woods and along the road which hugs the banks of the Esk just out of Egton Bridge, towards Glaisdale. A weir tumbles towards an old mill where a series of stepping stones lead to an island in the river.

ESK DALE
MAP REF: 85NZ7407

Esk Dale is the largest of the dales within the North York Moors National Park and differs from the others because it stretches from west to east.

The River Esk rises at Esklets, a hollow in the moors between Westerdale and Farndale, and then twists and turns under many bridges along the floor of the dale, flowing east until it reaches the North Sea at Whitby. It is a premier salmon river and public fishing for salmon and trout (with the necessary licences) is available along certain stretches. There is boating at Ruswarp.

All the Esk's main tributaries rise in high moorland to the south and flow northwards, to enter the Esk in something akin to herring-bone fashion. The largest tributary is the Murk Esk which joins the Esk at Grosmont. This features some spectacular waterfalls, although Sleddale Beck and Baysdale Beck, both joining near its source, are major contributors.

The landscape of Esk Dale is dramatic and there are some stunning viewpoints from the surrounding moors which are clothed with purple heather in August. The scenic Whitby to Middlesbrough (BR) railway line, with stations at most villages, is popular with visitors, and steam trains of the private North York Moors Railway join the line at Grosmont.

No main road threads through Eskdale, but minor roads descend into the villages, and are noted for their steep hills and narrow twisting routes. Limber Hill at Glaisdale, for example, has a gradient of 1-in-3 while the lanes into Littlebeck are as steep or even steeper. Like so many others, Lealholm Bank has wonderful views from the summit while the roads along the side of the dale are full of interest. There is a thrilling drive from Key Green near Egton Bridge into Grosmont. Great care is needed when driving in Esk Dale, especially during the summer when farm vehicles are on the move, and many of these roads are not suitable for coaches and caravans.

Esk Dale's villages are unspoilt. Surrounded by a scattering of sturdy farms, many of which offer bed-and-breakfast, they have lovely stone houses, with inns, post offices and shops. There are cricket pitches too and quoits is a popular game.

This is good walking country, with plenty to interest the naturalist, the photographer and the artist.

FADMOOR
SEE GILLAMOOR

FARNDALE
MAP REF: 89SE6697

Farndale is a long, remote valley which reaches deep into the centre of the Moors north of Kirkbymoorside. It contains the hamlets of Church Houses, Low Mill and Lowna, with a scattering of farms and cottages. Some are ancient cruck houses with thatched roofs, and the winding, narrow lanes provide a picturesque circuit. The dale is famed for its wild daffodils. Every spring, around the middle of April, the banks of the gentle River Dove are covered with mile after mile of small yellow daffodils. They are the true wild daffodils native to Britain. Farndale's environment of low-lying damp pastures with sandy loam seems particularly conducive to their growth. Yorkshire folk often call these daffodils 'Lenten Lilies' because they bloom around that season. The flowers, once threatened by plundering visitors, are now protected by law and 2,000 acres of Farndale are designated as a local nature reserve.

Farndale is the setting for several local legends. They include Sarkless Kitty who drowned after a sad love affair; the Farndale Hob whose mischief caused a farmer to move house and the local witch who could turn herself into a black dog.

Poor Kitty loved a wealthy farmer's son but when she became pregnant he abandoned her. Kitty pleaded for a meeting but the young man didn't turn up. A horseman said he had seen Kitty's lover riding in the opposite direction and, in a fit of sorrow, she leapt naked into the flood. Her body was later found near an old ford; ironically it lay beside her beloved who had also perished in the river. He had ridden into Kirkbymoorside to buy Kitty a wedding ring, but had drowned on the way to meet her. The lovers were buried at the roadside but on the anniversary of her death, the ghost of the naked (sarkless) Kitty haunted the area. The river began to claim other victims too until a Quaker couple living nearby secretly exhumed the bodies and re-buried them in a Quaker burial ground; the hauntings and drownings then stopped.

◄ Sheep farming still provides a relatively important economic backbone to the Farndale community

FORGE VALLEY
MAP REF: 93SE9886

Some of the most impressive scenery around Scarborough can be found in Forge Valley, a deep, tree-lined dale with the River Derwent flowing gently along its floor.

Known for its profusion of ash and other deciduous trees, the valley contrasts vividly with the surrounding conifer forests. Its name may come from the establishment of a medieval forge by the monks of Rievaulx Abbey, although there was a foundry here in 1798.

Forge Valley is a National Nature Reserve containing a wealth of wildlife and lies on the route of the Derwent Way, one of the local long-distance walks.

FRYUP DALES
MAP REF: 85NZ7304

A drive around Little Fryup Dale and Great Fryup Dale makes a pleasant diversion when exploring Esk Dale. Danby Castle stands at the entrance to Little Fryup and from here there is a pleasant journey along Crossley Sides, where bilberries ripen in late August. A pair of narrow roads lead to Great Fryup Dale near Furnace Farm and Wheat Bank and it is fair to say there is little more here than peace and tranquillity, for Fryup is a very scattered community of sturdy houses and farms. High in Great Fryup Dale there is the quaintly named Fryup Street, a tiny lane between a few quiet dwellings.

The eastern road into Great Fryup

be magical and children would play around them. One old lady gave a graphic account of seeing a little green man here, while another claimed she had found a fairy bairn (a fairy child) in a hayfield.

FYLINGDALES
MAP REF: 86NZ9003

There is no village of Fylingdales. The name applies to a spacious stretch of moorland and an adjoining coastal area which lies inland near Robin Hood's Bay. The hamlet of Raw, and the village of Fylingthorpe with its views and steep hills can be included, along with many farms and houses and some dramatic and lovely countryside.

Fylingdales Moor rises to almost

▲ A peacefully serene picture beside the River Derwent in the Forge valley; a National Nature Reserve since 1980

Situated at the northern end of Forge Valley is the hamlet of Everley, and this marks the start of a remarkable early 19th-century drainage scheme. The Derwent used to flood wide areas around Pickering and Malton until Sir George Cayley of Brompton devised a way to prevent this happening by cutting an overflow channel for the Derwent. Known as the Sea Cut, his waterway slices through the landscape like a canal and was constructed between 1800 and 1810. A sluice allows the normal waters to take their course, but floodwater is diverted to the North Sea through Scalby.

Dale once had six gates in its first mile. A stone commemorating their removal reads: 'Six gates in next mile a nuisance proved. Helped by kind donors, tenants and others had them removed. USE WELL TIME SAVED.'

Fryup's odd name causes amusement and speculation. It might be derived from Friga, an old English personal name, while the 'up' or 'hop' means a small valley.

The dales meet at Fairy Cross Plain, a name which goes back more than 200 years. 'Cross' refers to the meeting place of two tracks, while 'fairy' is a reminder that this was the legendary haunt of fairies, who were supposed to make butter at night. Fairy rings, formed naturally on the ground by toadstools, were thought to

1,000ft above sea-level. Crossed by many tracks it lies between the A169 and the A171 and has two remarkable landmarks; one very ancient and the other very modern.

Seventh-century Lilla Cross, one of the country's oldest Christian relics, stands almost in the shadow of the Ballistic Missile Early Warning Station on Fylingdales Moor. The ancient stone cross, reached by a 2-mile moorland walk, commemorates a Christian, Lilla, who died in AD626 while saving the life of the heathen King of Northumbria, Edwin. As a result Edwin became a Christian and built a church where the present York Minster stands.

The three radomes, resembling giant golf balls, of the Early Warning

Station, completed in 1962, are between 140 and 150ft in diameter, with an inter-connecting tunnel. They have formed one of the most dramatic moorland landmarks in Britain for 30 years but their space-age geometry is to be replaced from 1992, by a single, seven-storey, truncated, triangular pyramid on a two-storey rectangular base. Each of its three sloping faces will be about 100ft square, bristling with over 2,500 small antennae. The three golf balls will gradually be demolished from late 1992 and the area restored as moorland.

On a bend in the nearby A169, Ellerbeck is a popular beauty-spot and car-parking area, with views of the North York Moors Railway at Fen Bog, where a 40-acre nature reserve is famous for its bog plants and communities. The Lyke Wake Walk crosses the main road at Ellerbeck, and many of its walkers are met by support parties here.

▲ The sign of the Plough Inn, Fadmoor

GILLAMOOR AND FADMOOR
MAP REF: 90SE6889

These tiny moorland villages, with less than a mile separating them, are both on the southern edge of the National Park a few miles north of Kirkbymoorside. They are villages through which it is best to stroll, not drive. The influx of visitors to neighbouring and more prominent areas has spilled into these quiet places and each now caters for tourists – if only in a small way – and a walk will reveal many delights.

Gillamoor is perhaps best known for its Surprise View. When leaving the village on the road towards Farndale, there is an abrupt left turn which reveals a magnificent view across the moors, the River Dove and the southerly tip of Farndale. This is one occasion when walking is recommended, because the narrow road and sharp turn makes parking dangerous or even impossible.

Gillamoor contains a three-faced sundial and some fine old houses, one of which used to contain a witch-post. Often made from rowan and decorated with carvings of the cross, these were intended to ward off evil spirits. The church, with a Jacobean altar table, is

▲ The village of Gilling East

of interest because it was rebuilt in 1802 by one man, James Smith. The east and north walls have no windows and its sturdy structure was designed to withstand the tough climate of the moors.

GILLING EAST
MAP REF: 95SE6177

A charming and delightfully compact village in mellow stone, Gilling East is dominated by its castle, approached by a long, steep drive. After long associations with the Fairfax family, the castle is now owned by Ampleforth College. It dates from the 14th century but, after many alterations and owners between the 15th and 18th centuries, it is now a preparatory school for about 120 boys.

The castle's Great Chamber and impressive gardens are open to the public. The magnificent Elizabethan Great Chamber is used by the boys as their refectory. Completed in 1585, it is noted for its oak panelling, its frieze, the windows and ceiling. The panelling is superb. Large oak panels are divided into lozenges and triangles, and inlaid with a variety of patterns. No two are alike. When the College bought the castle in 1929, this panelling was sold separately to Randolph Hearst, the American newspaper magnate. Happily, Ampleforth College managed to re-purchase it in 1952 for restoration to its original position.

The village's history dates back to Norman times when it was known as 'Ghellinges'. The parish church contains portions believed to date from that period. There is some medieval glass in the chancel windows and a fine memorial to Thomas Fairfax.

Although principally of the early 18th century, much of Gilling Castle dates from the Elizabethan period ▼

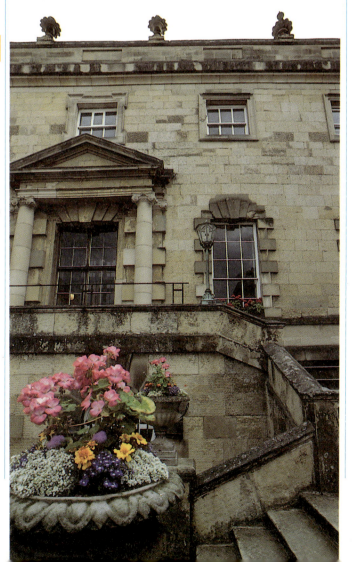

GLAISDALE
MAP REF: 85NZ7705

An old guide described the village as having 'many natural charms', and went on, 'It is among meandering streams and wooded vales, and around for miles are the beautiful moors'. This is still a good description today, for Glaisdale is a sprawling village built on a succession of steep hillsides. There are pleasant walks in the local woods and on the moors.

The path through East Arncliffe Wood to Egton Bridge is delightful. There is an old 'wishing stone' on the way. This is a rock, through the middle of which grew a tree (now dead). Walk around the tree nine times and your wish should come true! Other pleasant walks include the climb up Glaisdale Nab from the ford near the railway station, and the long trek via an ancient 'trod' (paved track), past an imposing school and along the daleside.

Traffic from Egton comes via Limber Hill (gradient 1-in-3) and across the River Esk on a metal bridge. Almost concealed between the metal bridge and a huge railway bridge above is tiny Beggar's Bridge, built in 1619 by Tom Ferris. Tom courted an Egton girl but the swollen river often prevented them meeting. Furthermore, her father thought Tom was too poor. Determined to be a success, Tom went to sea, fought against the Armada and made a fortune. He was made Mayor of Hull and Warden of Trinity House, and returned to build this lovely and graceful pack-horse bridge. He also left a legacy for Glaisdale and Lastingham churches.

Between 1866 and 1876, Glaisdale's iron-ore helped establish Middlesbrough as a major steel town, but there are few signs of its brief industrial role. Charming Glaisdale Dale, running south-west from St Thomas' Church, contained a thriving weaving industry in the 16th and 17th centuries.

Hart Hall Farm is the setting for the tale of the Hart Hall Hob (see page 63), and the Glaisdale and Lealholm Society for the Prosecution of Felons still exists, possibly the only such society still surviving in England.

GOATHLAND
MAP REF: 86NZ8301

One of the most picturesque villages in the North York Moors, Goathland nestles among the heather some 500ft above sea level. Just off the Whitby to Pickering road, and with a station for the North York Moors Railway, it has superb stone houses, excellent hotels and interesting shops. The wide grass verges are shorn to perfection by wandering sheep. Please do not be tempted to feed the sheep, which may even attempt to enter your car in their search for tit-bits. Although they will eat out of visitors' hands, unsuitable or even dangerous food may be given to the annoyance of farmers.

Goathland's name is not linked with goats, but may relate to 'Goda', a Scandinavian settler, or the Swedish 'Goths' or even 'Godeland', meaning God's Land. In 1117, St Mary's Hermitage was established at Godeland. The present church with its interesting font, pulpit and altar stone, is also dedicated to St Mary. Nearby is the old village pound where stray livestock were penned until the owners had paid a fine. It was in use until 1924.

A fine centre for exploration, Goathland is surrounded by extensive moorland, and wooded valleys with lovely waterfalls are within easy reach by foot. One well-known waterfall, 70ft Mallyan Spout, is reached by a footpath which leads from the green beside the Mallyan Spout Hotel. There is a steep but exciting climb down to the waterfall, with Nelly Ayre Foss upstream.

▲ Mallyan Spout, one of many waterfalls around Goathland

The village is the home of the Goathland Plough Stots, a sword dance team whose displays in the locality have their origins in the settlement in the area by Viking raiders over 1,000 years ago. Close to the village are camping and caravan sites, and Wheeldale Lodge Youth Hostel is nearby. One of the finest remaining portions of a Roman road in Britain, Wade's Causeway crosses Wheeldale Moor near the Youth Hostel.

GOLDSBOROUGH AND KETTLENESS
MAP REF: 86NZ8414

Perched near the edge of high cliffs north-west of Whitby, Goldsborough is a lonely, windswept hamlet with a little pub and a history dating back to the Romans who established a chain of defensive signal stations along this stretch of coastline.

The site of Goldsborough's Roman station is beside the lane leading down to Kettleness. In the 5th century it was ransacked and its occupants apparently killed as excavations in 1919 revealed skulls, clothing, coins and animal bones, and the bones of a man with a dog at his side. The station had an outer defence consisting of a 12ft-wide ditch. Within this was a 5ft-thick wall, only the foundations of which remain.

Kettleness, half a mile away with open sea views, comprises a few cottages and a coastguard station. Jutting into the North Sea is the 400ft-high Kettleness Point while the Cleveland Way long-distance footpath skirts the cliff top. In 1829 the cliff

The single-arched Beggar's Bridge over the River Esk at Glaisdale. It was built by fortune-hunting Tom Ferris to symbolise his love for the girl he eventually married ▼

▲ Having plunged over Mallyan Spout, the West Beck tumbles down among limestone boulders on its way to join the River Esk near Grosmont

slipped into the sea, taking with it the entire hamlet of Kettleness. It must have been a gentle slide, however, because the inhabitants had time to reach an alum ship standing off-shore although their homes and the alum works were lost.

In 1857, fossilised ichthyosaurus and plesiosaurus remains were found here and the area has its share of legends and folklore. Near Goldsborough are two standing stones about 100ft apart, each called Wade's Stone. The giant Wade is said to be buried between them. At Kettleness, fairies known as 'bogles' were once said to wash their clothing in Claymoor Well, beating it with bats known as 'bittles'.

GREAT AYTON
MAP REF: 83NZ5511

Situated on the pretty River Leven with its weirs and flower-bedecked banks, Great Ayton is a village of contrast, its old stone-built cottages mingling with more modern houses. It is affectionately known by the locals as 'Canny Yatton'.

Tucked beneath the northern edge of the North York Moors, it lies just outside the National Park but within

The village of Great Ayton stretches along both sides of the River Leven ▼

the county of North Yorkshire. The A173 runs through the centre and the village's proximity to Middlesbrough means that it is popular with day visitors from Teesside and other parts of the north-east. Its crafts-people, shops, cafés, inns and small businesses are now also welcoming visitors from a wider area, largely thanks to Great Ayton's most famous son, Captain James Cook. His school is now the Captain Cook Museum. Regrettably, the retirement cottage of Cook's parents was removed stone by stone in 1935 and rebuilt in Melbourne, Australia. An obelisk now marks the site.

In 1827 the 50ft Cook Monument was erected on Easby Moor and can be seen from miles around. The grave of Cook's mother and those of five of his brothers and sisters can be found in Great Ayton's All Saints' churchyard.

The village has two churches, the old All Saints with some Saxon and Norman relics, and the new Christ Church with a tower and a spire. It is also known for its long association with the Society of Friends, or Quakers. Overlooking the High Green is the well-known Friends' School, one of eight Quaker schools in England. Co-educational, its 200 pupils come from all over the world although today not all are Quakers.

Somewhat symbolically, the Cook Heritage Trail, linking five places associated with Cook, begins in front of this school.

STONE CAUSEWAY

In many parts of the North York Moors, particularly in and around Eskdale, stone-flagged causeways are prominent features across the moors, through woods, in villages and alongside roads. Over 150 miles of them have been traced, probably only a fraction of what once existed. Many doubtless remain unmapped. Other moorland areas in England have them, but they are most prolific in the North York Moors, the South Pennines and the Peak District; all areas where packhorse routes crossed boggy moors.

Although it is almost impossible to date these causeways, it seems probable that many originated in medieval times, possibly pioneered by monasteries like Whitby, Rievaulx and Byland, to ease travel between them and their outlying granges, to collect and export wool, and, with Rievaulx, to bring fish from its Teesmouth fisheries. Monasteries would have the resources to quarry, transport and lay the stone flags.

Many are named on maps – Monks' Path, Quakers' Way, Smugglers' Way, Paved Causeway, Pannierman's Way – suggesting that after the Dissolution there was probably a much more widespread use of these routes, while others may have been newly created. Industrial growth, with the transport of coal, charcoal, lime, ironstone, and salt, as well as wool and cloth, across the moors throughout the year created a demand for such tracks capable of withstanding regular use by trains of 30 or 40 laden packhorses in single file, led by one or two panniermen. Centuries of such use have hollowed many sandstone flags of the causeways, but, happily, some new causeways are being laid or old ones restored, by the National Park Authority, for the benefit of today's walkers.

Wade's Causeway, which crosses the edge of Wheeldale Moor, south-west of Goathland, was constructed by the Roman army almost 2,000 years ago. One of the best-preserved stretches of Roman road in Britain, it is now in the care of the Department of the Environment. About 1¼ miles long and 16ft across, with a raised centre, or agger, to facilitate drainage, its present rough appearance is misleading, being merely the foundation for a final surface of small pebbles or gravel which has long-since vanished. Some kerbstones survive, as well as a few drainage culverts near the northern end.

Built originally as part of a route from Malton, via Cawthorn Camps, crossing the Esk near Grosmont, to the signal station on the coast at Goldsborough, near Kettleness, the road lay hidden for centuries. It was rediscovered in 1914.

Our ancestors believed it was built by a giant called Wade, to link his castles at Mulgrave and Pickering. The reality of its Roman origin, however, confirms it as a remarkable feat of engineering in a nearly straight alignment across a boggy moor, 600ft above sea-level. Access to it is free.

A rather time-worn section of Wade's Causeway. Only the rough foundation layer of the road is visible today ▼

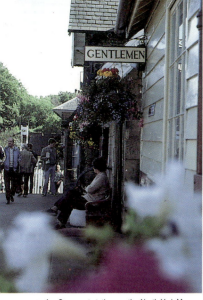

▲ Grosmont station, on the North York Moors Railway. The present line was opened in 1865

GROSMONT
MAP REF: 86NZ8205

The Romans built a road through Grosmont and a fort to protect it. The village remains strategically placed at the junctions of the Rivers Esk and Murk Esk, and two railways – British Rail's Whitby to Middlesbrough line and the private North York Moors Railway. Approaches by motor vehicle involve narrow roads and steep hills but the views are impressive and the countryside is lovely.

There is little evidence of Grosmont's ancient history. Around 1200, Johanna Fossard founded a priory here. Supported by the French priory of Grandimont, it was known as Grosmont Priory by 1394, but no trace remains.

The village's more recent history involves the railways and the iron-ore industry. During the building of the Whitby to Pickering railway in 1836, a rich ironstone seam was discovered at Grosmont. Extending towards the coast near Skinningrove, it was of the finest quality and a village was built here to house the many miners needed.

Thus Grosmont helped establish the iron and steel industry on Teesside; 100,000 tons of ore were mined

Looking up Grosmont's main street from the railway crossing ▼

annually and the new railway carried it to Whitby for shipment. The mine closed in 1871 but for nearly another century the village maintained its industrial tradition with a brickworks.

However, Grosmont no longer has any industries. Its scenic location attracts visitors, but its popularity owes much to the North York Moors Railway whose terminus and locomotive shed is here. The railway uses the beautiful route of George Stephenson's line, built in 1836 as a horse-drawn service. In 1845 George Hudson of York introduced a steam locomotive, but the gradient from Grosmont through Beck Hole to Goathland, which was 1-in-10 in places, was so steep that the coaches were hauled up by rope. A drum, 10ft in diameter, was located at Incline Top near Goathland Station and used a 5½in thick rope to haul the coaches up the final stretch. Novelist Charles Dickens used that line, which he called 'a quaint old railway' and today steam trains of the North York Moors Railway pass through Ellerbeck and then along the original route through Newton Dale.

GUISBOROUGH
MAP REF: 83NZ6115

A fine market town with red-roofed buildings of local stone, Guisborough is situated beneath the tree-lined northern edge of the North York Moors. It used to be the capital town of the Cleveland district of the North Riding of Yorkshire, but since 1974 has been part of the new county of Cleveland.

The town retains its many links with North Yorkshire. Its location makes it a good centre for exploration of both the moors and the coast, while its thriving markets (Thursdays and Saturdays) draw customers from many moorland communities.

The town has much to offer. There is an old market cross with a sundial and a 15th-century church containing the unique Brus Cenotaph, linking the local Brus family to the Scottish king Robert the Bruce whose grandfather was buried at Guisborough Priory. Its fine ruins are accessible from the town centre and are noted for the beautiful 56ft arch of the east window framing a view of the Cleveland Hills. The priory, once one of the richest in Yorkshire and the north of England, was founded in 1119 by Robert de Brus for the Augustinian order. A ghost of a Black Monk is supposed to inspect the ruins once a year, at midnight at the first new moon, letting a vanished drawbridge down over an invisible moat.

▲ Gisborough Hall, ½ mile east of the Augustinian priory, was built in 1857 for Admiral Chaloner and enlarged in 1902

The beautiful grounds of Gisborough Hall are noted for their huge old trees. One curiosity is that the family name of Lord Gisborough, and indeed Gisborough Moor behind the town, omit the first letter 'u' which appears in the town's name.

Sir Thomas Chaloner of Guisborough introduced alum mining to this area in about 1595. Having recognised the presence of alum on the North York Moors, he travelled to Italy and stole the secrets of how to mine it from the Pope! He is said to have smuggled some of the Pope's experienced workmen into his mines, subsequently being excommunicated.

Nearby, Tockett's Mill is Cleveland's last working watermill. Dating from the middle of the last century, it is open on Bank Holidays and Sundays during the summer, when milling takes place and stone-ground flour is for sale.

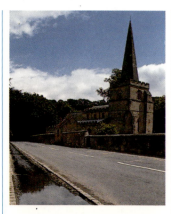

HACKNESS
MAP REF: 93SE9690

It would be difficult to find a more interesting and more beautiful village. Lying deep in the Derwent valley with its Hall, houses and buildings of mellow stone, and a clear stream rippling beside the road, Hackness is surrounded by leafy woods and lofty moors. The curiously-named villages of Broxa and Silpho are on the hills above, with the steep, winding climb to Silpho affording fine views.

The poet William Mason described Hackness as 'A nest of sister vales, o'er hung with hills of varied form and foliage.' Several valleys and streams converge here, such as the romantically-named Whisperdales, while the surrounding hills boast acres of Forestry Commission conifers with splendid walks and a drive open to the public. One valley is so deep that part of it is said never to see the sun between October and March.

Hackness has a history too. A monastery was founded here in AD680 by nuns from St Hilda's abbey at Whitby, and the foundations of the present church of St Peter, with heavy oak pews, were laid in about 1050. It has a 13th-century tower, a 15th-century spire and a magnificent font with a tall oak cover carved in 1480. There is a Saxon cross too, made around AD720 to commemorate an abbess of Hackness. Hackness Hall, built in 1791 by Carr of York is the seat of Lord Derwent. Unfortunately it is not open to the public.

Sculptor Matthew Noble, who exhibited many works at the Royal Academy and carved some of London's best-known statues, was born here and is buried at the nearby village of Brompton.

HAMBLETON HILLS
MAP REF: 94SE5186

The Hambleton Hills form the western edge of the North York Moors, roughly from the area around Sutton Bank and north to the moorland peak called Black Hambleton. To the west,

the villages and hamlets of these hills look across the Vale of York towards the Pennines; to the east and running along the ridge of moorland behind is the route of the old Hambleton Drove Road which now forms part of the Cleveland Way long-distance footpath. The foothills between the path and the boundary of the National Park contain several small, remote villages and there are some on the moors too. They include Thimbleby, Nether Silton, Over Silton, Kepwick, Cowesby, Kirby Knowle, Boltby and Thirlby, with Felixkirk lying below and Old Byland and Cold Kirby on the plain above.

Standing on the moor near Thimbleby is the Hanging Stone – a huge mass of rock 931ft above sea-level, and Nun House – a farm built on the site of a former nunnery. Arthur Mee, in his *King's England* series, said Over Silton was 'a place of far horizons'. The small church of St Mary contains the tiniest of fonts and some Norman stonework.

At Nether Silton, a tall stone pillar in a field near an old manor house presents a puzzle. Facing across the Vale of Mowbray, it bears this sequence of letters:

HTGOMHS
TBBWOTGWWG
TWOTEWAHH
ATCLABWHEY
AD1765
AWPSAYAA

They are thought to be the first letters of the following words: 'Here the grand old manor house stood; the black beams were oak, the great walls were good; the walls of the east wing are hidden here; a thatched cottage like a barn was here erected year AD1765; a wide porch spans a yard and alcove.'

Boltby is a charming place in idyllic surroundings. Strong stone houses crowd beside a rippling stream while Felixkirk's church is one of the few dedicated to St Felix. It has Norman portions and the top of the tower is 400 years old.

Old Byland is a grey-stone village high on the plateau above Sutton Bank. Known by this name since 1541, it was to a site nearby that monks came in 1143 to establish an abbey. But the bells of Rievaulx disturbed them, and eventually they moved into the valley near Wass and founded Byland Abbey.

Cold Kirby is windswept on its lonely site. Dialstone Farm was one of four inns on the ancient drovers' road and there is a fine view of this old track from here.

HARWOOD DALE
MAP REF: 93SE9695

Deep among the pine forests, this small village lies inland from the A171 between Whitby and Scarborough. Harwood Dale is both the name of the village and the valley in which it stands. The forest to the north is called Harwood Dale Forest while to the south is Broxa Forest, with Langdale Forest over to the west.

The present church of St Margaret was built in 1862 close to the village, but a mile north-west, just off the road, is the ruin of the earlier St Margaret's. This was built in 1643 by Sir Thomas Posthumus Hoby and Lady Hoby of Hackness Hall.

There is a fine view towards the sea from the top of Reasty Bank which climbs on to Broxa Moor. There is a car park too, and the beginning of a nature trail and forest walk. The Silpho Forest Trail is a short 2-mile walk past a Bronze Age burial mound. The demanding Reasty to Allerston Forest Walk covers 16 miles. As it is not circular, careful planning is needed. Forestry Commission leaflets are available for both these walks. The Derwent Way skirts this forest along the banks of the Derwent between Langdale End and High Langdale End.

The moors around Harwood Dale, whether afforested or not, are noted for the number of standing stones, stone circles, howes and tumuli they contain.

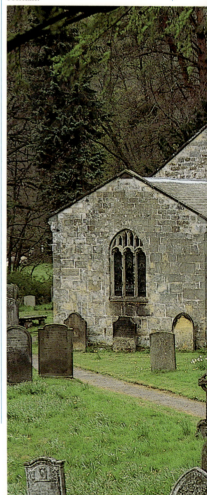

On Standing Stones Rigg, about 1½ miles from the village and about ½ mile south-west of the A171, is a circle 32ft in diameter. It originally comprised 24 standing stones, each some 2ft to 4ft high and a burial chamber was probably sited in the centre. Four stones from the centre can be seen in Scarborough Museum.

HAWNBY

MAP REF: 89SE5489

After John Wesley crossed Snilesworth Moor in July 1757 he wrote, 'I rode through one of the pleasantest parts of England to Hawnby.' His route from Osmotherley took him through lonely farmyards, up and down steep hills and across tumbling moorland streams with fords, all spiced with an abundance of heather and

▲ The pinnacled 19th-century tower of All Saints' Church looks down upon Helmsley and the daffodil-banked Borough Beck

▲ The Parable of the Seed taken from the Bible and set in stained glass in Norman All Saints' Church, Hawnby ▼

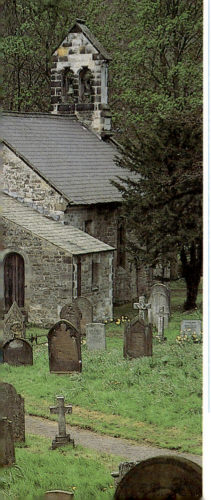

breathtaking views.

Today that route is surfaced for modern traffic, although coaches are banned, but it has plenty of moorland picnic areas and parking spaces.

Known as a stronghold of Methodism, tiny Hawnby with its knot of red-roofed stone cottages clings precariously to a lofty hillside which overlooks the River Rye. The little church of All Saints stands among a tumble of tombstones in the valley beside the River Rye. It claims no treasures, although a church has been here since the 12th century. There is some Norman stonework and an interesting stone cross can be seen near the font.

Arden Hall, seat of the Earls of Mexborough, is hidden among nearby woods and the elegant Queen Anne house occupies the site of a Benedictine nunnery. There is a Nun's Well in the garden and Mary, Queen of Scots, is said to have spent a night here whilst on her travels.

HELMSLEY

MAP REF: 95SE6183

Nestling in a corner of upper Ryedale, Helmsley is one of the most attractive of North Yorkshire's small country towns. Roads from Cleveland, York, Scarborough and Thirsk converge upon its wide, welcoming market place, dominated by the prominent memorial of 1867 to the 2nd Earl of Feversham.

The town's handsome buildings, mainly constructed of the local pale limestone, with pantile roofs, form a pleasing setting for the busy Friday market. Some half-timbering in the former Rectory House adjoining the Black Swan, at Canon's Garth, and at the old Manor House in Castlegate, suggests 16th-century origins, but much of Helmsley, as part of the Feversham estate, was rebuilt last century.

Borough Beck, which enters Helmsley from the north, and flows alongside a green, gives a village feel to this part of the town, and is daffodil garlanded in spring, by Castlegate, before it joins the River Rye which marks Helmsley's southern boundary.

Helmsley Castle was founded in the early 12th century but was extensively added to about 1200, with a remodelling of the west range by Sir Edward Manners in Tudor times. The Dukes of Buckingham held the Helmsley estate in the 17th century, until it was bought by a London banker, Sir Thomas Duncombe, from whom the Fevershams are descended.

The mansion of Duncombe Park, probably designed by Vanbrugh but built by the amateur architect William Wakefield in the early 18th century, was largely destroyed by fire in 1879 and rebuilt to the original designs a few years later. The present Earl of Feversham has recently renovated the house and opened it to the public. The 600 acres of parkland, including the superb terrace with classical temples at each end, represent a bold, early landscaping enterprise of 1720–30.

Wordsworth and his sister Dorothy probably stayed at Helmsley's Black Swan on their way to Brompton for William's wedding in October 1802. Dorothy's diary notes that they 'slept at a very nice inn and were well treated'. Today's visitors have a choice of good accommodation, including a purpose-built Youth Hostel. The North York Moors National Park headquarters are in the Old Vicarage, Bondgate, and Helmsley is the starting-point for two long-distance footpaths; the Cleveland Way and the Ebor Way. A good Tourist Information Centre is housed in the Town Hall.

A festival of music and the arts, part of the Ryedale and Helmsley Festival, is held in the town each summer.

HINDERWELL AND PORT MULGRAVE
MAP REF: 85NZ7916

Once a major community in this corner of Yorkshire, Hinderwell is now a quiet village less than a mile from the sea.

Its name comes from ancient links with St Hilda, abbess of Whitby. During the last century, it was known as Hilderwell and has been variously called Hylderwell, Hildrewell and Hyndrewell before assuming its present name. St Hilda's Well, in the churchyard, is said to have been blessed by the saint, who maintained a cell here so that she could pray in solitude away from the pressures of Whitby Abbey.

Some delightful countryside and rugged coastal scenery surrounds Hinderwell, and of some interest is the disused, decaying miniature harbour at Port Mulgrave, reached from the village of plain, cliff-top houses by a steep descent. Built last century to cater for the iron-ore boom, it handled 3,000 tons of ore every week and was reached through a mile-long tunnel which emerged from the cliff. The mouth of that tunnel is now sealed.

HOLE OF HORCUM
MAP REF: 92SE8493

The mysterious Hole of Horcum is a huge hollow in Levisham Moor. Large enough to contain two farms and their fields, and to provide the watershed of Levisham Beck, it is little wonder that our primitive ancestors believed it was the work of the devil or a giant.

One legend relates how the giant Wade scooped out the earth to throw at his wife Bell. Another is that the devil picked up a huge handful of earth and cast it across the moors to form 800ft-high Blakey Topping. Horcum's natural amphitheatre actually originated through the eroding action of springs over thousands of years. It can be admired from the A169 between Pickering and Whitby, and the best place to stop is the car park at the top of the steep and twisting Saltersgate Bank. The eastern rim of this great bowl has become popular with hang gliders, as well as sightseers and hikers. Trains on the North York Moors Railway steam through nearby Newton Dale and these can be seen from vantage points on the neighbouring hills.

Remote and lonely Saltersgate Inn at the foot of the hill was once a farm, which became an inn on the new turnpike road about 1770, and subsequently an important halt for coaches. Sometimes marooned in winter by moorland blizzards, it boasts

▲ The vast natural hollow that is the Hole of Horcum, sits green upon Levisham Moor like an enigmatic, oversized footprint

a peat fire which is supposed to have been kept alight since it was lit in 1801, and at one time was used for making buttered turf cakes. The inn was also the haunt of smugglers and one is said to be buried under the hearth where the famous peat fire still burns today.

HOVINGHAM
MAP REF: 80SE6675

Hovingham is an attractive, well-kept estate village with houses and hotels of local stone and a pretty stream. It lies on the Roman road from Boroughbridge to Malton near the wooded edge of the Howardian Hills. Its history goes back a long way and

during the construction of Hovingham Hall part of a Roman bath house, two tessellated pavements, some pottery and coins were discovered.

The Hall, built between 1745 and 1755, has a most unusual entrance because the builder, Sir Thomas Worsley, loved horses: an archway leads off the village green into the riding school and stables. The Worsleys are descended from Cromwell and Katherine Worsley of Hovingham is the present Duchess of Kent. The house has another somewhat odd feature, a ballroom on the upper floor. Its lawn is actually the village cricket field and an annual festival of cricket is held there.

Although the parish church of All Saints was largely rebuilt in 1860, the tower is Anglo-Saxon and there is a Norman window and some stones dating from around AD1000.

HUTTON-LE-HOLE
MAP REF: 90SE7089

One of the showpieces of the Moors, Hutton-le-Hole's houses, inn and shops surround a spacious and undulating village green divided by a clean moorland stream, once crossed by fords. There are now tidy bridges and well-kept gardens to uphold Hutton's claim to be one of the prettiest villages in Yorkshire. The grass is beautifully shorn by moorland sheep which freely roam among the sturdy stone cottages.

Near the car park on the road to Lastingham is an old cattle pound, while the tiny church, well-kept as a result of 40 years' fund-raising by the villagers, contains oak furniture by woodcarver Thompson of Kilburn.

A major attraction here is the fascinating Ryedale Folk Museum located in the centre of Hutton-le-Hole. From small beginnings in a cottage, it has expanded out-of-doors to include a completely reconstructed medieval thatched cruck house from Danby, an Elizabethan manor house from Harome, other cottages and barns, an ancient glassworks, a blacksmith's shop and displays depicting a wide range of local crafts and customs. Children love the witch in her hovel, while indoors there are items – ranging from witch-posts to kitchen utensils – collected from old moorland farms and cottages.

Common land hereabouts is administered by the ancient Spaunton Court Leet and Court Baron with View of Frankpledge, one of the few surviving Courts Leet (see page 56–7).

▲ The 100ft-high keep of Scarborough Castle, built by Henry II

CASTLES

Centuries ago, defence of the high plateau of the North Yorkshire Moors with its virtually inaccessible dales was confined to the periphery of the area – as the castles at Helmsley, Pickering, Scarborough and Danby testify.

The extensive remains of Scarborough Castle stand high on the 300ft cliff which separates the north and south bays. With the sea on three sides and just a narrow tongue of land joining it to the town on the fourth, it held a strong position.

It was built in about 1136 by William de Gros on the site of an old Roman signal station and when Henry II took it over the 100ft-high keep was added. This was often put to the test as Scarborough saw a lot of military action. In 1312 unpopular Piers Gaveston, favourite of Edward II, defended it against his enemies the barons but was forced to surrender through starvation. Two hundred years later, during the Pilgrimage of Grace in 1536, Robert Aske and his army lay siege to the castle but Sir Ralph Evers successfully defended it for the king. While Queen Mary held the crown the castle was taken by means of subterfuge. Thomas Stafford and some of his men gained entrance by disguising themselves and although they were able to hold it for a few days, it was soon retaken by the Queen's troops. Throughout the Civil War the castle was constantly under threat. The longest siege lasted a year with the starving Royalist garrison eventually having to surrender.

Neither Helmsley nor Pickering castles saw the action which beset Scarborough but both are interesting with extensive ruins. The existing castle at Helmsley was built in the 12th century by Walter L'Espec and is remarkable for its defensive earthworks. These consist of two ditches with a double bank which surround the original keep and curtain wall and towers added in the 13th century. The great hall and buttery were another addition a century later. The west range was extensively remodelled and added to around 1570, decorated with Tudor panelling and plasterwork, thus creating a comfortable home within the fortress.

Pickering Castle, a motte and bailey castle, consists of a keep standing on a high mound (motte) which is surrounded by a ditch, the space between this and the outer walls being known as the bailey. The castle was closely associated with royalty and most of the kings of England visited it when hunting in Pickering Forest. It also served as the administrative centre of the area and was used as a prison after the Civil War, during which it suffered considerable damage.

Overlooking the Esk Valley in the north is Danby Castle, built in the early part of the 14th century by the Latimers. Catherine Parr may have lived here as the wife of John, Lord Latimer, before she became Henry VIII's last wife in 1543. The castle now forms part of a farmhouse and is not open to the public, although a letter to the farmer may make a visit possible for groups such as school parties.

Other castles are known to have been built at Castleton, Cropton, Goathland, Kildale, Roxby, Whorlton and Kirkbymoorside, but in most cases no traces of these remain.

▲ An attractive private house of local stone, Hovingham
▼ The old school house, Hutton-le-Hole

RECALLING THE PAST

The Ryedale Folk Museum in Hutton-le-Hole opened in 1964 when the personal collections of bygones belonging to Mr B Frank and Mr R W Crosland were amalgamated for public display in a range of 18th-century farm buildings bequeathed for the purpose by Mr Crosland's sisters. Their niece helped the enterprise with a generous gift of money. Mr Frank was made curator and under his expert guidance, together with the advice of the museum's trustees, the venture has gone from strength to strength.

The exhibits, augmented by a combination of gifts and purchases, chiefly depict the life of the people of the North York Moors and Rye Dale from early times, most particularly during the 17th, 18th and 19th centuries.

▼ A witch at the Ryedale Folk Museum

Houses and buildings from local villages have also been brought to the 2½-acre site and re-erected with painstaking authenticity. They include the thatched Manor House from Harome, where the lord of the manor lived and held his meetings and courts, dating from about 1600, and the 500-year-old Cruck House from Stangend, Danby. This was a yeoman's cottage, built with the cruck-frame construction typical of the area and a thatched roof. Inside the house there is a witch-post, kept to ward off evil spirits. Made from mountain ash, it has a cross carved into the top as well as various other symbols whoses significance has been lost. There are also small holes; one big enough to hold a small coin, the other – slightly smaller – plugged with sheep's wool. The meaning of these is unknown. The post usually stood by the left-hand side of the fireplace supporting the smoke hood. There is also a stone box in the wall by the fire where salt was stored to keep it dry. This precious commodity, usually in short supply, was essential for preserving food. Spices were often kept in a similar way.

Another cottage, from Harome, is about 200 years old. Here there are two cooking ranges, one designed to burn peat which was obtained from the moors, the other made for the use of coal and wood. A fully equipped period dairy complete with wooden bowls, churns, butter pats and other utensils can be seen here.

Other buildings which recreate the past include a crofter's cottage, an iron foundry, a blacksmith's shop, a saddler's shop and a joiner and wheelwright's shop. All are fully equipped with the traditional furniture, tools and implements appropriate to the various occupants and their trades. One unique reconstruction is the 16th-century glass furnace which was discovered in Rosedale, then carefully excavated and brought to the museum.

The exhibits and buildings of the Ryedale Folk Museum make it easier for the visitor to imagine life as it was on and around the moors in times gone by. With the poor roads and transport the villages were isolated and more or less self-sufficient. Only a limited range of goods could be obtained from the outside world so people engaged in a variety of trades in order that their communities would want for nothing.

Life was hard for the villagers but they had their own entertainments to provide relief from work; dancing to the music of the fiddle and concertina and, in season, enjoying the mummers' play, maypole and morris dancing. There were also games to be played such as quoits and draughts. After a hard day's work they would sit by the fire and tell stories, safe in the knowledge that the witch-post was protecting them from evil spirits.

HUTTON RUDBY

MAP REF: 82NZ4606

Strictly speaking, there are two villages here. Rudby lies on one side of the meandering River Leven and Hutton Rudby on the other. They are separated by a wooded glen and linked by an attractive stone bridge.

This is a most attractive area which draws day visitors from Middlesbrough and Teesside. The river winds through the wooded banks and tumbles over a weir as it flows below houses perched on top of the cliffs. There are some pleasant walks in this vicinity; one follows the river bank on the Hutton Rudby side before turning high into the village and on to the spacious wooded green bordered on both sides by rows of pretty cottages.

The church, which sits on the banks of the River Leven at Rudby, dates back to the 13th century and has a good deal of 14th-century stonework.

There is some 15th-century stained glass depicting a shield, and the pulpit is Elizabethan. Access to the church is through an impressive oak lych gate.

Some nearby villages should not be missed by the visitor to the area. Crathorne is now by-passed by the A19, and contains an old watermill and some delightful white-walled cottages.

KETTLENESS

SEE GOLDSBOROUGH

KILBURN

MAP REF: 94SE5179

Travellers approaching North Yorkshire from the south by road or rail, or even by aircraft, can hardly fail to see the giant shape of the Kilburn White Horse cut from the turf on the side of Roulston Scar, about a mile south of Sutton Bank Top. The only turf-cut figure in the north of

England, it is almost 105yds long by 75yds high. Headmaster of the village school, John Hodgson, designed it with his pupils and 33 local volunteers completed the cutting in 1857. Gallons of whitewash were used to paint the original horse but now chalk chippings from the Yorkshire Wolds are used. Natural erosion, the weather and thoughtless people walking across the surface all cause damage, and a registered charity has been formed to maintain the horse.

Kilburn village is charming, with pretty gardens and a stream, while stacks of weathering oak provide a clue to the work of the village's famous craftsman – Robert Thompson. He died in 1955 but his old home, a half-timbered house, is now a showroom for fine woodcarving and craftsmanship in oak (see also page 32–3).

▲ Kildale Hall, near Kildale village

Maturing oak timber for Robert Thompson's Craftsmen Ltd, Kilburn ▼

▲ Kirkbymoorside Church is predominantly 18th century, with some medieval work

KILDALE
MAP REF: 83NZ6009

In ancient times a lake covered the land now occupied by Kildale – a small, quiet village tucked among trees on a plain in the north-west corner of the Moors. Standing on the upper reaches of the River Leven, Kildale continues to be served by the Whitby to Middlesbrough railway line, and the Cleveland Way footpath passes through.

Kildale's past is known to have included Danish settlers; four skeletons with swords, daggers and a battle-axe were found in 1868 during rebuilding of the church. Records also include references to a castle, but little trace of this remains.

In about 1200 a nunnery was founded in Baysdale, a short distance over the hills from Kildale, and in 1312 the Friars of the Holy Cross built a monastery here. However, they were asked to leave by the Archbishop of York because they failed to secure his permission to conduct their services. It is known that a chapel here was dedicated to St Hilda (and not St Kilda as some suggest). Kildale's name probably comes from 'Ketildale', Ketil being a northern name.

The noted Percy family, whose coat of arms can be seen on huge tombstones in St Cuthbert's Church porch, were Lords of the Manor of Kildale. Their mansion has now gone, but Percy Rigg and Percy Cross on the Moors recall their importance.

KIRKBYMOORSIDE
MAP REF: 90SE6986

Kirkbymoorside is pleasantly located almost midway between Pickering and Helmsley but is by-passed by the A170. This carries most of the passing traffic but is seen as a mixed blessing as it does tend to isolate the town from casual tourist trade. Even with a small industrial complex on the outskirts, this is a very peaceful market town.

Its position at the southern edge of the North York Moors, and its range of hotels, shops and small restaurants, make Kirkbymoorside a useful centre for touring. There is a thriving market every Wednesday and its community halls are used for art, flower and produce shows, as well as antique fairs and other events. The town's brass band performs regularly.

Kirkbymoorside shows little evidence of its long history. Two castles have come and gone with little to mark their passing, except that the stones of one were used to build the tollbooth in the town centre. The church, almost hidden behind the market place, possesses some Norman masonry, fragments of a Saxon cross, an old Mass dial and some medieval artefacts.

One well-known resident was George Villiers, the 2nd Duke of Buckingham (1628-1687). Rich and powerful, he was said to be one of the most notorious and dazzling courtiers of the time, but died in shame after a life of drunkenness, violence and general misbehaviour. Legend says he lay dying in the worst room of the worst inn in Kirkbymoorside, but this is not so. He died in one of the best houses in the town next door to the King's Head Inn. It was occupied by one of his tenants. There are a number of stories about his demise. One is that he fell from his horse while hunting in Bilsdale, and another says he caught a severe chill and was taken ill while riding. The parish register records his death simply: '1687, George Vilaus, lord dooke of bookingham.' His intestines were buried at Helmsley, and his body taken to London for burial beside his father in Westminster Abbey.

Known locally as 'Kirby', one of the town's problems is how to spell its name. It means 'church-by-the-moorside' but there are disputes about the presence of the second 'k'!

KIRKDALE

MAP REF: 90SE6686

Kirkdale is fascinating. It contains neither village nor hamlet, but there is a tiny 7th-century minster, a cave more than 70,000 years old and a river which disappears underground in the summer.

The little dale can be reached by leaving the A170 between Helmsley and Kirkbymoorside where signposts point to 'St Gregory's Minster', about a mile away. After travelling down steep hills to a wide ford, the sturdy outline of the church can be seen among trees. The first Kirkdale Minster was built around AD654 and dedicated to St Gregory the Great, the first monk to become Pope and the man who sent St Augustine to England.

▼ St Gregory's Minster, Kirkdale

Above the doorway, carved on a 7ft slab of stone, is a Saxon sundial, the most complete example of its kind in the world. Showing the eight hours of a Saxon day, it bears the longest known inscription from those times. From this we know the church was a ruin before 1066 and that it was rebuilt by Orm, son of Gamal. One name on the sundial is Brand, believed to be the first parish priest to be recorded by name. The church is now used for Anglican services.

Kirkdale Cave, which lies in the wooded cliff above the ford, was discovered in 1821 by a quarryman who came across the sealed entrance by chance. Once inside he found it to be full of old bones and thinking them to be of no value, threw many away. However, fortunately he showed some to a local doctor who recognised their importance. Expert examination revealed that the cave had been the haunt of hyenas and the remains belonged to their prey – animals which had lived some 70,000 years before Christ. They were species which no longer lived wild in the British Isles but proved that this corner of England had once enjoyed a warm, sub-tropical climate. The bones were those of spotted hyena, slender-nosed rhinoceros, woolly rhinoceros, hippopotamus, giant deer, European bison, straight-tusked elephant, mammoth and lion. The remains are now in several museums.

An extensive cave system is believed to exist beneath this area, which probably explains the occasional disappearance of the Hodge Beck, which flows through a gorge on one side of the graveyard. Legend has it that a goose once walked two miles underground from Kirkdale Cave into Kirkbymoorside.

LASTINGHAM

MAP REF: 90SE7290

One of the most attractive and interesting villages on the moors, Lastingham's place in the history of Christian England is assured. Today tourists, pilgrims and experts are drawn to its fine church, but they also enjoy the natural charm of this welcoming spot. Venerable Bede's comment in AD700 that it was 'among steep and solitary hills' is still true today.

It was here in AD654 that Cedd, a monk from Lindisfarne, was given land upon which to found a monastery. Unfortunately, he died of the plague before it was finished, but his younger brother, Chad, succeeded him as Abbot of Lastingham (later becoming Bishop of York and then of Lichfield) and the monastery flourished. The brothers became saints whose feast day is 2 March.

However, the Danes destroyed the monastery in AD866, and it lay in ruins until 1078, when Stephen, Abbot of Whitby, asked William the Conqueror if he could restore it. William consented and Stephen began by building a crypt as a shrine for St Cedd. However, Stephen moved to York in 1086 to establish St Mary's Abbey so the monastery was never completed.

The crypt, with chancel, nave and two side aisles, is a complete church in its own right and is used for special services; it is entered through St Mary's Parish Church. Apart from some levelling of the floor and some plasterwork, it has not been changed since 1068 and contains a wealth of interesting stonework, including an altar. St Mary's has a bier dating to before the Reformation.

Lastingham is very small, but a walk around it will reveal several well-

heads, one of which is dedicated to St Cedd, as well as an hotel, a restaurant, a post office-cum-shop and a cosy village inn. Near the summit of the hill leading towards Appleton-le-Moors is Lidsty Cross, erected in 1897 to commemorate Queen Victoria's Diamond Jubilee. Elizabeth II's Coronation seat beside it provides a welcome rest with superb views.

LEALHOLM
MAP REF: 85NZ7607

Over the past 20 years or so Lealholm has blossomed from being one of the quieter villages of Esk Dale into a busy Mecca for tourists, complete with toilets, a car park, garden centre and shops.

This is due to several factors: a splendid and spacious village green beside the River Esk with lovely cottages, shops, tea-rooms and an inn; stepping-stones across the river nearby; and lovely views from the surrounding moors. The view from the top of Lealholm Bank and the adjoining lanes is particularly impressive. A foreign writer said of Lealholm, 'Elsewhere, you have to go in search of beautiful views; here, they come and offer themselves to be looked at.'

Steep and winding hills drop into Lealholm from all sides, and of especial interest to naturalists (although privately owned) is Crunkley Gill, a deep and dramatic ravine which extends upstream from the village. It is said to be the biggest rock-garden in England, for it is rich with trees, ferns, flowers and rare plants. They

▲ Partly concealed by trees, St Mary's sits peacefully in Levisham valley

grow on the banks of the River Esk as it tumbles over rocks and boulders in this delightful gorge. There is no public access to the ravine.

The Whitby to Middlesbrough railway line, with a halt at Lealholm, runs along the northern side of the valley and half-way up Lealholm Bank are two churches. The modern Catholic church stands on a hillside site, while the red-roofed Anglican church has a very small tower, only 6ft wide at the base.

LEVISHAM AND LOCKTON
MAP REF: 92SE8390

A pair of tiny villages high on the moors north of Pickering, Levisham and Lockton were once known as 'the twin towns of the moors'. With their remote farms, sturdy stone cottages and neat appearance, they are more like hamlets than towns. As the

proverbial crow flies, they are less than a mile apart.

That mile, however, involves a deep and spectacular valley with winding hills and a route said by one traveller to be 'a breakneck descent and two distressing climbs'. Levisham Beck, which rises in the Hole of Horcum, flows along this valley and at its foot there is a bridge with a watermill and a small waterfall.

Almost hidden away near the bridge is the little church of St Mary. This dates from the 11th century and although the church was largely rebuilt in the 19th century there are some Norman remains.

Lockton's church has a squat, 15th-century tower, with a medieval nave and chancel and a 14th-century arch.

Nearby is Killingnoble Scar, so called because it was once the haunt of peregrine falcons kept by James I for hawking. In 1612 the local people were charged with the duty of 'looking after the birds for the King's use'.

At the foot of the Scar a pool called Newton Dale Well was the scene, long ago, of a Midsummer day fair and a blessing the well ceremony. Because of the health-giving properties of the water, a spa complex was proposed for this site, but it never reached fruition.

Two tortuous and scenic miles out of Levisham, deep in Newton Dale, is Levisham Station – now on the North York Moors Railway – beyond which lies Cropton Forest where there are some lovely walks. There are also impressive walks from Levisham along the Beck into the Hole of Horcum or on to Levisham Moor, rich with tumuli and earthworks.

Tiny, pretty Levisham faces Lockton across a gorge in the plateau of the Tabular Hills ▼

LITTLEBECK
MAP REF: 86NZ8804

Strong nerves and good brakes are required on the descents into Littlebeck. The lanes are very narrow with sharp bends and extreme gradients from whichever direction it is approached. One route leaves the A169 as it drops down Blue Bank into Sleights near Whitby, and another way is to take one of two small roads leading off the B1416 which climbs out of Ruswarp towards Scarborough.

This entrancing hamlet is set deep in a wooded valley which extends south from Esk Dale. Some delightful houses surround a quiet pool in the stream – also called Little Beck.

One little-known local custom is the annual Rose Queen ceremony, held in August, in which a local girl is crowned Queen and floated on a raft in the stream. It was in this stream that a man called John Reeves drowned himself in 1679 after betraying the 82-year-old Catholic priest, Nicholas Postgate. The pool is now called Devil's Dump.

Beside the B1416 above Littlebeck is a location called Red Gates. From here a track leads to Falling Foss, a lovely 40ft waterfall in a sylvan setting, which is at its most dramatic in times of flood. There is a car park and picnic site nearby.

The surrounding rocks are thick with ferns, mosses and woodland plants and tucked away nearby is the home of George Chubb carved out of solid rock in 1780. It will accommodate about 20 people and even includes stone armchairs.

Higher up the valley is the delightful open area known as Maybeck with walks and sights to treasure, complete with another picnic site and car park.

The tempered waters of Little Beck flowing through the sheltered greenery of Little Beck Wood ▼

LOFTUS
MAP REF: 84NZ7118

Once a North Riding market town, Loftus is now part of the new county of Cleveland. Its weekly market has ended and today Loftus retains overtones of its recent industrial past. Its history dates back to Roman times and before William the Conqueror's Harrying of the North, when it was laid waste, Loftus was a thriving township. The gradual return of prosperity began with alum mining and continued with the iron-ore industry which established Skinningrove as a major iron- and steel-producing complex.

The town's dependence upon heavy industry, rather than agriculture, has meant that Loftus (spelt as Lofthouse until the last century) has endured many peaks and troughs in its commercial life. Recently the potash mine at Boulby has brought some work to the area and new projects offer some pleasant shopping facilities. There is also a superb sports centre with a swimming pool, squash courts, saunas and a jacuzzi.

The coast behind Loftus is dramatic. Here the Cleveland Way crosses the cliffs by Hummersea Scar and continues along the coast to Boulby. Boulby Cliff, almost 700ft high, is the highest point on the east coast of England and from here there are excellent views.

A nice walk through Ness Hag Wood beside Kilton Beck leads to Liverton Mill. Legend says the woods here contained a serpent which ate young maidens but one day a brave fellow called Scaw came by and smote it with his trusty sword, ridding the area of this terror. He married a wealthy maiden whose life had been threatened by the serpent and Handale Priory is supposed to have contained his coffin. A nearby spinney was named Scaw Wood in his honour.

On the plateau south of Loftus, Liverton Church (usually locked, but key-holders' addresses are given on the notice-board) contains a spectacular Norman chancel arch.

LOW DALBY
MAP REF: 92SE8587

If there is a secret village in North Yorkshire, it is probably Low Dalby. Nestling in a fold in the hills beside rows of conifers, it is now a thriving centre for the tourist boom which has developed locally because of the recreational value of the forests.

The Forestry Commission began planting conifers in the North York Moors in 1920 and there are now some 50,000 acres of plantations within the National Park. Low Dalby lies within the large Allerston Forest which comprises many smaller plantations, including Dalby Forest. Much of this forest land is open to the public.

Afforestation has made use of poor land which would otherwise lie idle and has created many jobs. Specially constructed forest villages at Low Dalby, Wykeham Moor and Darncombe house Forestry Commission employees and their families.

Since afforestation, the recreational potential of forests has been recognised and encouraged by the Forestry Commission. At Low Dalby, the Commission has established a Forest Visitor Centre. Here, a whole range of information is available, from details about the work of the Commission and its foresters to illustrated guides about the wildlife which is supported here.

To encourage visitors, there is a forest drive (toll road), forest trails, camping and caravan sites and forest cabin accommodation for holidaymakers. The recommended walks vary from about a mile up to 6 or 7 miles, and the forests have several picnic sites and view points.

Dalby Forest Drive (with a small toll)

COURTS LEET

Courts Leet date back to feudal times when the administration of certain aspects of the law was vested in the lord of the manor. A manor – also known as a lordship, or hundred – was the name given to the sub-divisions of a county or shire, each of which had its own court. The word Leet first appeared in Domesday Book, meaning a territorial and jurisdictional area in East Anglia. But by the 14th century the term had spread throughout England and referred specifically to courts over which the Sheriff had no jurisdiction: virtually a royal court which the lord administered for his own profit.

Nevertheless, the tenants of each manor had rights to a certain amount of common land – although this usually consisted of land of little use to the lord anyway – and an important function of the Court was to ensure these rights were upheld. Other obligations included the maintenance of roads, ditches and fences, the appointment of local officers, the judgment of petty offences, as well as various administrative duties.

However, the Enclosure Acts of

emerges at Langdale End near Hackness, and motor rallies frequently use the forest tracks as special stages.

Visitors to this area must take immense care not to start fires.

LYTHE AND SANDSEND
MAP REF: 86NZ8413

Lythe Bank is a very steep hill which takes the A174 from Lythe down to Sandsend where the road runs literally along the edge of the sea. There are wonderful sea views from the top and a fine sandy beach, devoid of amusement arcades, at Sandsend below.

Lythe, on the hill, is a small village, but there is a nice inn and adequate car parking. Its sturdy, cliff-top church is worth a visit. Founded in Saxon times, it has endured several restorations and has proved strong enough to withstand the fierce North Sea storms. Seven sailors are buried here who died in the sea below during World War I. They have never been identified.

One of Lythe's noted priests was later to become Cardinal, and then Saint, John Fisher. His stand against Henry VIII at the Reformation cost him his life.

▲ The village of Sandsend stretches up the small beck on both sides, understandably avoiding full exposure to the sea

In the village there is a tiny blacksmith's shop whose anvil can be seen through the window. Here is practised an old custom known as Firing the Stiddy (anvil); it celebrates notable events in the family of the Marquis of Normanby of Mulgrave Castle. This fine building (Georgian and later) stands in a wooded ravine adjoining the village. The grounds – open to the public, on foot only, on Wednesdays, Saturdays and Sundays, but not during May – contain the ruins of Foss Castle dating back to the Conquest, and there are places with evocative names such as Devil's Bridge, Wizard's Glen, the Waterfall and Eagles' Nest.

Charles Dickens enjoyed a holiday at Mulgrave Castle and it has accommodated many notable people, including members of the Royal Family. Legend says that one of the early inhabitants of Foss Castle was the Saxon giant Wade and his wife Bell (see Wade's Causeway).

Like the A174, Mulgrave Woods descend into Sandsend. Once the site of a Roman cement works, this cluster of pretty houses by the sea is aptly named, as they mark the end of 2½ miles of beach stretching from Whitby. However, this is a holiday centre in its own right with hotels, inns, boarding houses and holiday cottages. A superb cliff-top golf course and 2½ miles of fields separates the village from Whitby. Jet was once mined here and there were alum works which closed in 1867. A railway used to cling to the cliffs here too, but this closed in the late 1950s and some of its tunnels, cuttings and embankments form part of the long-distance Cleveland Way walk and the Sandsend Trail, which is a two-mile waymarked walk through this area of former industry, whose scars are now softened by nature.

▲ Officers and jury of the Spaunton Manor Court Leet in 1908

the early 19th century saw the steady decline of the Courts as, with the abolition of common land, one of their main purposes disappeared. By 1946 most had ceased to function and their responsibilities passed to the County Courts. However, some do remain and the North York Moors can claim four of the 38 still in existence throughout England; probably representing the greatest concentration in such a small area in the country. These operate at Spaunton, Danby, Fyling and Whitby Laithes – although the territory of the latter had become so small that its jurisdiction now embraces only grass verges.

The nominal head of the Court Leet is still known as the 'Lord of the Manor' although these days he does not necessarily have to be present at meetings, usually held annually in October, or maybe even every alternate year. In days gone by the Courts met twice a year and all the residents of the district attended. The administration of the Court is left to the Steward, or 'seneschal'. At present there is one lord of the manor for the Courts Leet of both Fyling and Whitby Laithes, but at Danby there is a bailiff as well as a steward and he supervises proceedings. A jury of 12 attends and any fines are fixed by the 'affeeror'. Encroachment fines relating to common land are really the only power the Courts have today. For example, if the County Council erect a sign on common land the Court is entitled to exact a fine.

MOUNT GRACE PRIORY

MAP REF: 88SE4498

The full name of this spacious and beautiful ruin is 'The House of the Assumption of the Blessed Virgin Mary and St Nicholas of Mount Grace in Ingleby'. Almost everyone calls it Mount Grace Priory and it is to be found just off the western edge of the North York Moors. Open to the public, it is located close to the Cleveland Tontine Inn where the dual carriageway of the A19 meets the A172 from Stokesley.

This is the largest and best-preserved of all the English Carthusian houses and the only one in Yorkshire. It was founded at the end of the 14th century by a nephew of Richard II, Thomas Holland, who was Duke of Surrey and Earl of Kent.

The spacious ruins provide a striking reminder of the austere lives and the strict rule followed by the resident monks. Having taken a vow of silence, each lived alone in a tiny two-storey cell with a fireplace and a ladder to the upper floor. They lived, ate and prayed in these cells, only 22ft square, being allowed out only by permission of the prior. Each of the 15 cells had a small garden separated from the one next door by high walls, and each monk was given his meals through a square hole in the wall, angled so he could not see who brought it. One such cell has been reconstructed and furnished to show what it may have been like in medieval times. There is also an impressive exhibition explaining and illustrating the history of Mount Grace Priory.

In 1420, the priory was extended. More cells were built, bringing the total to 20, and a tower and transepts were added to the priory church.

In the woods above, on the route of the Cleveland Way where there are splendid views across the Vale of York towards the Pennines, is the Chapel of Our Lady of Mount Grace. This is becoming an increasingly popular place of pilgrimage for Roman Catholics. Described in 1642 as having four walls but no roof or shelter, it has now been restored. Access is from Osmotherley.

OLD BYLAND

MAP REF: 95SE5485

The name is rather confusing. It is old compared to the hamlet of Byland near the present ruins of Byland Abbey near Wass. Old Byland is on the limestone plateau west of Rievaulx Abbey, and the original monastic site of Byland Abbey was in Ryedale, just north of Rievaulx. The Byland monks evicted the original villagers from the

▲ The heavily-carved market cross on the green is a poignant reminder of Osmotherley's greater past importance

chosen site and rehoused them in a 'new' village – now Old Byland – in the middle of the 12th century, and built a church for them. This survives today, a strange structure with a stumpy tower over the south porch, lower than the nave roof. There is an Anglo-Danish sundial on the tower's east wall.

Village houses stand well back from a spacious green, preserving the original monks' layout. Trees, shrubs, and flowers add a special charm, and around the village is the planned landscape of Parliamentary enclosures of late Georgian times, with straight roads and field boundaries.

OSMOTHERLEY

MAP REF: 88SE4597

The old name for the village was Osmunderly, probably coming from the Old Norse meaning 'Osmund's Ley', a ley being a clearing. There is little likelihood of Osmotherley's origins having anything to do with the tale of a drowning prince (see Roseberry Topping).

One of the chief attractions for visitors to the village is a large area of open National Trust moorland which borders Cod Beck at a point known as the Sheepwash. This is about a mile from the village, on the road towards Swainby, and there is space for car parking. The area is popular with families who can picnic, paddle in the stream and explore the moors. It is adjacent to Cod Beck Reservoir, a quiet, man-made stretch of inland water which is administered by Yorkshire Water.

Just beyond, on the narrow road towards Swainby is a natural gap called Scarth Nick. Shaped like a V, it was carved by meltwater during the Ice Age, and provides beautiful views over Cleveland.

Osmotherley is an attractive mixture of lovely old stone cottages and stylish modern houses in a lofty situation on the edge of the moors. Once it was a small but busy market town and in the centre is a heavily carved market cross. Next to it is a squat stone table standing on short stone legs. This is probably an old market stall.

John Wesley, the 18th-century founder of Methodism, once stood upon this table to deliver a sermon and one of the first Methodist chapels in the moors was built in a cobbled alley in the village. It bears the date 1754 above the door.

The Anglican church has a 15th-century tower and porch, a long nave with medieval walls, Norman foundations and a Norman font. The foundations of a Saxon apse were found during renovations in 1892.

The Catholic Lady Chapel (see Mount Grace Priory) is nearby and Mass is also said in the Old Hall.

There are fine walks in the surrounding countryside. The Lyke Wake Walk begins nearby and the Cleveland Way passes through. A famous 300-year-old drovers' inn called The Chequers Inn was situated on the road to Hawnby, 800ft above sea level. Now a farmhouse, it has a sign which says, 'Be not in haste; Step in and taste – Ale tomorrow for nothing.' In 1960 this sign vanished, but was found at Northallerton and replaced in 1984.

PICKERING

MAP REF: 91SE7983

Pickering is known as the 'Gateway to the Moors' and its position on the crossroads of the Malton to Whitby and the Helmsley to Scarborough roads amply justifies this title. A thriving market town, it is the focal point of a large rural area.

Monday is market day when the town centre is busy with open-air trading at colourful stalls. At the bottom of the gently-sloping market place, once the village green, is the terminus of the North York Moors Railway, and an olde-worlde atmosphere is created as steam engines hiss and whistle only yards from the market stalls.

Overlooking the market place, with its wide range of shops, inns and small business premises, is the huge parish church of St Peter and St Paul whose walls bear a unique gallery of 15th-century paintings. Discovered in 1851, they were promptly concealed beneath whitewash because the vicar thought they would encourage idolatry. Happily, they were rediscovered in 1878. They depict scenes from the Bible, from history and from legend, ranging from St George slaying the dragon to the martyrdom of St Thomas à Becket.

The Beck Isle Museum of Rural Life is housed in the building where Marshall planned England's first agricultural institute. Beside the river in the town centre, it houses a fascinating collection of artefacts of rural life. These include a cottage kitchen, cobbler's shop, dairy, barber's and even a Victorian pub bar.

Almost opposite is Beckside Crafts Centre, an example of the new enterprises which are flourishing in the town. A few minutes' walk away is the Kirk Theatre, formerly a Methodist chapel but now a venue for concerts and other events, and along the road past the Railway Station is the Moorland Trout Farm and Lake. Open seven days a week from March to November, visitors can hire everything they need to catch beautiful trout. There is also a shop

▲ The 13th-century spire of St Peter and St Paul's, obvious above Pickering's main street

Pickering station on the North York Moors Railway ▼

and a small restaurant.

Almost concealed high above the town is Pickering Castle which probably dates back to the Conquest. It is claimed that every English king who reigned between 1100 and 1400 stayed here to hunt in nearby Blansby Park, and some parts of the old Royal Forest of Pickering still belong to Her Majesty the Queen.

Just outside the town, on the road to Malton, is Flamingoland Zoo and a large nursery and garden centre.

PORT MULGRAVE

SEE HINDERWELL

RAVENSCAR

MAP REF: 87NZ9801

The southern tip of the large bay which contains the village of Robin Hood's Bay is called South Cheek or Old Peak. Originally, it was simply the Peak, but confusion with the Peak District of Derbyshire led to the adoption of the South Cheek name. The face of the cliff known as Old Peak was altered forever by alum quarries, worked between 1640 and 1862.

Now the area is better known as Ravenscar. There is a small community of houses, an information centre, tea rooms and the huge Raven Hall Hotel with mock battlements and a dramatic cliff-side golf course. The hotel was built as a private house in 1774.

Overgrown roads are the only evidence of a plan in the 1890s to turn the area into a holiday resort. Beach walks and cliff treks are a feature of this area, while the Cleveland Way passes through the village. Ravenscar is also the finishing point of the challenging 40-mile Lyke Wake Walk from Osmotherley.

Walks along the rocky beach are dangerous due to the fast-rising tide and should be undertaken only as the tide is ebbing; even then, limited time is available. Bathing is dangerous too, but the splendour of this coastline is unrivalled. The cliffs rise to 585ft and tradition says the Danes hoisted a flag bearing a raven's image. In the 3rd and 4th centuries there was a Roman fort here.

The scramble down the South Cheek cliff below the hotel to the boulder-strewn beach is worth the effort, and the area provides splendid views of Robin Hood's Bay.

Much of the coast and undercliff here is now owned by the National Trust, whose information centre and shops form the starting-point for a waymarked track which passes various sites of former industry, including the recently excavated old alum works.

▲ Walkers near Goathland enjoying the verdant countryside

WALKING THE MOORS

The North York Moors area provides some superb walking country, with something to offer all tastes and capabilities. There are so many paths and tracks that the walker can choose between the difficult and not so difficult, the long or the short. He can walk for hours across open moorland, plan his walk through attractive villages and green valleys, or follow a route close to the sea.

Public rights of way are clearly signposted and are marked on Ordnance Survey maps. A public footpath can be used by anyone on foot but a bridleway can also be used by horse riders. Bridleways can be used by pedal cyclists as well, subject to local authority orders and byelaws, but the cyclist must give way to walkers and horses. Apart from the usual signs marking footpaths and bridleways at roadsides, the National Park Authority marks footpaths with yellow arrows and bridleways with blue arrows.

When planning a walk along the shore it is essential to check the times of the tides.

Some well-known long distance walks are entirely or partially within the National Park (see page 75).

One of the best ways of exploring and learning about a particular area is to join a guided walk. Information about these walks can be obtained at the National Park Office in Helmsley or at any information centre.

At some of the stations along the Esk Valley railway walks are mapped out so that you can follow a route to the next station or complete a circular tour.

Whatever type of walk is embarked upon comfortable and waterproof clothing and footwear should be worn. The weather in the valleys can be very different from that on the moors and is liable to change quickly. It is a good idea to take something to drink and eat as it may be difficult to find refreshment on the way.

Wherever you go always follow The Country Code:
Keep to paths, especially across farmland.
Guard against all risks of fire.
Fasten all gates.
Avoid damaging hedges, fences and walls.
Protect wildlife, wild plants and trees.
Safeguard water supplies.
Keep dogs under proper control.
Leave no litter.
Respect the life of the country-side.

RIEVAULX
MAP REF: 95SE5785

In his *King's England* series, Arthur Mee described Rievaulx Abbey as being 'among the rarest treasures of our countryside' while St Aelred, one of its abbots, wrote that Rievaulx provided 'a marvellous freedom from the tumult of the world'. Dorothy Wordsworth, sister of 19th-century poet William Wordsworth, said she could have 'stayed in this solemn spot until evening, without a thought of moving'. Turner painted the abbey and today's visitors are entranced by its serene splendour.

Pronounced 'Reevo', it was founded in 1132. The first Cistercian house in Yorkshire, it became the mother church of the Order in England.

The most imposing of the Cistercian houses, its church has the earliest Cistercian nave in Britain (1140), but the aisles and triforium were not completed until a century later.

During the building the monks lived in rough shelters. They floated huge stones from local quarries along the River Rye, dug canals and dammed the river to provide deep water at the point of work on the abbey walls.

As the abbey grew, trade developed. Its interests included fishing, agriculture and the woollen industry and within 50 years it owned more than 6,000 acres of land and over 14,000 sheep. The abbey had 140 monks with 240 lay brothers and 260 hired workmen.

At the Reformation the walls were razed to the ground and many local buildings are constructed with material taken from them. Lead from the roof was buried and nearly 400 years later it was found and used in the restoration of the Five Sisters Window at York Minster.

The abbey is now in the care of English Heritage, and attracts some 200,000 visitors each year.

Looking down upon the abbey is Rievaulx Terrace (NT), a beautiful example of landscape gardening completed in 1758. With a lawn ½ mile long, there are two classical temples and superb views. Entrance is from the Helmsley to Stokesley road but there is a nice walk from Helmsley to Rievaulx following part of the Cleveland Way.

Tiny Rievaulx village, perched on a wooded hillside, has some pretty thatched cottages. One was occupied by ancestors of Lord Wilson of Rievaulx, previously Sir Harold Wilson who was Labour Prime Minister for two terms (1964 to 1970 and 1974 to 1976).

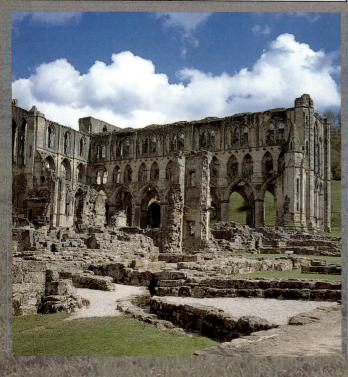

◀ The splendour that was once the pride of the Cistercian Order, Rievaulx Abbey

▲ Robin Hood's Bay is a maze of steep little streets and passages with houses on a diversity of levels

ROBIN HOOD'S BAY
MAP REF: 87NZ9505

Whether Robin Hood is fact or fiction, there is no evidence to link him with this cliff-hanging coastal village, known as Robbyn Huddes Bay in Tudor times. Locals prefer the old name, Bay Town, which really applies to the close-clustered cottages, houses and other buildings near the shore at the bottom of a tortuously steep hill which forms the main street. Called New Road, this was new around 1780 when the village thrived on fishing. Almost a century later 174 boats were registered here.

Cobbled slopes, flights of steps, narrow alleys and streets stitch together ledges, terraces and groups of usually small stone cottages, pink-pantiled and glowing in the sunshine. Many, together with numerous inns, had cellars; almost certainly used for storing brandy, tobacco, silk and tea during the smuggling days of the 18th and 19th centuries.

Visitors must park their cars in the large car park at the top of the hill. Be warned – the climb back up the hill is fairly demanding. Geologists and rock-pool enthusiasts will appreciate the long, curving beach with its interesting rock formations, but should beware the fast-rising tide. A mile inland is St Stephen's old church, a splendid period-piece, little-changed from when it was built in 1821.

Robin Hood's Bay features as Bramblewick in Leo Walmsley's book *Three Rivers*, later filmed as *The Turn of the Tide*. He lived in King Street between 1894 and 1913.

ROSEBERRY TOPPING
MAP REF: 83NZ5712

The boundary between the counties of North Yorkshire and Cleveland runs across the cone-shaped summit of this conspicuous landmark. However, it lies entirely within the North York Moors National Park and much of the hill has been in National Trust hands since 1985.

There is a car park with a picnic site and the convenience of a local inn at the nearby little village of Newton-under-Roseberry.

Roseberry Topping resembles a small mountain. A shade over 1,000ft, it dominates the surrounding area and offers a short but stiff climb for those who wish to tackle its slopes. The reward is the magnificent view from the summit.

The word 'topping' is used for peaks in the North York Moors; it comes from the Danish 'toppen' meaning peak, or summit. This peak has also been called Odinsburg, however, after Odin, the Norse god of creation.

It is linked to a legend which tells how the mother of baby Prince Oswy of Northumbria dreamt he would drown on a certain day. She asked his maid to take him to the top of Roseberry Topping, away from any water but the maid fell asleep and the child wandered off, only to be found lying face down in a spring on the hillside. His mother died from grief and the legend says they are buried side-by-side at Osmotherley, so called because Os-by-his-mother-lay.

Local people watch the summit of Roseberry Topping for signs of bad weather. A verse says, 'When Roseberry Topping wears a cap, Cleveland must beware a clap'. In other words, mist on the hill means bad weather.

ROSEDALE
MAP REF: 91SE7295

Rosedale is a long and pleasant valley which extends from the centre of the moors to the south-east. The River Seven, fed by moorland streams, flows along the dale and to the east are the conifers of Cropton Forest. All around are the splendid moors with some very steep hills, remarkable scenery and outstanding views.

Huge rhododendron bushes brighten the route from Lastingham and deer are known to leap out in front of passing cars. Off this road, about ¾ mile into Cropton Forest, is a Forest Office and Spiers House caravan and camping site with splendid walks and drives. There are other camping and caravan sites around the village of Rosedale Abbey as this area is becoming increasingly popular with visitors.

Rosedale Abbey is the largest community in the dale. A small priory for Cistercian nuns was founded here in 1158 but was dismantled during the Dissolution of the Monasteries in 1535. A short tower and staircase near St Lawrence's Church are all that remain, and a curious round sundial, which may have belonged to it, adorns a nearby building.

Another of Rosedale's vanished landmarks is its famous chimney, which has given its name to Chimney Bank – a twisting climb, with gradients of 1-in-3 – leading past the White Horse Farm Hotel on to the moor. At the summit there used to be a 100ft-tall chimney, a relic of last century's iron-ore boom in Rosedale. Visible for miles, it was declared unsafe and demolished in 1972.

Memories and reminders of that short but intensive burst of industry remain in the dale. Huge quantities of iron-ore were found and the first mine opened in 1851, yielding three million tons between 1856 and 1885. Other mines followed, transforming this peaceful valley into a bustling industrial complex. The population rose from 500 to 5,000, but by the 1920s the boom was declining and the mines closed after the General Strike of 1926.

The route of a remarkable railway, used to move the ore around the rim of the dale, and to provide a link with the main line at Battersby and thence to ironworks in Durham, now provides a scenic footpath from which to see the dale. It passes impressive groups of calcining kilns, where ore was roasted to reduce its weight.

The quiet village of Rosedale Abbey clusters by its green ▼

Background: serene, distinctive, and sandstone-capped, the cone of Roseberry Topping

picturesque scenery.

The river then meanders leisurely across low-lying land as it is joined by rivers flowing from the moors and other becks and streams. North of Malton, the Rye enters the River Derwent at Rye Mouth. The Derwent's long route takes it into the Ouse south of Selby and then the Humber.

The lanes of lower Rye Dale meander like the river to link a patchwork of tiny villages and hamlets. If they lack the splendour of the moors and dales, they offer instead tranquillity and a good deal of interest.

Harome has a delightful thatched inn while the quiet streets of Nunnington overlook its splendid Hall which contains a remarkable collection of miniature rooms. Built on the site of a nunnery, this fine 17th-century manor is maintained by the National Trust and is open to the public. The church, dating from the 13th century, is worth a visit and there are good views from Caulkleys Bank.

Stonegrave's tiny Minster was founded in AD727 and contains a fascinating Saxon cross. Nearby Stonegrave House, home of the late Sir Herbert Read, the poet, art

▲ Looking out over the rooftops of the steeply ordered fishing village of Runswick Bay

The old town of Malton was burnt down by Archbishop Thurstan around 1138 ▶

RUNSWICK BAY
MAP REF: 85NZ8016

One of North Yorkshire's delightful fishing villages, Runswick Bay is a collection of pretty red-roofed cottages which cling to the cliff in a most remarkable way. It is only a mile or so from the A174 Whitby to Guisborough coast road and is easily by-passed.

Its evident attractions draw tourists and this has resulted in shops, hotels, restaurants, holiday cottages and a car park at the bottom of a very steep hill.

There is a fine, sandy beach which stretches around the bay in which Runswick reclines, and in common with all these bays, visitors must beware of the fast-rising tides. Nonetheless, the sheltered waters do attract pleasure craft and there is usually a line of fishing cobles on the shore near the car park; a reminder that a fishing industry continues to operate from these shores. The lifeboat, always standing by, is a reminder of the prevailing danger of the sea. In 1901 the village women launched the heavy lifeboat themselves to save their fishermen husbands whose cobles had been caught in a storm.

RYE DALE
MAP REF: 95SE5982

One of Yorkshire's more gentle dales, Rye Dale emerges from the moors near Helmsley then broadens into a wide valley as it extends towards Malton. It has given its name to Ryedale District, the largest local authority area in England. This is based upon Malton and extends far beyond the boundaries of the dale after which it is named.

The Rye rises on Snilesworth Moor in the Cleveland Hills, flows through wooded countryside near Hawnby and past the historic ruins of Rievaulx Abbey until it reaches Helmsley via Duncombe Park. This part of its journey takes it through very

historian and author, is occasionally open to the public for the benefit of the Red Cross.

Oswaldkirk's ancient church, with Norman walls and Saxon foundations, has links with antiquarian Roger Dodsworth whose work is in the Bodleian Library. He was born here in 1585 and baptised in this church. Dedicated to St Oswald, this is one of the few villages named after the patron saint of its parish church. The modern Catholic church is a complete contrast.

Middleton church, near Pickering, has a Saxon doorway, some Norman features, and contains marvellous old crosses, while Slingsby has a 17th-century castle which was never completed or occupied. The villages of

▲ Seventeenth-century Nunnington Hall

Barton-le-Street and Appleton-le-Street are reminders that a Roman road ('stratum') passed this way into Malton ('Derventio').

Kirby Misperton, between Pickering and Malton, is the home of Flamingoland with a popular zoo and pleasure park.

Malton, with its Roman history and museum, is peaceful now that the A64 by-passes it. It is a welcoming market town (market day is on Saturday), with a wide range of shops and hotels. Heavily dependent upon agriculture, its cattle market on Tuesdays and Fridays is the third largest in Britain. Norton, separated from Malton by the River Derwent, is known for its racing stables.

SALTBURN

MAP REF: 84NZ6621

This modest seaside resort originated in medieval times as a place where salt was 'panned' by the burn, or beck, which flows into the North Sea, for trading inland. By the early 19th century it was a small fishing hamlet, sheltered by the huge bulk of Huntcliff. Old Saltburn still clusters round the Ship Inn, supposedly favoured by smugglers.

Victorian Saltburn came with the railway from 1861, when the Quaker ironmaster Henry Pease of Darlington provided the impetus for the development of the town for leisure and seaside relaxation. A simple pier was added, hotels and boarding-houses built above a steep-sided valley where there are now attractive, semi-formal gardens.

A late Victorian atmosphere still prevails, and no brash amusement arcades disturb the sea-front peace, where fine sands are cleansed by every tide. The Cleveland Way passes through before climbing Huntcliff, where the Romans had a signal station. The railway still carries passengers here from Darlington, as it has done for 130 years.

SANDSEND

SEE LYTHE

FOLKLORE

Hobs, or hobgoblins, were Yorkshire's equivalent to the Irish leprechaun or the Norwegian troll. They usually preferred to work on farms and in dairies and although they sometimes drank the cream or stopped the butter forming, they were essentially friendly, helpful little people.

Hobs were adept at avoiding prying eyes and resented anyone who used unfair means to catch them at work. They apparently had an aversion to clothes (although modesty prevailed at certain times) and considered them a hindrance as they bustled about their work. It seemed that the mere suggestion of clothes could turn them into nasty, vindictive and dangerous creatures.

Most villages had their own hob at some time but many of the stories have been forgotten and except for the occasional name –

A troll or hob, an ugly dwarf-like little man with long hair, illustrated by Florence Harrison in *The Fairy Ring* ▼

Hob of the Hasty Bank, Hob of Bransdale, Dale Town Hob of Hawnby, Hob of Studford, Hob of Egton High Moor, or a landmark or farm – Hob Holes, Hob Cave, Hob Hill, Hob Green, Hob Thrush Grange, the majority have disappeared into oblivion. However, there are three stories associated with the area which have remained prominent in Yorkshire folklore. These concern the hobs of Glaisdale Hart Hall, Runswick Bay and Farndale.

The hob of Glaisdale Hart Hall worked hard on agricultural tasks around the farm at night and was always on the look-out for extra work. One evening the opportunity arose. A farm wagon, loaded with hay, got stuck in a field and all efforts by the farmer and his men to free it failed. They considered unloading the hay but night fell so they abandoned the idea. There was no alternative but to leave the wagon where it was and take a chance on the hay getting soaked by rain.

Once the men were out of the way the hob set to work and when the farmer came down the next morning he found that the hay had all been safely stacked.

After this one of the farm hands was determined to see the hob and so when he next heard the sound of him threshing the corn inside the barn, he peeped through a crack in the wall. Surprised to see the little fellow almost naked, he persuaded the staff at Hart Hall to make the hob some clothes, which they did, and left out as a thank-offering. However, the hob was not at all pleased with the gift because he realised he had been spied on and he left the Hall for ever.

The hob at Hob Holes on the coast at Runswick Bay was supposed to have the power to cure whooping cough. He used to be called on by mothers who took their stricken children into his cave, uttering the words 'Hob Hole Hob, ma bairn's getten t'kink cough; tak' it off, tak' it off'. Whether it was the sea air or the hob's power is in question, but it usually seemed to work.

Bob o' Hurst of Farndale was another happy, hard-working little hob who took it upon himself to replace a farm worker called Ralph, who was killed in a blizzard on the moors. The hob always worked speedily and efficiently around the farm at night – and the grateful farmer left him cream with bread and butter each evening. Several years later Bob o' Hurst was still working there when the farmer's grandson inherited the property and he in turn continued to supply the hob with cream and food.

However, the grandson remarried and the hob turned to mischief when his mean new wife left skimmed milk instead of cream. The hob made the farmer's life so unbearable, that he eventually decided to move.

On the way to their new farm the couple met a neighbour who said 'Ah see thoo's flittin'. A voice piped up from the back of the cart, 'Aye we's flittin'. There sat the hob. The farmer defeated, sighed, 'Well, if thoo's theer, flittin' with us, we may as well gan yam (home) ageean!'

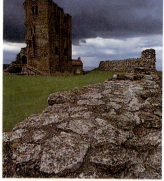

▲ Battle-wearied Scarborough Castle

SCALBY
MAP REF: 93TA0190

Scalby was once a village in its own right but is now a suburb of Scarborough with a large complex of seaside entertainment at Scalby Mills. This used to be the site of an old mill but there is now a giant fun park with shops, cafés, bars and paddling pools.

Nonetheless, reminders of Scalby's rural past remain. Inland is the church of St Lawrence with some late 12th- and 13th-century stonework and a 17th-century tower. Another link with the past is the Derwent Sea Cut. This artificial river was cut by hand between 1800 and 1810 to relieve flooding by the River Derwent. The channel reaches the coast at Scalby, near Scarborough, and is also known as the Scalby Cut (see Brompton).

While Scalby is separated from Scarborough by the North Cliff golf course, it is linked by a walk along the North Bay Promenade and by the miniature railway line which runs to Scalby Mills from Northstead Manor Gardens.

Scalby's development, directly linked to Scarborough's success as a holiday resort, has occurred since World War II, but its scenery and sheltered position on the coast of Scarborough's North Bay make it an ideal holiday base. There is a youth hostel and a touring caravan park and the Cleveland Way passes through the area. The countryside attracts naturalists and geologists and there are pleasant walks through Raincliffe Woods and into the hills behind Scalby where the National Park boundary meets the village. The woods are a continuation of the Forge Valley woodlands and towards the east, on the edge of Scarborough, is a small natural lake, Throxenby Mere.

SCALING RESERVOIR
MAP REF: 85NZ7412

Scaling Reservoir is the largest area of inland water within the North York Moors, and as it dates from about 1957, is a comparatively modern man-made lake. It is not very deep, about 30ft at most, and in the 1976 drought this fell to a mere 15ft – many large trout dying as a result. However, the reservoir has matured into a beautiful moorland lake, rich in many forms of wildlife, especially birds which favour reservoirs and inland waterways.

One peculiarity is that the county boundary between North Yorkshire and Cleveland runs north to south through the centre of the reservoir, but the lake lies within the National Park. Administered by Northumbrian Water, it offers water sports and fishing with worm or fly, as well as facilities for observing birds and other wildlife.

A parking area and picnic site has been provided and there are some excellent walks around the hamlet of Scaling and upon the surrounding moors. There is a picturesque drive through Roxby Woods down to the coast or into Staithes.

SCARBOROUGH
MAP REF: 81TA0488

The Victorians described Scarborough as 'the Queen of Watering Places' and it is England's oldest holiday resort.

There is something for nearly everyone; almost every taste and age group is catered for. It has two bays with golden sands separated by a castle-topped headland; there are modern theatres and cinemas; magnificent hotels and simple boarding houses; restaurants and shops, a busy harbour; noisy amusement arcades and quiet tea dances. There is the colourful bustle of the sea front, the gracious splendour of the Spa and the calm dignity of parks and gardens.

Add to this a quaint old market in the town centre, some very modern shops and a surrounding landscape which is beautiful by any standards and the result is a place to which visitors can return time and time again, yet always find something new.

Scarborough has a long history. The remains of very early man were found near Scarborough in 1949 and Bronze Age relics have been found at the castle. The Romans had a signalling station there and in AD966 the Vikings

South Beach, Scarborough, stretching down towards the town and castle ▼

used the natural harbour. It was the Viking leader, Thorgils Skardi, who ordered this settlement to be made, and who gave his name to the town, 'Skardiburgh'.

Invaders made use of nature's fortress behind the harbour, and on that site, in 1136, William le Gros began to construct the present castle. Piers Gaveston, favourite of Edward II, surrendered here to the Earl of Pembroke in 1312 and was executed the same year. Robert Aske, leader of the Pilgrimage of Grace, laid siege to it in 1536. Sir Thomas Stafford seized it in a revolt against 'Bloody' Queen Mary in 1557 only to lose it and his cause a few days later. The Parliamentarians took it in 1645 after a hard battle in which nearby St Mary's Church suffered serious damage. Three centuries later the castle came under attack once more when German cruisers bombarded the town in 1914.

Scarborough's modern appeal owes much to a Mrs Farrow. In 1620 she noticed that some spring water was different from the usual, with an acid taste, and soon its health-giving reputation attracted visitors from afar. In 1660 a Dr Wittie of Scarborough strongly recommended the beneficial properties of sea bathing which brought people to the town. Scarborough's success as a spa, or

watering place and resort, had started and in 1698 the first Spaw House was built.

Here the people could drink the water, but it was the Victorians who made the town the Queen of Watering Places. They built the present Spa (dropping the letter 'w'), a magnificent complex of buildings restored in 1981, welcomed the railway, constructed a promenade, built hotels, shops and theatres, landscaped the gardens and brought style to the Yorkshire coast.

The Theatre in the Round hosts the world premieres of plays by local playwright Alan Ayckbourn. There is an Open Air Theatre, a Royal Opera House and a Floral Hall with top entertainers. The Spa Complex offers dances from gentle waltzes to discos, while the seafront competes with amusements and bingo. On several afternoons in the summer there is a realistic mock battle with warships and aircraft in Peasholm Park, and for children there is the magic of Kinderland's playpark, with a spectacular waterchute nearby at Waterscene.

SINNINGTON
MAP REF: 91SE7485

Midway between Kirkbymoorside and Pickering, Sinnington is now bypassed by the A170, much to its advantage. Here, the gentle River Seven leaves its moorland background and the valley of Rosedale for the open, fertile vale country to the south. The main, and most attractive, part of the village has charming groups of houses well spaced out and facing inwards across a broad green, with the river chattering over its pebbly bed down the western side. A tiny packhorse bridge in the middle of the green presumably once had significance but now spans a dry watercourse. Stately trees cast a useful shade on summer days.

Beyond the northern corner of the green the church has Norman doorways and some Norman windows as well as pre-Conquest sculptures. To its north is the barn of Sinnington Hall. This seems to have been the great hall of a medieval manor house, added to and given new windows in the 15th century, and still presenting architectural historians with some puzzles to solve.

SLEIGHTS
MAP REF: 86NZ8607

In Whitby's more prosperous days the wealthy built their grand houses at Sleights where the River Esk moves at a leisurely pace in a cosy hollow of Esk Dale, away from the bleakness of the moors.

It is by no means a tourist's village but is a good centre in which to stay for sightseeing and touring other areas. Buses and trains serve Sleights and the main A169 passes through.

Sleights means 'flat land near water'. Modern Sleights is built on a hillside but the road from the village runs through Briggswath to Ruswarp beside the Esk, where there is boating. A striking bridge carries the A169 across the Esk above Sleights Station and provides marvellous views along the valley. Going through Sleights towards Pickering, this road climbs Blue Bank, the first road to be surfaced in the district. In 1759 it first linked Whitby to Saltersgate and by 1788 there was

Boating on the tree-fringed River Esk at Sleights. Rising on Westerdale Moor it enters the sea at Whitby ▼

a twice-weekly cart service to Pickering and York. The car park at the summit of Blue Bank gives incredible views of Whitby and the sea.

About 1½ miles upstream is a ruined chapel associated with Whitby's ancient custom of Planting the Penny Hedge, known as the Horngarth Ceremony. In 1159 three hunters drove a boar into the chapel which was the home of a hermit who protected the animal. The hunters beat the monk who subsequently died, but before dying he imposed a penance on those men.

At sunrise on the Eve of the Ascension every year they had to collect short staves from a wood on Eskdaleside, the cost of which had not to exceed one penny. They then had to go to Whitby and at 9am set their staves in the harbour mud, weaving them in the form of a small barrier to withstand three tides. If it failed, the lands of those men would be forfeited to the abbot of Whitby Abbey, or his successors. That ceremony is still conducted at Whitby annually.

At Sleights Lane End, near the junction of the A171 and A169, there is a commemorative plaque which records the first enemy aircraft shot down in England during World War II. It was a Heinkel bomber which fell nearby on 3 February 1940. The British pilot was Peter Townsend, later Group Captain Peter Townsend, known for his romance with HRH The Princess Margaret.

ON A WING AND A PRAYER

The site of the Yorkshire Gliding Club at Sutton Bank is packed with visitors most weekends, craning their necks to watch gliders soaring in the sky. It is an ideal spot for gliding, for thanks to geological changes during the Ice Age, the hills were cut away by glaciers, leaving steep-sided cliff faces, which help to provide the 'up-draught' necessary to keep the sleek, high-performance machines aloft. The gliders make use of the 10-mile edge to maintain their altitude for long periods as they meander from one end of the escarpment to the other. On good days – that is when the weather permits – the gliders encounter the right conditions which allow them to

take advantage of wind currents and cloud formations to soar on the lift of thermals. Often reaching 5,000ft from a cable launch powered by a winch, the experienced gliders can stay up for as long as they want or can even fly away from the site, often landing in a farmer's field many miles away. There are also flights launched with the help of 'tug' aircraft. The club altitude record stands at 30,200ft.

Visitors are welcome, and at weekends short trial flights can be arranged. The club holds residential courses from April to September and these provide an unusual holiday. There is always the chance of 'going solo', and a social life is there to be enjoyed at the end of the day in the circular club house.

Waiting to soar on the thermals . . . ▶

STAITHES
MAP REF: 85NZ7818

There are two parts to Staithes. The modern village stands beside the A174 as it runs along the coast to Whitby, but old Staithes is concealed below the cliffs. Coaches are forbidden to descend the steep hill into the old part and access for visitors' cars is restricted. There is a car park at the hill top.

This is an 'olde worlde' fishing community with old cottages apparently piled one on top of the other in a glorious jumble as they crowd around the tiny harbour. Narrow alleys and steep steps divide the buildings and there is no room for gardens, so it seems as if the houses huddle together as protection against the sea.

Indeed, houses have been swept away. In 1953, the Cod and Lobster Inn, which stands on the edge of the waves, was severely damaged and on a past occasion 13 houses were claimed by the sea. Staithes is constantly threatened by it as the nearby lifeboat house testifies.

Tourists are catered for here, but there are no amusement arcades, dodgems or bingo halls and the village has managed to retain its own vital character. Indeed, it is a haven for resident artists and the curious and traditional Staithes bonnets can still

be seen. The village's connection with Captain Cook, one of the world's greatest seamen, however, gives it extra interest. He was apprenticed to a grocer and draper on the seafront at the age of 17.

There is one oddity about Staithes. It has no Anglican parish church, although there is a Catholic one. The reason may be that in its early days it was merely a landing place, a 'staithe', for nearby Seaton, now part of Hinderwell.

STOKESLEY
MAP REF: 82NZ5208

Stokesley is a thriving North Yorkshire market town with a market every Friday. Lying so close to Middlesbrough, it has a great deal of affinity with Teesside and yet it stands on a plain just beyond the north-western edge of the moors. It serves both the moors and Teesside.

The A172 now by-passes Stokesley and this has removed from its main street the former large volume of heavy vehicles and through-traffic, thus allowing the town to become more leisurely and attractive. It might have also taken away some of the trade which is so important for a small town.

Stokesley does not lay claim to any particular beauty or history yet the area behind the main street, along the

River Leven, is pretty with its little bridges and flowered grassy banks and it cannot be denied that Stokesley is a gracious town with some fine late-Georgian brick houses. A particularly good grouping surrounds a green at the western end of the High Street.

The church has some medieval portions, including a 600-year-old door, but it was largely rebuilt in the 18th century. It stands in a corner near a large open area known as the Plain. This provides ample parking space for shoppers and visitors, except on Fridays when the produce market is held there. A thriving and growing livestock market is also held every Tuesday at the Auction Mart in Station Road.

One event which brings many people to Stokesley is the mammoth Stokesley Show, organised by the town's Agricultural Society. Held on the Saturday following the third Thursday in September, it occupies the Show Field on the edge of the town. This is its permanent home, the field having been purchased by the Society in 1955. The show boasts attendances of around 20,000 with visitors coming to see a huge range of livestock and agricultural and horticultural products and equipment, as well as the demonstration of associated crafts, skills and trades.

On the Wednesday preceeding the show and for the following four days, the town is taken over by Stokesley Fair. Noisy fairground vehicles and stalls literally bring the town to a halt. Apart from these four days, Stokesley is a quiet, unassuming town and a convenient base for exploring the northern edge of the moors.

Closely packed Georgian houses and a war memorial fringe the West Green in the small market town of Stokesley ▼

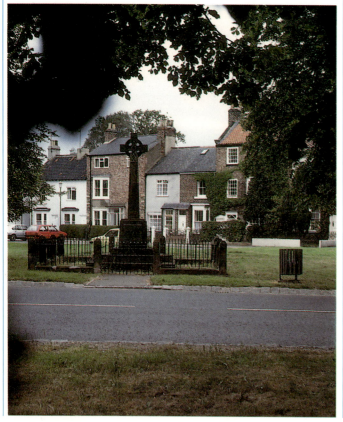

▲ Twin headlands wrap protective arms around Staithes harbour

SUTTON BANK
MAP REF: 94SE5182

There can be little doubt that the top of the escarpment known as Sutton Bank affords the finest view in Yorkshire, if not in England. The view stretches from the Pennines in the west, into Cleveland in the north and across to York in the south.

There is a large car park, a telescope and a guide to the points in sight, and a National Park Information Centre is situated here too, with books and information about the area, as well as a picnic area, refreshments and toilets. Information is available on the Sutton Bank Nature Trails and the White Horse Walk, which both start from here, each taking about two hours.

The A170 crosses Sutton Bank about 6 miles from Thirsk and climbs to the summit of Whitestonecliff over a distance of a mile, with gradients of 1-in-5, 1-in-4 and 1-in-5 again. It holds no terrors for local drivers, but strangers have problems climbing it. Caravans have been forbidden to use it since 1984.

There is a wealth of interest here. Nearby was a noted racecourse where the annual Hambleton Races were staged, and there are still racing stables here. Soaring gliders from the Yorkshire Gliding Club fill the sky when the conditions are right because the cliffs funnel the prevailing westerly winds into strong up-currents. The airfield lies a few minutes' walk from the car park along the cliff top. Visitors are asked not to walk on the airfield, but should use the footpath.

Bilberries grow here too and make lovely pies!

Another winding footpath, part of the nature trail, descends the steep slopes to Lake Gormire. This pretty lake, ⅓-mile in circumference, can be seen from the summit and is remarkable because there are no streams flowing in or out of it. It is a natural lake rich with wildlife and probably dates from glacial times. One legend says it is bottomless, while another claims it hides a complete village.

The Cleveland Way passes along the summit, and the old Hambleton Drovers' Road used by cattle en route from Scotland to Malton and York also passed this way.

SWAINBY
MAP REF: 82NZ4702

Although Swainby has all the appearances of a modern village, it dates back to the 14th century, and possibly earlier. When nearby Whorlton was attacked by a plague, the people moved away and settled here, but it is probable that this was already a community.

Signs of its ancient history were obliterated when it became a village for jet- and ironstone-miners last century.

Houses were built and some are still known as Miners' Cottages. The miners used donkeys for carrying their belongings and grazed them on nearby Live Moor. Those who lived in the neighbouring district came into Swainby to spend their money, a fact still marked by the Miners' Arms.

Swainby, with its fine parish church, occupies a flat area beneath the moors. Behind the village is Scarth Nick, a gap in the hills where a steep, twisting climb leads on to the moors near Osmotherley where there is good walking country. The route of the Cleveland Way footpath crosses Scarth Nick and the start of the Lyke Wake Walk is also nearby. An old drovers' road climbed onto the moors from Swainby via Scarth Nick.

Leading into the moors behind Swainby is Scugdale, a quiet valley with a hamlet called Huthwaite. This tiny dale, less than 3 miles long, has produced two remarkable people.

One was Elizabeth Harland who died in 1812, having lived until she was 105, and the other was a giant of a man, Henry Cooper. By 1890 he was 8ft 6in tall, and the world's tallest living man. He worked as a farm labourer before joining Barnum and Bailey's Circus, married a tall woman from the circus, and died aged 32.

The clock towerette in the busy Market Place at Thirsk ▶

THIRSK
MAP REF: 94SE4282

Thirsk and the surrounding countryside have become known as Herriot Country thanks to the books of James Herriot, and the television series. The town is visited by those seeking the famous veterinary surgeon, his premises, and the countryside which inspired his books.

But there is a good deal more in Thirsk. It is a busy town in two parts, the old and the new. The new, 18th-century part, has a fine cobbled market place surrounded by stores, restaurants, antique shops and some fine coaching inns. There are delightful alleys leading to a variety of craft shops and small business premises. The Clock Tower, erected in 1896, is a focal point and stands near the Bull Ring. This cobbled area is used as a coach park but bulls were tethered here prior to being baited well into the 18th century.

The old part of Thirsk is centred around St James' Green which was once the market place. In the 11th century a castle stood near Cod Beck, which flows prettily through the town, but that has long since gone.

The parish church of St Mary is magnificent. Known as 'the Cathedral of the North' because of its splendour, the tower was started in 1410 and it took 50 years to complete the church. There is an impressive roof and some delicate tracery in the battlements which furnish the walls, and one of its bells came from Fountains Abbey. The altar stone is from Byland Abbey.

In Kirkgate, on the approach to the church, is the town museum. It was once the home of Thomas Lord, born in 1775, founder of Lord's Cricket Ground in London. Thirsk Racecourse was opened in 1854.

▲ This delightful thatched cottage overlooking Thornton Beck in Thornton Dale is justifiably one of Yorkshire's most-photographed houses

THORNTON DALE
MAP REF: 92SE8383

The boundary of the National Park loops southwards near Pickering to include this attractive village. Even though the A170 runs through the centre, Thornton Dale has retained its charm and is a Mecca for visitors.

As long ago as 1907 it was voted the most beautiful village in Yorkshire, a title which may still apply. Its shops, inns, cafés and a lovely forge all provide excuses for staying, and there are lovely walks beside the bubbling streams and through the village lanes. There is a spacious car park in the grounds of the hall, a fine Tudor building which is now a residential home (but with a public bar).

Just off the A170, beside the bridge which crosses the stream near the parish church of All Saints, is one of the most photographed homes in Britain. So beautifully proportioned is this fine, thatched cottage that it appears on calendars, chocolate boxes and magazine covers, as well as advertisements. The frontage is usually bright with flowers and it makes an unforgettable picture.

Roxby Castle used to stand a mile or so along the road to Pickering. This was home of the Cholmleys. Sir Richard Cholmley was known as the 'Great Black Knight of the North' at the time of Elizabeth I and is buried in the parish church. Also buried there is Matthew Grimes who died in

1875 aged 96. He stood guard over Napoleon at St Helena and helped carry the emperor to his grave.

Other features of the village include a 600-year-old market cross and a set of stocks on the green; 12 almshouses completed in 1670 and an old grammar school founded in 1657. There are pleasant walks through Ellerburn towards Dalby Forest.

Thornton Dale is often called Thornton-le-Dale and there are still arguments about its correct name.

UGTHORPE
MAP REF: 85NZ7911

In its remote situation on the moors above Whitby, Ugthorpe is more a place of pilgrimage than a tourist attraction. It is a small village with an old windmill and some sturdy stone houses and farms.

The village is perhaps best known for its adherence to the Roman Catholic faith. It was one of the few villages to maintain a resident Catholic priest throughout the Reformation when Catholics were

▼ Terraced cottages on the single, undulating main street of Thornton Dale

being persecuted. Priests' hiding places have been found in some of Ugthorpe's old buildings, including an oak-panelled Elizabethan farmhouse which was once the hall. A chimney in a stable contained a priest hole.

Ugthorpe's part in the survival of the ancient faith came about because during the Reformation priests who had been trained and ordained overseas were secretly brought back by sea. They came ashore near Whitby and were then smuggled into 'safe houses' at Ugthorpe before taking up appointments in the north.

Father Nicholas Postgate, martyred at York in 1679, lived at the Hermitage which is near Ugthorpe and ministered locally in his disguise as a gardener. The present Catholic Church of St Anne was opened in 1857 by Cardinal Wiseman, the first Archbishop of Westminster. The much smaller Anglican Christ Church which stands opposite was opened in the same year.

▲ Hunter's Sty packhorse bridge over the young River Esk at Westerdale. The structure probably dates from as early as the 13th century

Anglican Christ Church, a strange encounter in historically Catholic Ugthorpe ▼

UPSALL
MAP REF: 94SE4587

This tiny place, tucked among leafy lanes on the wooded slopes of the Hambleton Hills, has had three castles. One is ruined, one was burnt to the ground in 1918 and the other is still used as a home. Near the entrance to the latter is a fine forge built in 1859 whose entrance is shaped like a giant horseshoe and which bears the words 'Upsall Town'. The roads hereabouts afford marvellous views across to the Pennines and over the Vale of York.

The first castle was built in the 14th century by the Scropes, an ancient Yorkshire noble family, and is known for its 'Crock of Upsall Gold' legend. Finding his castle in ruins, Scrope dreamt that if he stood on London Bridge he would become rich. So he walked the 250 miles to London and stood for hours on the famous bridge. Nothing happened and he began to think he had been fooled. However, a stranger appeared and told Scrope he had had a strange dream; he had dreamt there was a crock of gold under an elderberry tree at Upsall Castle – a place he did not know. Scrope hurried back to Upsall, found the gold and regained his place in society.

On the plain below, near Felixkirk, is Nevison House, the supposed home of highwayman William Nevison, nicknamed Swift Nick by Charles II.

WASS
MAP REF: 95SE5579

Peaceful Wass reclines within the most southerly tip of the North York Moors and is reached by narrow, winding lanes between Coxwold and

▼ An attractive stone cottage, Wass

Ampleforth. One route is to turn off the A170 at Tom Smith's Cross, then descend the steep Wass Bank with its wonderful views of Byland Abbey.

Tom Smith's Cross, marks the point where several minor roads enter the A170 on the summit of its long descent into Helmsley. Tom Smith was reputedly a highwayman who was gibbetted and the stone base of his gibbet is said to be here.

From Wass there is an exhilarating walk from the crossroads through Elm Hagg Wood to an observatory above Oldstead. Another route leads through the woods and emerges on to a leafy lane just beyond Byland.

WESTERDALE
MAP REF: 84SE6605

This remote, beautiful valley marks the head of Eskdale. The River Esk is born on the slopes of Westerdale Moor and flows northwards before swinging into its eastwards course above Castleton. Westerdale village is a small cluster of modest stone cottages along both sides of a short street. Nearby, Hunter's Sty is a medieval packhorse bridge, over-restored last century and now heavily shaded by trees. Roads climb the surrounding moors, north-westwards to Kildale, southwards to Hutton-le-Hole, north-eastwards to Castleton; and roadside crosses testify to a long use of these ancient routes. Major J Fairfax-Blakeborough, author of many books on rural life and sport, as well as contributing regular columns to northern newspapers for more than 50 years, lived for most of his life at Low House, on the Castleton road, until his death in 1976, aged 92.

▲ Steps and houses tumble down towards the harbour at Whitby, where the River Esk flows out into the North Sea

WHITBY
MAP REF: 86NZ8911

Whitby's place in the religious, maritime and literary history of England is assured. As an English town it is unique. Moors embrace it on three sides, to the north it faces the hostile North Sea; which, until the mid-18th-century arrival of the turnpike road from Pickering, was its main channel of communication with the outside world. Victorian times brought the railway, linking it to Pickering, York, Middlesbrough and Scarborough. Only the Esk Valley line from Middlesbrough now operates.

The River Esk bisects Whitby creating two very different towns. Old Town is to the east, where the starkly beautiful ruins of Whitby Abbey crown the clifftop. Here, in the 7th-century predecessor, the abbess Hilda ruled, and in the Synod of Whitby in AD664 the date of Easter was determined. Here, the cowherd Caedmon sang of the Creation, and English poetry was born. Caedmon is commemorated by a large stone cross at the top of the famous 199 Steps, the old way to the parish church of St Mary's. The church is homely, lovable and quite unique, not architecturally but as a social document of growth during Whitby's prosperous days between 1697 and 1818. The Victorians scarcely touched it.

Far below, along Church Street, are the shops selling souvenirs, books, jet, junk, antiques, and kippers. Close-clustered cottages crowd behind in yards, or face the street; here lived the fisherfolk, whalers, mariners and men who built and repaired the wooden ships that sailed distant seas and brought prosperity. Across the harbour, spanned now by an iron swing bridge manned for two hours each side of high water, is the present Fish Quay, always fascinating. Behind is the paraphernalia of holiday-making, amusement arcades, bingo saloons, assorted souvenir shops and sea-food stalls. Above the swing bridge a larger harbour, used by timber-importing ships, adjoins a large, modern marina. Narrow streets, with a variety of more modern shops, climb to the hotels, boarding-houses and gardens of George Hudson's planned development when he brought the railway to Whitby in the 1840s. Near the whalebone arch the modernised spa complex looks towards the sea.

Waterfront and hillside views are constant rewards along alleys, down steep steps, across textured roofs loud with gulls. Tourism has overtaken fishing as Whitby's chief industry, and there is a wide variety of accommodation. Car parking is, however, always a problem, although the modern high-level bridge ½ mile up river does help to keep out the north-south through-traffic, as well as providing a sensational view of this two-in-one town, which inspired Bram Stoker's *Dracula*, at the end of last century. Frank Meadow Sutcliffe's magnificent photographs, displayed in the Sutcliffe Gallery, evoke the same period, and are a source of delight to thousands of visitors.

WHORLTON
MAP REF: 82NZ4802

There is no village at Whorlton now, only a farm, a melancholy church ruinous since 1875, and a sturdily impressive gatehouse; part of a 14th-century enlargement to an important 12th-century castle. Above its huge entrance are shields bearing the arms of the Meynell, d'Arcy and Gray families. Latimers also lived there at one time, and for a few years at the end of Henry VIII's reign it passed to the Crown.

In the 1560s, when it belonged to the Lennox family, Margaret, Countess of Lennox, is known to have written from here to Mary, Queen of Scots, proposing that she marry her son, Lord Darnley, which she did in 1565. The son of that marriage became James VI of Scotland and James I of England, the first of the Stuart kings. Whorlton can therefore lay claim to a significant role in the history of both kingdoms.

The gatehouse, now owned by Viscount Ingleby, is scheduled as an Ancient Monument, and is freely accessible. So, too, is the nearby church of The Holy Cross, whose chancel is still used as a burial chapel. Inside is a curious stone recess containing a rare, beautiful oaken effigy, probably of Nicholas de Meynell, and dates from the early 14th century.

Whorlton's sudden demise is explained by the arrival in 1428 of the

TRADITIONAL BUILDINGS

It is doubtful if any farmhouse, house, cottage or village in the North York Moors today remotely resembles its appearance two centuries ago. Rebuilding, renovation, or so-called restoration has ensured that. However, it is possible occasionally to glimpse what such buildings looked like.

The basic plan of a typical, pre-18th-century farmhouse of the region was that of a long-house. At its simplest this was single-storeyed, cruck-framed, with stone walls and a ling-thatched roof. The family lived at one end, with accommodation for livestock at the other. Between these areas a cross-passage ran from front to back, with doors from each side leading into the 'house' and the 'byre'. A larger farmhouse may have had an extra bay, and sometimes used loft space beneath the rafters for sleeping or storage.

Spout House, by the Sun Inn in Bilsdale, is an outstanding example of a 16th-century long-house that has survived remarkably intact. Faithfully

plague. The disease reduced the population to ten people, and the survivors left the village, moving a mile away to Swainby. Only the castle and church remained.

WYKEHAM
MAP REF: 93SE9683

This village of mellow stone houses justifies a halt, for there are pleasant walks nearby (the Derwent Way passes by) and a most interesting lych gate. The church, which replaced the earlier All Saints, was built in the 19th century and features the delightful oak carving of 'Mousey' Thompson. The remarkable lych gate is in fact the tower of an earlier chapel and stands apart from the main building. This gave rise to a legend that two sisters decided to build a church here, but quarrelled before it was completed. One built the tower and the other built the church at a discreet distance. The story is, however, pure fancy.

The truth is that there was a Cistercian nunnery at Wykeham in 1153, but it was destroyed by fire. Then, in the 14th century, John de Wykeham founded the chapel of St Mary and St Helen, but it fell into disrepair. In 1855, after the present church was built in 1853, the tower of the ancient chapel was restored and fashioned into this unique lych gate.

Modern Wykeham Abbey is a large house set in parkland and it occupies the site of the ancient nunnery. The seat of Viscount Downe, it is occasionally open to the public.

YARM
MAP REF: 80NZ4112

Standing within a horseshoe-shaped loop of the River Tees, Yarm used to be a North Riding market town. Before 1974 the river formed the boundary with County Durham but the local government changes of that year placed Yarm within the new county of Cleveland.

Nonetheless, it retains the aura of a Yorkshire market town, although the weekly market is no longer held. The long, main street with its cobbled verges and range of lovely old inns and Georgian buildings, plus a market hall dating from 1710, help to maintain that image. There is little doubt that Yarm, once a busy town and indeed a port and the lowest bridging point on the Tees until 1771, stepped into the shadows as Middlesbrough and Stockton rapidly developed.

However, Yarm has its place in history. It was here, on 12 February 1820, that five men met in the George and Dragon Inn in the High Street to discuss their request to Parliament to build a railway. The result was the world's first public railway from nearby Stockton to Darlington. Their initiative changed the world's transport system, and that historic meeting is commemorated by a plaque on the wall of the George and Dragon.

Another reminder of Yarm's railway history is the huge 43-arch viaduct which passes over the houses of the town. Built of brick and stone, it is one of the biggest viaducts in England.

The town does contain reminders of its earlier history. Known for its annual fair, which was once a cheese fair, Yarm's name comes from the Danish 'Jarum'. The church is part Norman, and there was a friary here in the 13th century. In Chapel Wynd is the fine octagonal chapel of 1763, often visited by John Wesley, who called it 'by far the most elegant in England'.

Yarm's position on the River Tees means it is prone to flooding, but a lowering of the river bed has reduced this danger.

Across the river is Eaglescliffe, with its junction on the Stockton to Darlington railway, and Egglescliffe, an elevated village with a green and views across Yarm.

---

restored by the National Park Authority, it is open to the public. A former cruck-framed cottage from Danby, dismantled in 1966, it has been re-erected at the Ryedale Folk Museum, Hutton-le-Hole.

Some villages along the northern edge of the Vale of Pickering, have cruck-framed buildings, although the crucks are hidden beneath later stonework. But the steep pitch of their roofs, identified as the inverted 'V' of cruck timbers at the gables, shows in Rose Cottage, White Cottage and Cliff Cottage at Beadlam, at Orchard House, Harome, as well as in cottages at Pockley, Rievaulx and in Farndale.

Their structure made it easy to extend and enlarge long-houses simply by adding one or more bays, or by incorporating rooms in the roof space. At Spaunton, a yeoman's house dated 1695, is a cruck-framed house, with cross-passage and three bays. Until 1913 it had a thatched roof, and it has now acquired dormer windows.

By the middle of the 18th

century timber was being replaced by stone – readily obtainable from quarries on the moorland edge – as the main building material. At the same time pantiles, introduced via Whitby and subsequently manufactured in tileries there and around Pickering, were replacing thatch. Most of the farmhouses seen today were built, or rebuilt, between 1740 and 1840, using the warm, yellow sandstone in the moorland areas and cool grey limestone in the southern uplands. Styles had changed. Houses became two-storeyed and more box-like in appearance, yet with associated structures added

lengthwise, still maintained a 'false' long-house (without the cross-passage) appearance.

In valleys such as Farndale, Bilsdale, Bransdale, Danby Dale and the Fryup Dales, isolated farmhouses, neatly spaced out along the valley length, are usually two-storeyed, with a byre attached to the lower end of the house, resulting in attractive, stepped roof lines. The more urbane, balanced formality of Georgian houses seen in a number of villages represents the end of traditional or vernacular architecture, and the arrival of railways introduced Welsh slate as roofing material.

A traditional cruck-framed cottage at Ryedale Folk Museum, Hutton-le-Hole ▶

◀ The elements have sculpted age-old rock outcrops into mysterious shapes and forms to create what are collectively known as Bride Stones

FACT FILE

CONTENTS

Places to Visit
Stately homes, castles, gardens, museums, theme parks and other attractions

Sports and Activities
Angling, cycling, golf, gliding, riding and trekking, sailing, walking, watersports

Craft Shops
A selection of workshops producing original items

Useful Information
Addresses, tourist information centres, market days, theatres and cinemas

Customs and Events
A calendar of festivals

PLACES TO VISIT

This is a selection of places to visit within the North York Moors. Each is listed under its nearest town or village, and where possible the entries correspond to those in the gazetteer section of the book.

The opening times given are intended to provide a rough guide only. Very often a place may just open for part of the day, or close for lunch. Also, although stated as open all year, many places are closed over Christmas and New Year. Full information should be obtained in advance of a visit, from a local tourist information centre (see pages 75–6).

Many places are owned either by The National Trust or are in the care of English Heritage, and if this is the case the entry is accompanied by the abbreviation NT or EH.

Telephone numbers are given in brackets.

BH = bank holiday
Etr = Easter

BYLAND ABBEY
SEE WASS

CASTLE HOWARD
SEE MALTON

COXWOLD
Newburgh Priory. *Country home with wild water garden.* Open mid-May to Aug, Wed and Sun.

Shandy Hall. *Former home of Laurence Sterne, with adjoining wild garden.* Open Jun to Sep, Wed and Sun. Other times by appointment.

DANBY
Botton Village. *Community of mentally handicapped adults. Visitors welcome; products from bakery, glassworks, and sawmill on sale.*

The Moors Centre, Lodge La. *Information on the North York Moors National Park with woodland grounds and children's area.* Open Apr to Oct, daily; Nov to Mar, Sun only.

EBBERSTON
Ebberston Hall. *Small 18th-century country house.* Open Etr to Sep, daily.

GILLING EAST
Gilling Castle. *Now a preparatory school for Ampleforth College, but gardens and great chamber open.* Chamber open during term time, Mon to Fri; garden open Jul to Sep, Mon to Fri.

GREAT AYTON

Captain Cook Schoolroom Museum, High St. *Maps, books etc connected with the explorer's life.* Open Etr to Oct, daily. Other times by appointment

GROSMONT

North York Moors Railway. *Runs to Pickering through Newtondale.* Open Etr to Oct, most days. Santa Specials in Dec.

GUISBOROUGH

Gisborough Priory (EH). *Augustinian foundation.* Open Apr to Sep, daily; Oct to Etr, Tue to Sun.

HELMSLEY

Helmsley Castle (EH). *Ruins within huge earthworks. Exhibition.* Open Etr to Sep, daily; Oct to Etr, Tue to Sun.

Duncombe Park. *Early 18th-century mansion set in 30-acre landscaped garden.* Open Etr to Sep, Sun to Thu.

HUTTON-LE-HOLE

Ryedale Folk Museum. *Reconstructed buildings, crafts, displays of rural life.* Open end Mar to Oct, daily.

KIRBY MISPERTON

Flamingoland Zoo and Family Funpark, Kirby Misperton Hall. *Rides, exhibitions, lake, animals.* Open Apr to Sep, daily.

MALTON

Castle Howard. *Early 18th-century Baroque house with large collection of 18th- to 20th-century costume.* Open daily, Mar-Nov.

Eden Camp Modern History Theme Museum. *Devoted to civilian life in World War II and housed in former PoW camp.* Open daily, Feb to Dec.

Malton Museum. *Local history.* Open all year.

MOUNT GRACE PRIORY

SEE OSMOTHERLEY

NUNNINGTON

Nunnington Hall (NT). *Large house with Carlisle collection of miniature rooms.* Open Apr, weekends only; Etr and May to Oct, Tue to Sun.

ORMESBY

Ormesby Hall (NT). *Mansion with good furniture and 18th-century paintings.* Open Apr, certain days; May to Sep, Wed, Thu, Sun and BHs; Oct, Wed and Sun.

OSMOTHERLEY

Mount Grace Priory (NT and EH), Staddle Bridge. *Beautiful Carthusian ruins.* Open Etr to Sep, daily; Oct to Etr, Tue to Sun.

PICKERING

Beck Isle Museum of Rural Life, Bridge St. *Regency building housing exhibitions of local life and customs.* Open Apr to Oct, daily.

North York Moors Railway, see Grosmont.

Pickering Castle (EH). *Ruins of former royal hunting lodge above the town.* Open Apr to Sep, daily; Oct to Etr, Tue to Sun.

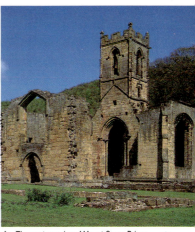

▲ The austere ruins of Mount Grace Priory, founded in 1398

RAVENSCAR

Staintondale Shire Horses, East Side Farm. *Working horses, carts and wagons.* Open May to Sep, Sun, Tue, Wed and Fri.

RIEVAULX

Rievaulx Abbey (EH). *Magnificent Cistercian ruins.* Open Apr to Sep, daily; Oct to Etr, Tue to Sun.

Rievaulx Terrace (NT). *Curving terrace overlooking the abbey. Mock Greek temples, frescoes and exhibition on English landscape design.* Open Apr to Oct, daily.

ROBIN HOOD'S BAY

Smuggling Experience, Bank Top. *A theme museum with sound, sights and smells of the 18th century.* Open Jan and Mar to Oct, daily.

SCARBOROUGH

Art Gallery, The Crescent. *Italianate villa with permanent collection.* Open in summer, daily; winter, Tue to Sun.

Rotunda Museum, Vernon Rd. *Regional archaeology and natural history.* Open summer, daily; winter, Tue to Sun.

Scarborough Castle (EH). *Substantial remains on headland above the town.* Open Apr to Sep, daily; Oct to Etr, Tue to Sun.

Woodend Museum, The Crescent. *Former home of the Sitwell family; books, paintings etc, plus a natural history museum.* Open summer, daily; winter, Tue to Sun.

THIRSK

Osgodby Hall, 5m E of Thirsk. *Jacobean manor house.* Open Etr to Sep, Wed and BH Mon.

Thirsk Museum, 16 Kirkgate. *Local life and industry exhibits.* Open Apr to Oct, daily.

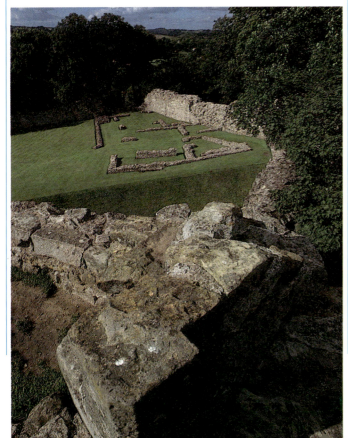

WASS

Byland Abbey (EH). *Haunting ruin with exhibition of carved stone and finds.* Open Etr to Sep, daily; Oct to Etr, Tue to Sun.

WHITBY

Captain Cook Memorial Museum, Grape La. *An 18th-century merchant's house where Cook lodged. Period furnishings etc.* Open end Apr to end Oct, daily.

Sutcliffe Gallery, 1 Flowergate. *Display of Frank Meadow Sutcliffe's maritime and rural photographs.* Open all year, Mon to Sat; also Sun in Jul and Aug.

Whitby Abbey (EH). *Benedictine ruins.* Open Apr to Sep, daily; Oct to Etr, Tue to Sun.

▼

Whitby Lifeboat Museum, Pier Rd. *Boats and models and local history of the RNLI.* Open summer, daily; winter, weekends only.

Whitby Museum, Pannett Park. *Cook, Whitby jet, whaling and ship-building exhibits.* Open all year, daily.

SPORTS AND ACTIVITIES

The following information is by no means comprehensive and further details can be obtained from the authorities and contacts given.

Addresses are listed under Useful Information on page 75.

ANGLING

The North York Moors area offers a wide range of freshwater fishing locations, as well as the possibility of sea fishing.

The River Esk is the principal salmon and sea trout fishery in Yorkshire and there are also the rivers Rye and Derwent and their tributaries.

Lakes and reservoirs include Lake Arden, Bilsdale; Cod Beck Reservoir, Osmotherley; Scaling Dam Reservoir; Lockwood Beck Reservoir; and Scarborough Mere.

A rod licence must be obtained to fish any water and to fish a particular water a permit is also needed. Full information may be obtained from Yorkshire Water or Northumbria Water Tees Division.

CYCLING

Bicycles can be hired at the following places.

Gillamoor. *Mountain Bike Hire,* Gales House (0751 31258).

Helmsley. *Footloose in North Yorkshire,* Borogate (0439 70886).

Scarborough. *Len Raine Cycles,* 25 Victoria Road (0723 365751).

Thirsk. *Dial-a-Bike,* Briar House, Pickhill (0845 567435).

Whitby. *Mountain Bike Tours,* Serenity Camping and Caravan Park, Hinderwell (0947 840523).

GLIDING

Stokesley. *Newcastle and Teeside Gliding Club,* Carlton Bank (0642 778234).

Sutton Bank. *Yorkshire Gliding Club* (0845 597237).

GOLF

The following clubs and courses welcome visitors.

Easingwold. *Easingwold,* Stillington Road, 1m S of Easingwold (0347 21964).

Filey. *Filey,* West Avenue (0723 513293).

Kirkbymoorside. *Kirkbymoorside,* Manor Vale (0751 31525).

Malton. *Malton & Norton,* Welham Park, Norton, 1m S of Malton (0653 692959).

Scarborough. *Scarborough North Cliff,* North Cliff Avenue, 2m N of town centre (0723 360786). *Scarborough South Cliff,* Deepdale Avenue (0723 374737).

Thirsk. *Thirsk & Northallerton.* Thornton-le-Street, 2m N of Thirsk (0845 522170).

Whitby. *Whitby,* Sandsend Road, Low Straggleton, 1½m NW of Whitby (0947 602768).

RIDING AND TREKKING

Helmsley. *Bilsdale Riding Centre,* Shaken Bridge Farm, Hawnby (04396 252).

Robin Hood's Bay. *Farsyde Stud and Riding Centre* (0947 880249).

Scarborough. *Snainton Riding Centre,* Station Rd, Snainton (0723 859218). *Wellfield Trekking Centre,* Staintondale Road, Ravenscar (0723 870182).

Sinnington. *Friar's Hill Riding Stables,* Friar's Hill (0751 32758).

Whitby. *Borrowby Equestrian Centre* (0947 840134).

▼ The West Beck, near Mallyan Spout

▲ Yacht bedecked shores at Scaling Dam reservoir

SAILING

SEE WATERSPORTS

WALKING

There are numerous opportunities for walking in the North York Moors, including various guided walks of up to five miles led by a National Park ranger.

Further information about these, and the series of Waymarked Walks, is available from the National Park at Helmsley, and other National Park Information Centres.

The following is a selection of the long-distance walks and trails in the area.

The **Cleveland Way**, marked with an acorn symbol, runs between Helmsley and Filey for 93 miles.

The **Lyke Wake Walk** is a 40-mile route from Osmotherley to Ravenscar.

The **Esk Valley Walk** follows the River Esk from source to mouth in 10 short, linking sections.

The **White Rose Walk**, 34 miles, joins the White Horse near Kilburn to Roseberry Topping in Cleveland.

The **Derwent Way**, 17 miles, follows the Derwent from its source on Fylingdales Moor to West Ayton.

The **Reasty to Allerton Forest Walk** is a 16-mile route through Forestry Commission land.

The comparatively calm waters of Scaling Dam provide a suitable playground for windsurfers ▶

Trails include:

Bridestones Moor Nature Trail. This 2-mile walk starts at the car park 3 miles north-east of Low Dalby.

Goathland Rail Trail. A 2-hour walk along the track bed of George Stephenson's original railway from Goathland to Grosmont.

May Beck Trail. A 3-hour walk from Maybeck.

Sutton Bank Nature Trail. A 2-hour walk along the escarpment edge, close to Lake Gormire.

WATERSPORTS

Dinghy Sailing. Scaling Dam Reservoir (0642 783262).

Rowing and Canoeing.
River Esk, Ruswarp (0947 604658).
Sleights (0947 810329).
Osmotherley (0609 82571).
Cropton (07515 228).

Facilities for inland sailing are also available at Scarborough.

There are several facilities for off-shore sailing along the coast, and enquiries should be made locally. Advice is also available from HM Coastguard (0723 372323 or 0947 602107).

CRAFT SHOPS

An abundance of craft workshops, markets and galleries ensures that wherever you go in the North York Moors there is the chance of finding a gift of local origin.

COXWOLD

Coxwold Pottery. *Handmade earthenware and stoneware.*

KILBURN

Robert Thompson's Craftsmen Ltd. *Oak furniture bearing the famous mouse.*

LEALHOLM

Forge Pottery. *Distinctive hand-thrown stoneware.*

WYKEHAM

Ankaret Cresswell. *Handwoven fabrics in natural fibres.*

USEFUL INFORMATION

ADDRESSES

English Heritage (EH), Bessie Surtees House, 41-44 Sandhill, Newcastle-upon-Tyne NE1 3JF (091-261 1585).

The National Trust (NT), Goddards, 27 Tadcaster Road, Dringhouses, York Y02 2QG (0904 702021).

Northumbrian Water Group, PO Box 4, Regent Centre, Gosforth, Newcastle upon Tyne NE3 3PX (091 284 3151).

North York Moors National Park, The Old Vicarage, Bondgate, Helmsley, York (0439 70657).

Yorkshire and Humberside Tourist Board, 312 Tadcaster Road, York YO2 2HF (0904 707961).

Yorkshire Water, 21 Park Square South, Leeds LS1 2QG (0532 440191).

Youth Hostels Association, Yorkshire Regional Group, 96 Main Street, Bingley, West Yorkshire BD16 2JH (0274 567697)

INFORMATION CENTRES

Those marked with an asterisk are not open during the winter.

Danby,* The Moors Centre, Lodge Lane (0287 660654).

Easingwold,* The Galtres, Chapel Lane (0347 21530).

▲ Malton cattle market

Great Ayton,* High Green (0642 722835).

Guisborough, South Cleveland Heritage Centre, Fountain St (0287 633801).

Helmsley, Town Hall (0439 70173).

Hutton-le-Hole,* Ryedale Folk Museum (07515 367).

Malton,* The Old Town Hall, Market Place (0653 600048).

Pickering, 7 Eastgate Square (0751 73791).

Scarborough, St Nicholas Cliff (0723 373333).

Sutton Bank,* Sutton Bank, near Thirsk (0845 597426).

Thirsk,* 14 Kirkgate (0845 522755).

Whitby, New Quay Road (0947 602674).

MARKET DAYS

Guisborough, Thursday, Saturday

Helmsley, Friday

Kirkbymoorside, Wednesday

Malton, Saturday

Northallterton, Wednesday, Saturday

Pickering, Monday

Stokesley, Friday

Thirsk, Monday

Whitby, Saturday

THEATRES AND CINEMAS

There are theatres at Pickering and Scarborough, and cinemas at Malton, Pickering and Scarborough.

CUSTOMS AND EVENTS

Although the events shown in this section usually take place in the months under which they appear, the actual dates of many vary from year to year.

Numerous other events such as fêtes, county shows, flower festivals and horse shows also crop up regularly in the area.

Full details of exactly what is happening where can be obtained from tourist information centres (see pages 75–6) or local newspapers.

JANUARY

Plough Stots Service, Goathland (Sunday after 6th). *Church service during which a plough is blessed. On the following Saturday there are traditional sword dances in the village.*

FEBRUARY

Shrovetide Skipping Festival, Scarborough (Shrove Tuesday). *Crowds skip along Foreshore Road.*

MAY

Planting the Penny Hedge, Whitby (morning of Ascension Eve). *Symbolic planting of a hedge in Whitby Harbour.*

JULY

Ryedale Festival, Helmsley (late July to early August).

Kilburn Feast, Kilburn (second week). *Four days of sports, quoits and a procession.*

AUGUST

Old Gooseberry Show, Egton Bridge (first Tuesday). *Open to anyone in the country, provided they become a member of the society.*

SEPTEMBER

Blessing the Boats, Whitby (first Sunday).

Boats of the Whitby fishing fleet ride at anchor within the safe haven of Whitby harbour. The austere abbey ruins crown the hill above the town ▼

Atlas

▲ Levisham Valley

The following pages contain a legend, key
map and atlas of the North York Moors,
three motor tours and sixteen coast and
countryside walks.

MAP SYMBOLS

THE GRID SYSTEM

The map references used in this book are based on the Ordnance Survey National Grid, correct to within 1000 metres. They comprise two letters and four figures, and are preceded by the atlas page number.
Thus the reference for Pickering appears 91 SE 7983

91 is the atlas page number

SE identifies the major (100km) grid square concerned (see diag)

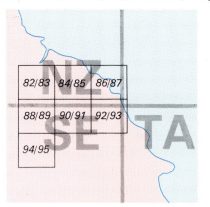

7983 locates the lower left-hand corner of the kilometre grid square in which Pickering appears

79 can be found along the bottom edge of the page, reading W to E

83 can be found along the right hand side of the page, reading S to N

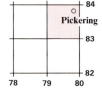

ATLAS 1:63,360 – 1" TO 1 MILE ROADS, RAILWAYS AND PATHS

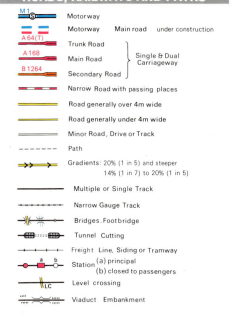

M1	Motorway
	Motorway Main road under construction
A 64(T)	Trunk Road
A 168	Main Road — Single & Dual Carriageway
B 1264	Secondary Road
	Narrow Road with passing places
	Road generally over 4m wide
	Road generally under 4m wide
	Minor Road, Drive or Track
	Path
	Gradients: 20% (1 in 5) and steeper / 14% (1 in 7) to 20% (1 in 5)
	Multiple or Single Track
	Narrow Gauge Track
	Bridges. Footbridge
	Tunnel Cutting
	Freight Line, Siding or Tramway
	Station (a) principal (b) closed to passengers
	Level crossing
	Viaduct Embankment

PUBLIC RIGHTS OF WAY

	Road used as a Public Path
	By-way open to all traffic
	Footpath
	Bridleway

Public rights of way indicated by these symbols have been derived from Definitive Maps as amended by later enactments or instruments held by Ordnance Survey on 1st December 1989 and are shown subject to the limitations imposed by the scale of mapping.
Later information may be obtained from the appropriate County Council.
The representation in this atlas of any other road track or path is no evidence of the existence of a right of way

Danger Area — MOD Ranges in the area. Danger! Observe warning notices

BOUNDARIES

	National		County
	National Park		District
NT	National Trust	NT	always open
		NT	opening restricted
FC	Forestry Commission		Pedestrians only – observe local signs

GENERAL FEATURES

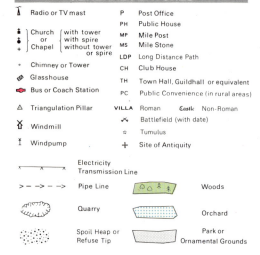

	Radio or TV mast	P	Post Office
	Church or Chapel with tower / with spire / without tower or spire	PH	Public House
		MP	Mile Post
		MS	Mile Stone
	Chimney or Tower	LDP	Long Distance Path
	Glasshouse	CH	Club House
	Bus or Coach Station	TH	Town Hall, Guildhall or equivalent
	Triangulation Pillar	PC	Public Convenience (in rural areas)
	Windmill	VILLA Roman Castle Non-Roman
	Windpump	Battlefield (with date)
		Tumulus
		Site of Antiquity
	Electricity Transmission Line	
	Pipe Line	Woods
	Quarry	Orchard
	Spoil Heap or Refuse Tip	Park or Ornamental Grounds

WATER FEATURES

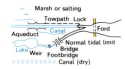

Marsh or salting / Towpath Lock / Aqueduct Canal Ford / Normal tidal limit / Lake Weir Bridge Footbridge / Canal (dry)

HEIGHTS AND ROCK FEATURES

outcrop cliff 500 scree 250

Contours are at 50 feet vertical interval

To convert feet to metres multiply by 0·3048

Heights shown close to a triangulation pillar refer to the station height at ground level and not necessarily to the summit

TOURS

2	Start point of tour		Featured tour
	Direction of tour	6	Point of Interest

TOURIST INFORMATION

	Camp Site		Nature reserve
	Caravan Site		Other tourist feature
	Information Centre		Preserved railway
	Parking Facilities		Racecourse
	Viewpoint		Wildlife park
	Picnic site		Museum
	Golf course or links		Nature or forest trail
	Castle		Ancient monument
	Cave		Places of interest
	Country park		Telephones: public or motoring organisations
	Garden	PC	Public Convenience
	Historic house		Youth Hostel
	Mountain Rescue Post		

Waymarked Path / Long Distance Path / Recreational Path

TOURS 1:250,000 – ¼" TO 1 MILE ROADS AND RAILWAYS

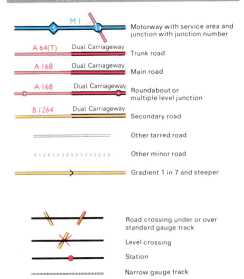

M1	Motorway with service area and junction with junction number
A 64 (T) Dual Carriageway	Trunk road
A 168 Dual Carriageway	Main road
A 168 Dual Carriageway	Roundabout or multiple level junction
B 1264 Dual Carriageway	Secondary road
	Other tarred road
	Other minor road
	Gradient 1 in 7 and steeper

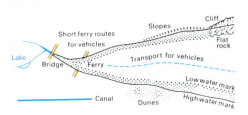

	Road crossing under or over standard gauge track
	Level crossing
	Station
	Narrow gauge track

WATER FEATURES

Cliff
Slopes
Flat rock
Short ferry routes for vehicles
Transport for vehicles
Lake
Bridge   Ferry
Low water mark
High water mark
Canal   Dunes

GENERAL FEATURES

Buildings

Wood

⊕ Civil aerodrome (with custom facilities)

ᛁ Radio or TV mast

ᛁ Lighthouse

ʕ ʔ Telephones : public or motoring organisations

ANTIQUITIES

⁘ Native fortress

------ Roman road (course of)

ꞔastle • Other antiquities

CANOVIVM • Roman antiquity

RELIEF

Feet	Metres	
		.274
		Heights in feet above mean sea level
3000	914	
2000	610	
1400	427	
1000	305	Contours at 200 ft intervals
600	183	
200	61	
0	0	To convert feet to metres multiply by 0.3048

WALKS

Start point of walk	Line of walk
Direction of walk	Alternative route
	③ Point of interest

WALKS 1:25,000 – 2½" TO 1 MILE ROADS, RAILWAYS AND PATHS

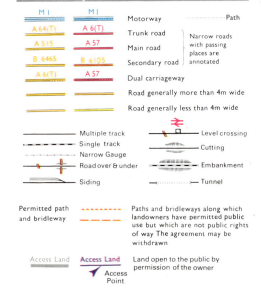

M1	M1	Motorway
A 64(T)	A 6(T)	Trunk road
A 515	A 57	Main road
B 6465	B 6105	Secondary road
A 6(T)	A 57	Dual carriageway
		Road generally more than 4m wide
		Road generally less than 4m wide

Path

Narrow roads with passing places are annotated

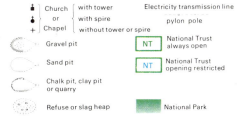

Multiple track		Level crossing
Single track		Cutting
Narrow Gauge		Embankment
Road over & under		Tunnel
Siding		

Permitted path and bridleway ---------- Paths and bridleways along which landowners have permitted public use but which are not public rights of way The agreement may be withdrawn

Access Land   Access Land Land open to the public by permission of the owner

↙ Access Point

GENERAL FEATURES

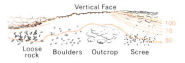

♦ Church	with tower	Electricity transmission line
♦ or	with spire	pylon pole
+ Chapel	without tower or spire	
Gravel pit		NT National Trust always open
Sand pit		NT National Trust opening restricted
Chalk pit, clay pit or quarry		
Refuse or slag heap		National Park

HEIGHTS AND ROCK FEATURES

Contours are at 10 metres vertical interval

50 } Determined { ground survey
285 } by { air survey

Surface heights are to the nearest metre above mean sea level Heights shown close to a triangulation pillar refer to the station height at ground level and not necessarily to the summit

Vertical Face
100
70
50
Loose rock   Boulders   Outcrop   Scree

PUBLIC RIGHTS OF WAY

Public rights of way shown on this Atlas may not be evident on the ground.

- - - - - - - - }	Public Paths {	Footpath
- - - - - -		Bridleway
+++++		By-way open to all traffic
-+-+-+-		Road used as a public path

Public rights of way indicated by these symbols have been derived from Definitive Maps as amended by later enactments or instruments held by Ordnance Survey between 1st October 1982 and 1st March 1985 and are shown subject to the limitations imposed by the scale of mapping.
Later information may be obtained from the appropriate County Council.

The representation on this map of any other road, track or path is no evidence of the existence of a right of way.

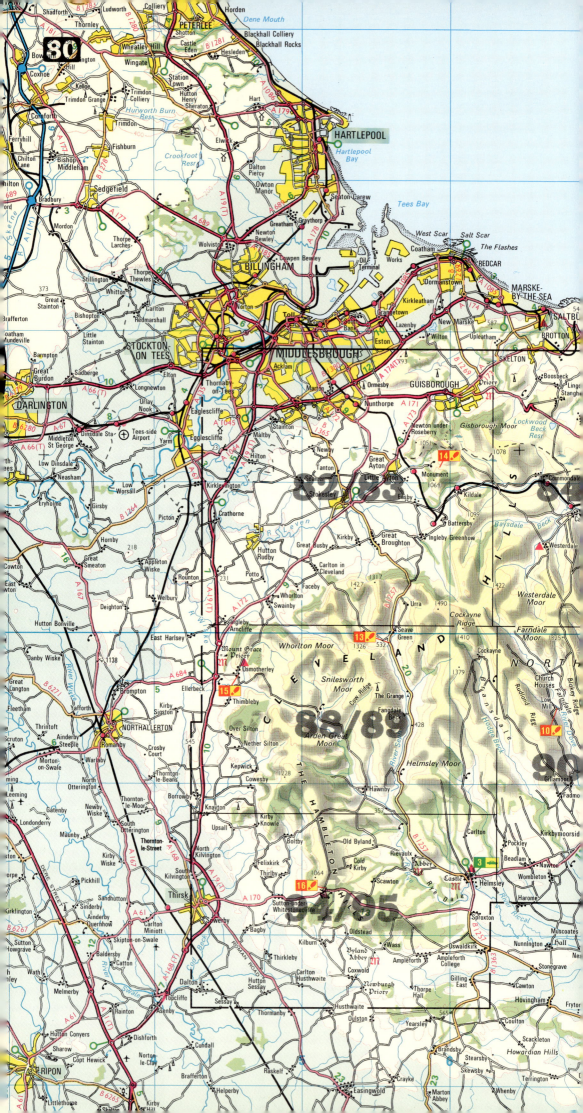

Key to Atlas pages

Distances in miles to PICKERING
Map Ref: 91 SE 7983

Bridlington	31	Leeds	49
Doncaster	70	London	232
Durham	69	Middlesbrough	41
Harrogate	49	Newcastle	78
Hull	44	York	25

NORTH YORK MOORS

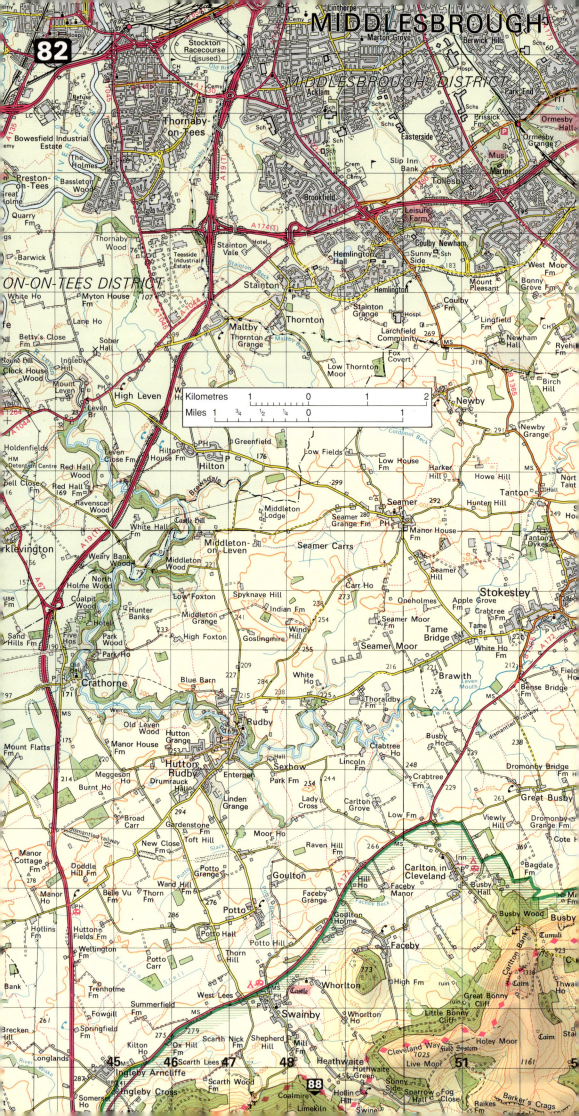

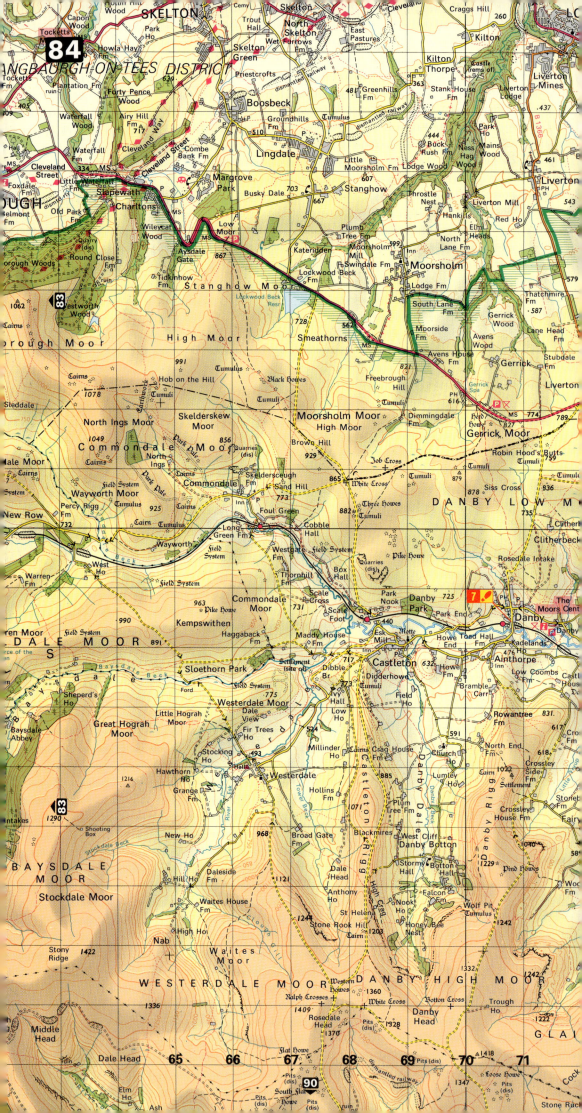

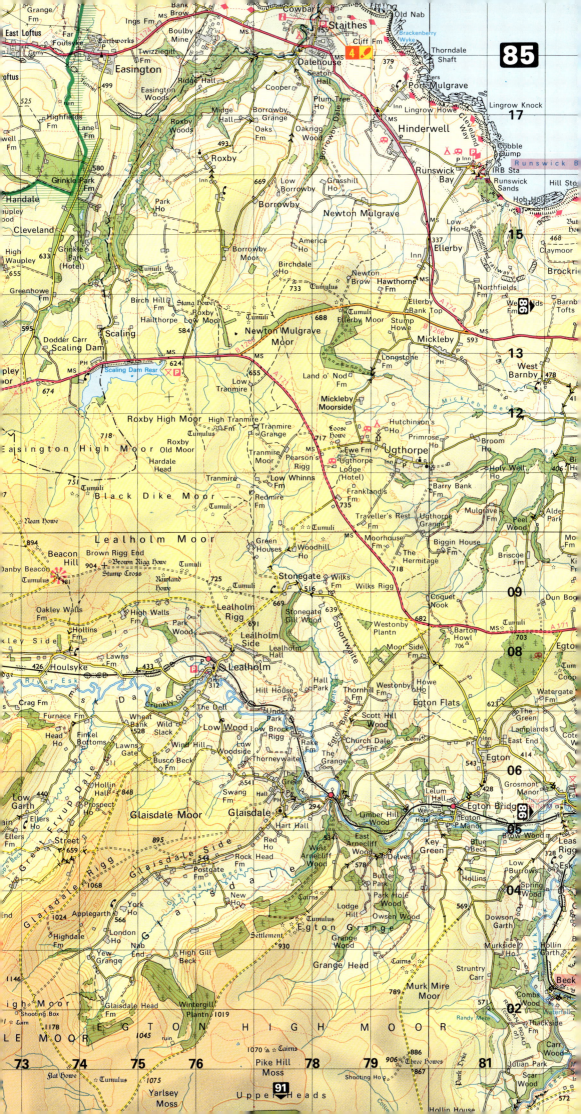

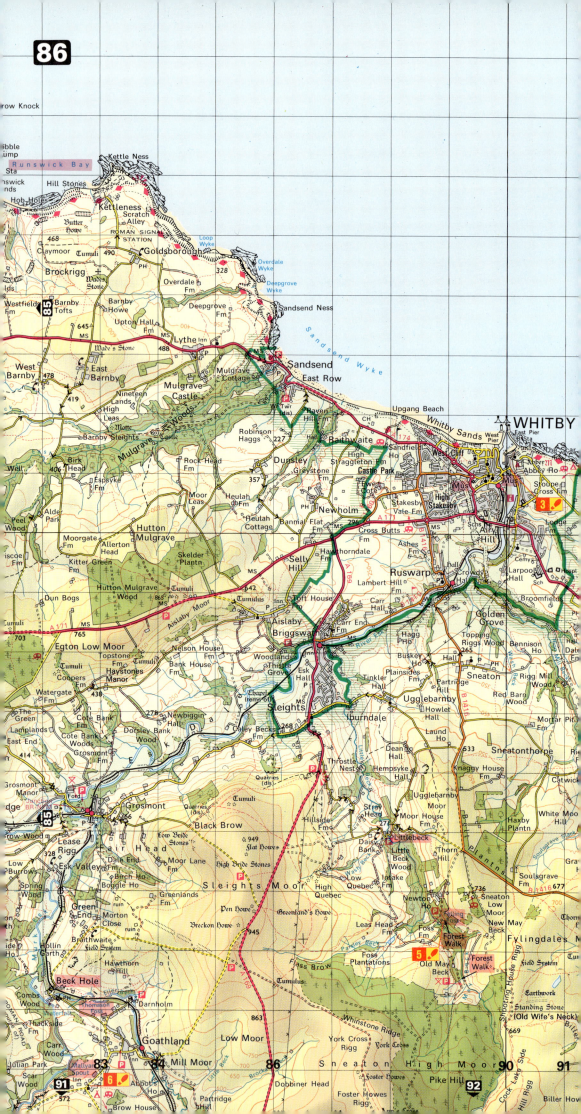

17

16

15

14

13

12

11

10

09

08

07

06

05

04

03

02

wick Nab

attwick
Bay

Black Nab

Cleveland Way

Highgate
Howe

use
es

Moat

Beacon
Hill

Widdy
Field

Hall 304

sacre

Gnipe
Howe

Long Lease

Maw Wyke
Hole

339

366

262

White Stone
Hole

MS

sker Hall
Fm

Hawsker Bottoms

dismantled railway

Low
sker

High
Hawsker

PH

Bottom
Ho

Homerell Hole

Mitten Hill Fm

444

462

T'awd Abba Well

443

Castle Chamber

Normanby

555

Smailes Moor
Fm

Ness Point or
North Cheek

562

High
Normanby

368

Raw

2

Robin Hood's Bay

Skerry
Hall

723

PH

Fylingthorpe

350

P

Mus

Park
Gate

Fyling Hall
(Sch)

179

Farsyde
Ho

Robin Hood's Bay

Latter
Gate Hills

Low
Fm

Boggle Hole

hwork

Tumuli

Standing
Stones

Ramsdale

Ramsdale Beck

Stoupe Beck
Sands

umulus

Oak Wood

Fyling
Park

Demesne
Fm

Stoupe Brow

25

Park Wall

Cottage Fm

Fyling Old Hall

Cleveland

Old Peak or
South Cheek

St Ives
Fm

Swallow Head
Fm

157

Way

Stoupe

Brock Hall
Fm

Kirk Moor

Howdale
Wood

Oxbank
Wood

Robin
Hood's Butts

Raven Hall
Hotel

Ravenscar

604

Thorney
Brow

Spring
Hill

Brow Moor

Brow

Blea Wyke
Point

Pond

Low Flask
Fm

Farm
Hotel

Howdale Moor

871

98

P

99

00

92

538

MS

94

95

96

93

Beacon Howes

757

Cook
Ho

Flask Inn

Tumuli

Stony Mart
Howes

Green Dike

570

Tumulus

Rigg

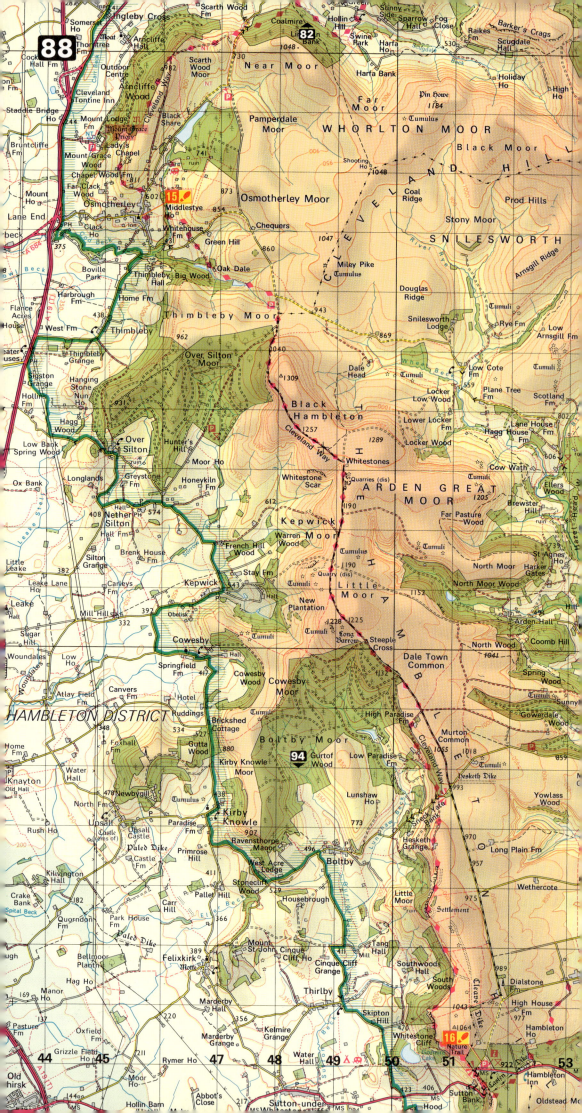

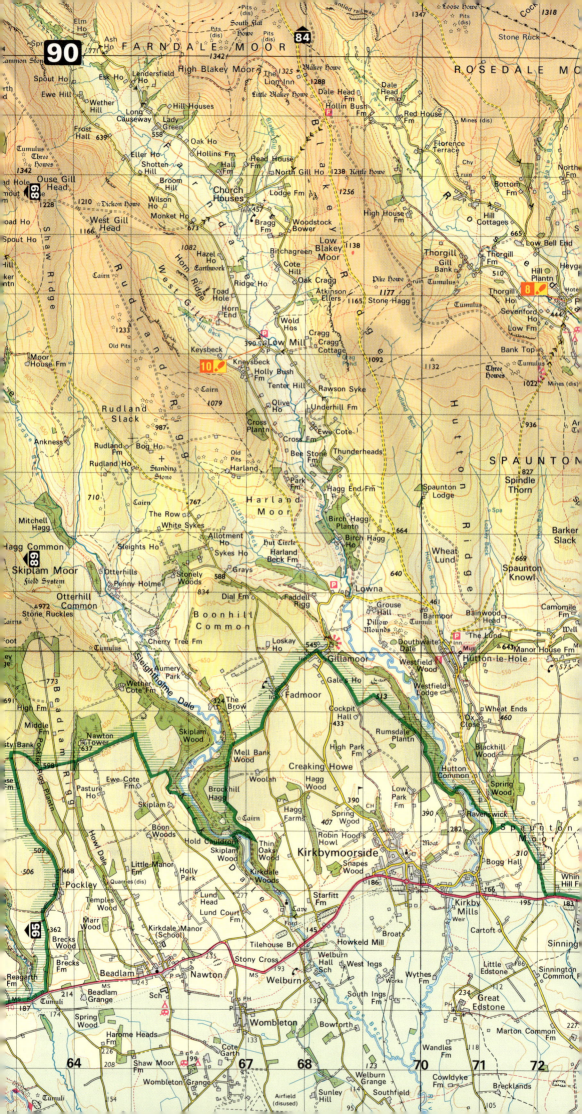

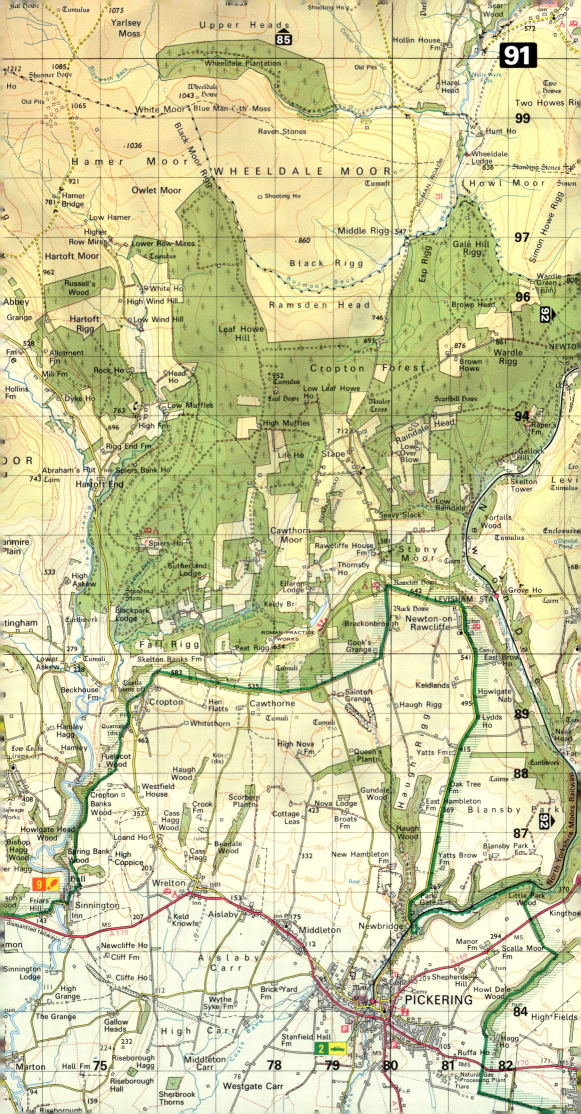

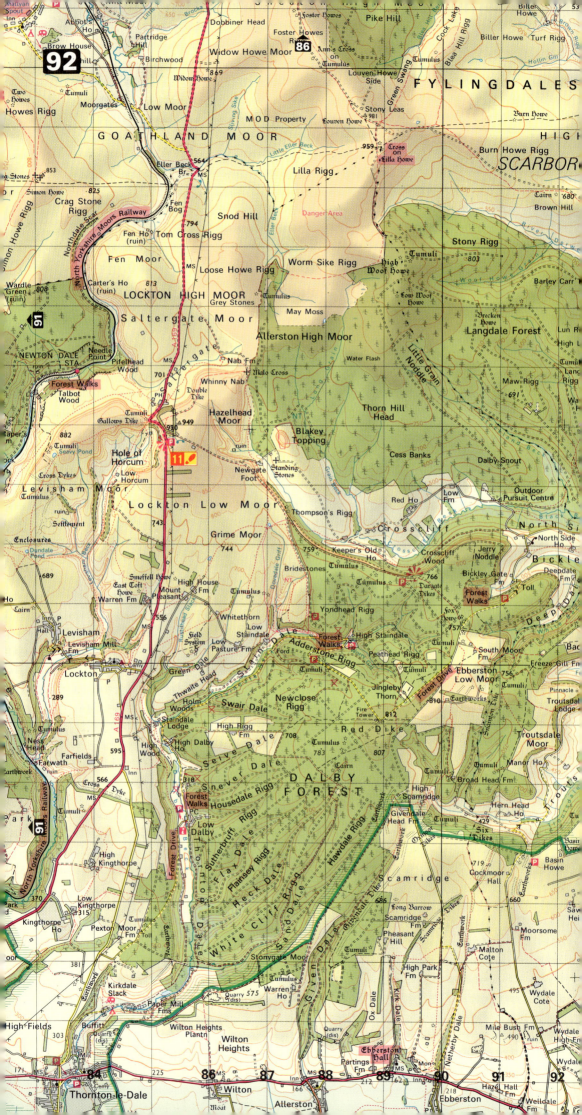

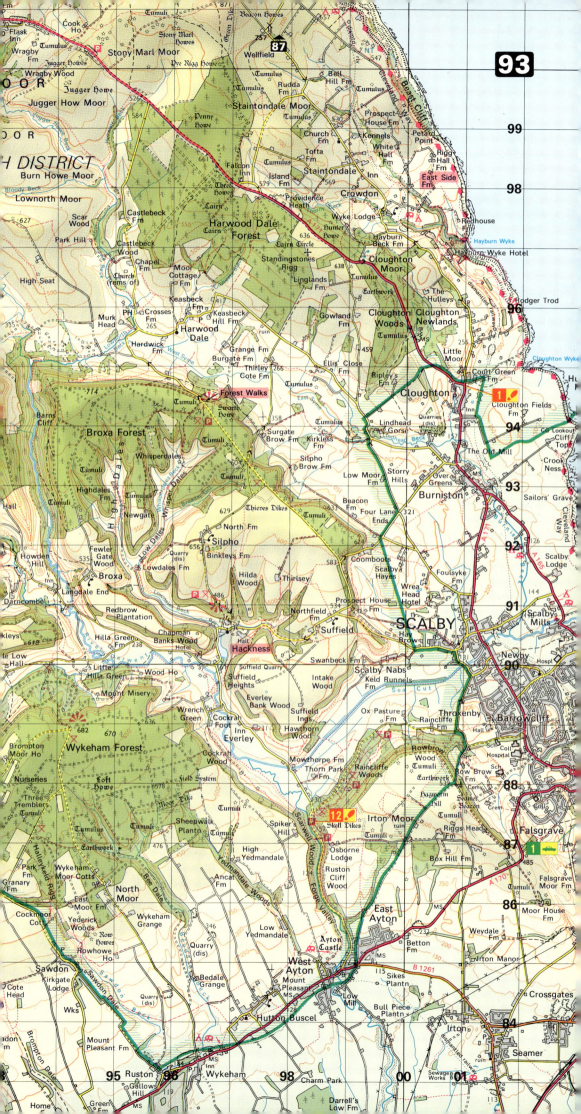

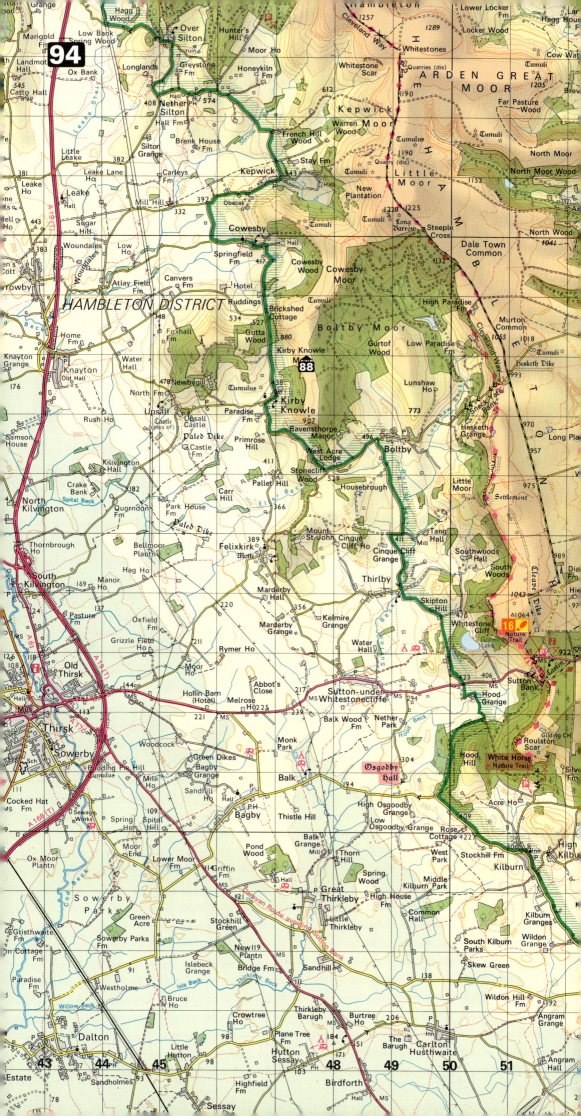

TOUR 1
COAST TO FOREST

The variety of the North York Moors National Park can be seen on this tour: the large resort of Scarborough and the small fishing village and port of Whitby; bleak moors, cool forests and picturesque villages.

ROUTE DIRECTIONS

*The drive starts from Scarborough*①.

Follow the signs North Bay then Whitby (A171) to leave on the A165. In 1 mile, at the roundabout, keep left and continue to Burniston. Here turn right on to the A171, signposted Whitby. At Cloughton bear left then pass through an afforested area before emerging on the desolate Fylingdales Moor. After 9½ miles turn right on to an unclassified road, signposted Fylingthorpe and Robin Hood's Bay. Descend a steep (1 in 4) hill with hairpin bends to reach the village of Fylingthorpe. Keep straight on to Robin Hood's Bay. The main thoroughfare is narrow and descends very steeply to the shore. From May to September there is restricted access for motor vehicles②.

From the village follow the signs Whitby along the B1447 to reach Hawsker. Bear right, and at the end of the village turn right on to the A171. Just over ¼ mile farther turn right again on to an unclassified road, signed Whitby Abbey. There are good coastal views before reaching the cliff-top ruins of Whitby Abbey.③.

Return for ¼ mile and turn right (no sign). At the foot of the descent turn right and later cross the swing bridge into the town centre of Whitby④.

Leave by the Teesside road, A171, and in 2 miles turn left on to the A169, signposted Pickering. Continue to Sleights. Beyond the village the road climbs on to Sleights Moor. Continue for 3 miles. Here a detour can be taken by turning right on to an unclassified road to Goathland⑤.

Continue with the main drive, following an undulating road over bleak moorland⑥.

Pass by the lonely Saltergate Inn then ascend. Pass, on the right, the natural amphitheatre known as the Hole of Horcum⑦.

In 4 miles, at the Fox and Rabbit Inn, turn left on to an unclassified road, signposted Thornton Dale. Two miles farther turn left, signed Low Dalby Forest Drive. Shortly join a Forestry Commission toll road. During periods of extremely dry weather the Forest Drive may be closed owing to the high fire risk.

If you wish to avoid the toll road continue to the picturesque village of Thornton Dale⑧.

Turn left on to the A170, signed Scarborough. The drive can be rejoined at Snainton. The main tour soon passes Low Dalby⑨.

Turn left at the visitor centre and continue on the Forest Drive. This passes through beautiful woodland scenery in the Dalby Forest. After 5 miles, at a fire tower, turn left and then in 2 miles leave the forest drive. In ¾ mile, at a T-junction, turn right, signposted Scarborough. Pass the Moorcock Inn at the hamlet of Langdale End, then in 1 mile turn sharp right signposted Troutsdale and Snainton. Proceed along an undulating and winding road through Troutsdale.

After 4 miles leave the valley, keeping left on the ascent. At Snainton turn left on to the A170, signposted Scarborough, and pass through Brompton⑩.

Continue to West Ayton, then cross the River Derwent and turn left on to an unclassified road, signed Forge Valley. The road follows the river through the thickly wooded Forge Valley.

In 1¾ miles turn right, signed Lady Edith's Drive. A short detour can be made by keeping forward at this junction for a nearby picnic site and viewpoint. Continue with the main drive through the Raincliffe Woods. Two miles farther pass a pond on the right, then in another mile, at a T-junction, turn right (A171), to re-enter Scarborough.

POINTS OF INTEREST

①Described by the Victorians as the 'Queen of Watering Places', Scarborough is England's oldest holiday resort. It has the Victorians to thank for the magnificent Spa complex, the promenade, and many of the shops, hotels and theatres.

②There is no hard evidence to link Robin Hood with this quaint seaside village, although the Bay does have a rich heritage of legends. It has fine beaches with rocky outcrops.

③First founded almost 13 centuries ago, most of the present ruins of St Hilda's Abbey are in the Early English style and date from the 13th century.

④Red roofed houses separated by narrow streets cover the steep valley sides on both banks of the River Esk at Whitby. The harbour still shelters a variety of boats, a reminder of the town's long seafaring past.

⑤Goathland is one of the most picturesque villages in the North York Moors, with superb stone houses. It has a station for the North York Moors Railway.

⑥To the left there are views of the Fylingdales Ballistic Missile Early Warning Station.

⑦Also known as Devil's Punchbowl, the Hole of Horcum is a huge natural hollow in Levisham Moor. The remote and lonely Saltersgate Inn has a peat fire which is supposed to have kept alight since it was lit in 1801.

⑧Among the most beautiful villages in Yorkshire, Thornton Dale has one of the most photographed homes in Britain, a charming thatched cottage. Other features include a 600-year-old market cross and 12 almshouses.

⑨Low Dalby is the thriving centre for the tourist boom which has developed locally because of the recreational value of the forests.

⑩Brompton has a special place in aviation history for it was here, in 1853, that Sir George Cayley devised a glider which flew 50yds.

TOUR 2
MOORLAND AND DALES

On this drive exhilarating high moorland with superb views contrasts with green dales and pretty villages. The many places well worth stopping to visit include the Moors Centre at Danby and the Ryedale Folk Museum.

ROUTE DIRECTIONS

The drive starts from Pickering ①.

Follow the Whitby road, A169, gradually climbing towards the moors. After 4¾ miles pass a turning on the left to Lockton. A detour can be made to visit the hilltop villages of Lockton and Levisham on the edge of the Tabular Hills ②.

Descend to the steep valley of Newton Dale. Continue the main tour, climbing to 920ft on Lockton Low Moor and passing on the left the Hole of Horcum ③.

Descend the Saltergate Inn. Continue on the A169 for 2¾ miles before turning left on to an unclassified road, signed Goathland ④.

Cross Goathland Moor before descending to Goathland. Bear right and pass the Mallyan Hotel to enter the village ⑤.

Follow signs for Whitby and cross the railway. Climb steeply on to the moors and after 2 miles turn left on to the A169. In another ¼ mile turn left again on to an unclassified road, signed Grosmont and Egton. The road crosses Sleights Moor. Later there are fine views to the right along Esk Dale. Descend steeply into Grosmont ⑥.

Proceed ahead over the level crossing and River Esk, and then ascend steeply (1 in 4) to reach Egton ⑦.

In the village bear right and, at the Wheatsheaf Inn, turn left, signed Glaisdale. Continue with the Castleton road and in 1 mile bear right. In another ¾ mile, at the T-junction, turn right for Lealholm. Recross the River Esk then turn left, signed Danby. Continue through Esk Dale for 3½ miles to reach the Moors Centre ⑧.

Keep left to reach the village of Danby ⑨.

Go over the staggered crossroads and continue to Castleton. Follow the Rosedale signs and in ½ mile bear left to climb along the 1,000ft-high Castleton Rigg. After 4 miles turn left, still signposted Rosedale ⑩.

Cross the plateau of Rosedale Moor for 4 miles and then descend into Rosedale before turning left for Rosedale Abbey ⑪.

At the end of the village turn right and ascend Rosedale Chimney Bank (1 in 3) ⑫.

Cross Spaunton Moor. After 3 miles, at the T-junction, turn right for Hutton-le-Hole ⑬.

Turn left on to the Kirkbymoorside road. In 2¾ miles, at a T-junction, turn left on to the A170, signed Scarborough. Return through the Vale of Pickering, passing through the villages of Wrelton, Aislaby and Middleton to Pickering.

POINTS OF INTEREST

① Pickering's now-ruined castle was used as a hunting lodge by English kings between 1100 and 1400. Although the site was fortified in pre-Conquest days, the present stone buildings date from the 12th century. The Castle saw action on several occasions but was not used during the Civil War. The town is the southern terminus of the North York Moors Railway.

② Lockton and Levisham are a pair of tiny villages separated by a deep and spectacular valley. Lockton's church has a squat, 15th-century tower, a medieval nave and chancel and a 14th-century arch.

③ The Hole of Horcum is a spectacular natural hollow that is popular with hang-gliders. See also Tour 1.

④ The Fylingdales Ballistic Missile Early Warning Station can be seen to the right of the A169.

⑤ Goathland has a station for the North York Moors Railway and there are several attractive waterfalls nearby. Mallyan Spout, 70ft, can be reached by a footpath which starts near the Mallyan Hotel. See also Tour 1.

⑥ The village of Grosmont developed in the 19th century to house miners for the local iron mining industry. The northern terminus of the North York Moors Railway is here.

⑦ Egton, from Egetune, meaning town of oaks, stands on the hill above Egton Bridge – one of Yorkshire's prettiest villages. The Egton Bridge Old Gooseberry Society holds a show of giant gooseberries every August.

⑧ The Centre is an information and interpretation centre for the North York Moors National Park.

⑨ Of interest in Danby are the remains of 14th-century Danby Castle and the high-arched Duck Bridge over the River Esk, built in 1386.

⑩ On the left pass a small medieval white cross known as Fat Betty with a separate round headstone sitting on top of the main 'body'. Coins used to be left under the top stone for poor travellers.

⑪ Rosedale became a busy mining centre after the discovery of ironstone in 1856. Next to the church are the scant remains of the 12th-century Cistercian nunnery after which the village of Rosedale Abbey was named.

⑫ Named after a previous landmark, a remnant of the iron industry, the view from the summit of Rosedale Chimney Bank, 1,022ft, is superb. The chimney was demolished in 1972 for safety reasons but the arches of iron kilns can still be seen on the right.

⑬ One of the showpieces of the Moors, Hutton-le-Hole's houses, inn and shops surround a spacious and undulating village green. A major attraction is the Ryedale Folk Museum.

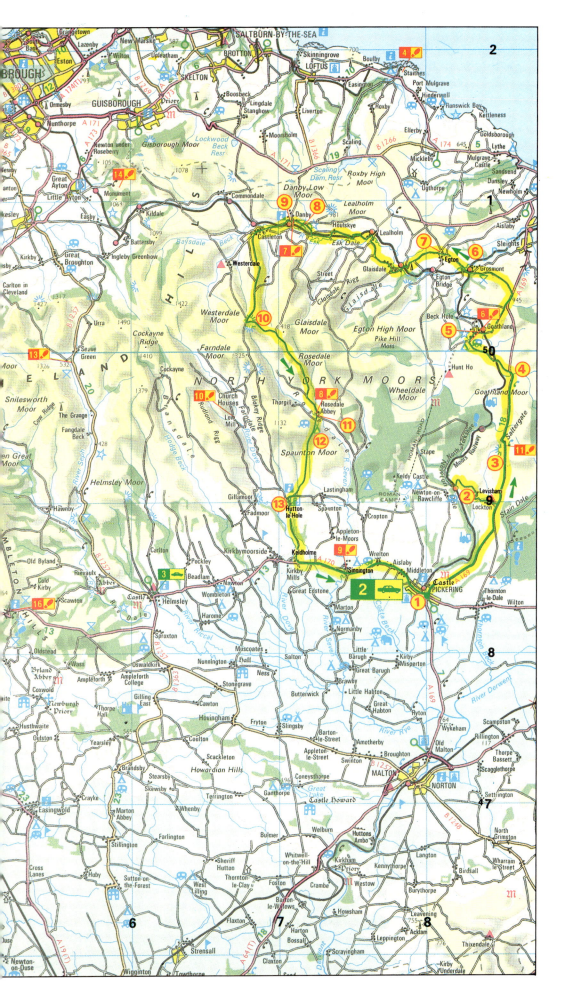

TOUR 3
ABBEYS AND PRIORIES

This drive through hilly country includes fine viewpoints and has a particular appeal for those interested in the rich Christian architectural heritage of the Moors area.

ROUTE DIRECTIONS

The drive starts from Helmsley ①.

Follow the signs Stokesley to leave by the B1257. Ascend and, in 1½ miles, turn left on to an unclassified road, signposted Scawton. Descend steeply through thick woodland before turning right by the near side of the river bridge, signed Rievaulx Abbey. Follow the River Rye to Rievaulx ②.

Continue with the unclassified road and ascend through the woods to the junction with the B1257. To the right is the entrance to Rievaulx Terrace ③.

To continue with the main drive turn left, signed Stokesley, and rejoin the B1257 which climbs to over 800ft, with fine views from the Newgate Bank Picnic Area. Descend into Bilsdale. Here the moors rise to over 1,100ft on both sides of the dale.

Pass through the hamlet of Chop Gate (pronounced 'Chop Yat') to reach the 842ft road summit of Clay Bank. To the east is Botton Head, 1,489ft, the highest point on the moors.

Descend through a forested area to Great Broughton. Two miles farther, at a roundabout, take the second exit to enter Stokesley. Leave by following signs to Thirsk (A172) and in ¾ mile turn right on to the A172. Follow the foot of the Cleveland Hills for 8 miles before branching left to join the A19. In ½ mile a road to the left can be taken to visit Mount Grace Priory ④.

Remain on the A19 for ½ mile then branch left on to the A684, signposted Northallerton, and continue to Northallerton ⑤.

Follow the signs Thirsk to leave by the A168. In 7 miles turn right on to the B1448 to enter Thirsk ⑥.

Follow the signs Scarborough to leave by the A170 and approach the escarpment of the Hambleton Hills. Beyond Sutton-under-Whitestonecliffe pass a turning, on the right, to Osgodby Hall ⑦.

Begin the steep ascent of Sutton Bank ⑧ with gradients of 1 in 4.

In just over ¼ mile turn right on to an unclassified road, signed White Horse Bank. One mile farther begin the descent of White Horse Bank (1 in 4). The huge figure of a horse was cut into the hillside in 1857. At the foot of the descent keep forward for the village of Kilburn ⑨.

Continue with the Coxwold road and in 1½ miles bear right, then at the T-junction turn left. Pass Shandy Hall before entering Coxwold ⑩.

At the crossroads turn left, signed Byland. Alternatively keep forward with the Oulston road to visit Newburgh Priory ⑪.

Continue with the main drive to Byland Abbey ⑫.

At the village of Wass turn right for Ampleforth ⑬.

At the end of the village bear right signposted Oswaldkirk and pass Roman Catholic Ampleforth College. Reach Oswaldkirk and keep forward, joining the B1363 signposted Helmsley. In ¼ mile turn left on to the B1257. At Sproxton turn right on to the A170, signposted Scarborough, for the return to Helmsley.

POINTS OF INTEREST

① Helmsley's handsome houses are built of local yellow stone with red pantile roofs. Ruined Helmsley Castle stands in the grounds of Duncombe Park.

② Many of the houses in the small village of Rievaulx were built with materials from the 12th-century Cistercian abbey, but despite this there are impressive remains of Rievaulx Abbey in a splendid setting.

③ Rievaulx Terrace is a 1½-mile-long grass terrace completed in 1758, with classical temples and superb views.

④ The spacious and beautiful ruin of Mount Grace Priory is the largest and best preserved of all English Carthusian houses and the only one in Yorkshire.

⑤ An important road and rail junction, the market town of Northallerton is situated on rising ground east of the River Wiske, outside the National Park.

⑥ Thirsk is an old market town astride the Cod Beck with a fine 14th-century church, some interesting historic houses and inns, and a well-known racecourse to the west.

⑦ A small, elegantly proportioned Jacobean manor house, Osgodby Hall retains several interesting features, including a walled forecourt and a 17th-century staircase.

⑧ The peak of the escarpment known as Sutton Bank affords the finest views in Yorkshire stretching from the Pennines in the west into Cleveland in the north and across to York in the south.

⑨ The village of Kilburn was the home of woodcarver Robert Thompson, 'The Mouseman of Kilburn'. Oak furniture is still hand-made by Robert Thompson's Craftsmen Ltd.

⑩ Rich with places of interest, Coxwold is small, compact and highly attractive. At one end of the village stands the literary shrine of Shandy Hall, the home of vicar and writer Laurence Sterne.

⑪ Standing in grounds containing wild water gardens, Newburgh Priory is a large 17th- and 18th-century house with some fine rooms.

⑫ The considerable remains of the Cistercian church and monastic buildings of Byland Abbey date mainly from the late 12th and early 13th century.

⑬ Known for its modern Benedictine Abbey and College, Ampleforth's main street stretches for almost a mile. St Hilda's Church has a 17th-century register, a Norman font and a 12th-century doorway.

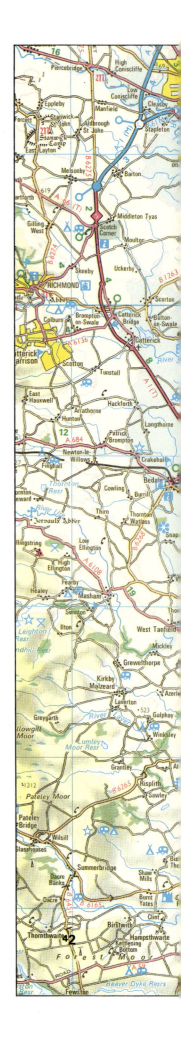

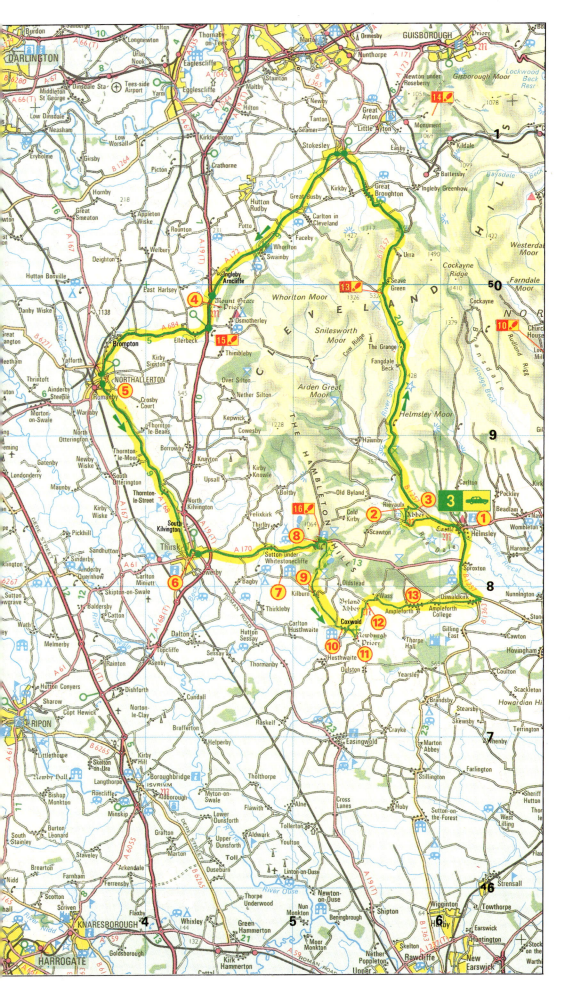

WALK 1

THE CLEVELAND WAY

One of the attractions of this easy walk is the shore at Cloughton Wyke and Hayburn Wyke. With children it would be wise to allow extra time to explore the boulder-strewn beaches. The route follows the Cleveland Way coastal footpath and returns along the track bed of the old Scarborough-to-Whitby railway.

ROUTE DIRECTIONS

Approx. 4 miles. Allow 2 to 2½ hours
Start from the lane that runs down by the side of Cober Hill, off the A171 (grid ref. TA012947). Parking is available at the bottom.

Go through the gate by the farm and follow the lane down to the cliff top at Salt Pans①.

Turn left to follow the Cleveland Way cliff path to Hayburn Wyke②.

At Hayburn Wyke the path drops down through the woodland, bearing right to reach the shore③.

Return from the shore by the same route and in 100yds, where the Cleveland Way turns left, continue straight ahead. Where tracks cross keep straight ahead, up steps. At the edge of the wood cross the stile and continue uphill through the field, gradually bearing left to pass in front of the Hayburn Wyke Hotel.

Continue a short distance up the road and turn left along the track bed of the old railway to return to Cloughton④.

Leave the railway at the bridge over the track bed and turn right to the car park.

POINTS OF INTEREST

① The sheltered inlet at Salt Pans is called Cloughton Wyke. The word 'wyke' is of Scandinavian origin and is used at several locations along the Yorkshire coast to denote a narrow inlet sheltered by headlands. The huge slabs of sandstone along the shore often show fine examples of ripplemarks, looking as fresh today as when they were made over 150 million years ago. These sandstones are in fact remnants of a huge river delta which then covered this part of north-east Yorkshire.

② The steep climb from Salt Pans brings you on to a section of the 110-mile Cleveland Way and gives extensive views south towards Scarborough, Filey and, on a clear day, the distant headland of Flamborough. A broad ledge well below the cliff edge but above sea level is a veritable jungle and a haven for wildlife. This tree-covered, boulder-strewn platform is known as the undercliff. Badger, fox and even deer are found here together with many smaller mammals, birds and insects. The plant growth is often luxurious, the trees and boulders giving shelter to a wide range of plants, particularly ferns.

③ Hayburn Wyke is a delightful and secluded bay with woodland coming right down to the shore and a twin waterfall. Much of the woodland here is a nature reserve managed by the National Trust and the Yorkshire Wildlife Trust.

The reserve is noted for beetles, a wide range of birds and varied flora including mosses and liverworts. Lias shales with fossil plant remains lie exposed along the stony beach.

④ The track bed of the old Scarborough-to-Whitby railway makes an ideal walking route and was acquired for this purpose by Scarborough Borough Council in 1975. Walkers can now follow the route from the outskirts of Scarborough to the viaduct over the River Esk at Whitby, a distance of some 20 miles. The route can also be used, as on this walk, for making shorter circular routes linking the coastal footpath.

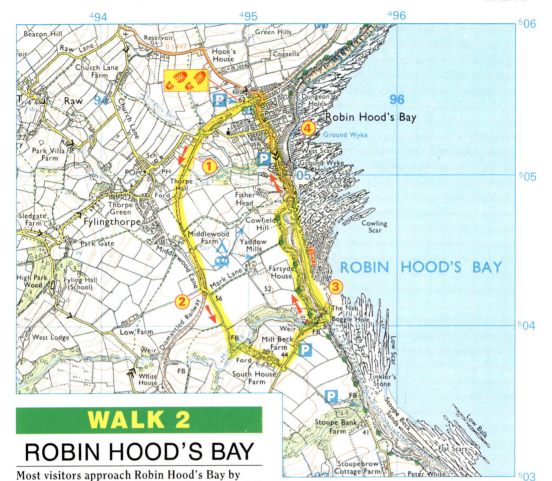

WALK 2
ROBIN HOOD'S BAY

Most visitors approach Robin Hood's Bay by road, park in the car park and walk down the hill into the old village. A more exciting approach is to walk along the beach from Boggle Hole.

ROUTE DIRECTIONS

Approx. 3 miles. Allow 2 to 2½ hours
Start from the old station car park (pay and display), on the north-western edge of Robin Hood's Bay village (grid ref. NZ949055).

Leave the car park by the lane at the opposite end to the main entrance. Join the road and turn right to Fylingthorpe and almost immediately opposite follow the track bed of the old Scarborough-to-Whitby railway line①.
  The bridge over Middlewood Lane has been removed. Drop down here to the road and continue ahead along the lane signed 'Unsuitable for Motor Vehicles'②.
  The lane drops steeply to a ford and footbridge and then climbs up between the buildings of South House Farm to join the road. Turn left down the road to Boggle Hole③.
  If the tide is out you can walk along the shore back to Robin Hood's Bay. If the tide is in, cross the footbridge by the Youth Hostel and follow the cliff-top path to the village④.
  When both routes meet New Road turn left through the village, climb the steep bank, and then continue for 400yds, turning left into the car park.

POINTS OF INTEREST

①The Scarborough-to-Whitby railway line was opened in 1885. In the short distance between Ravenscar and Robin Hood's Bay the line drops some 400ft and sweeps inland to avoid some of the steep-sided valleys draining into the bay. The track bed is now a walkway.
②The old railway continues southwards past Fyling Park. On local maps the word 'park' appears several times, a sure indication that there was a medieval deer park here. Earth embankments are the only evidence of it today.
③Boggle Hole was once a mill, one of several in the area, and is now a popular Youth Hostel. The word 'boggle' is a local name for a hob or goblin once said to frequent this

▲ Robin Hood's Bay viewed from the Cleveland Way footpath.

area. If the tide is out the bay's reefs are clearly visible. Formed from the oldest rocks in the area, they are a paradise for fossil hunters, and contain hundreds of fascinating rock pools. The bird life of the shore can be equally interesting, with several species of gull and wader.
④Wedged between cliffs and sea, the delightful fishing village of Robin Hood's Bay is a warren of steep streets and passageways, whose houses often seem to be built almost on top of one another. There is no real evidence to link the place with the famous Sherwood Forest outlaw whose name it bears, but centuries of fishermen's and smugglers' tales have ensured that Robin Hood's Bay has a folklore all of its own. Aspects of its history are illustrated in the small local museum, open in summer.

▲ St Mary's Church sitting solemnly amidst its graveyard.

WALK 3
EAST OF WHITBY

This two-in-one walk gives the option of a cliff-top walk from Whitby to Robin Hood's Bay, returning by bus, or a short easy walk never far from Whitby. In either case allow extra time to explore Whitby Abbey, the nearby parish church and some of the hidden alleys and courtyards of the old town. If intending to take the longer route, check the bus times in Whitby before setting off.

ROUTE DIRECTIONS

Approx. 4½ miles. Allow 2 to 2½ hours (a good half day for the longer walk)
Start from the swing bridge in the centre of Whitby (grid ref. NZ899111).

Go up Bridge Street and turn left to walk along Church Street and up to Whitby Abbey①.

From the abbey, cut through the car park and turn right to take the cliff path in front of the coastguard lookout②.

The path (signed the Cleveland Way) continues along the cliff and through a caravan site③.

Continue on the site road and cross a stile on to the Cleveland Way again to go along the cliff edge. Follow the path to the hilltop just beyond the Fog Horn Station and lighthouse. (Those walking to Robin Hood's Bay should continue on the coast path.) Most of the remainder of the circular route is on tarmac and some may prefer simply to retrace their steps to Whitby.

If completing the circular route, follow the tarmac lane from the lighthouse via Brook House to the road and turn right. Continue, with views ahead of Whitby Abbey. Just past the track to Knowles Farm (on the right) look for a narrow path on the left which goes towards New Gardens. Go through a gate and continue straight ahead, joining a narrow road. Where this bends right, continue straight ahead along a narrow path to join the road. Turn left downhill and right along the harbourside④.

From the harbour return to the town centre.

POINTS OF INTEREST

① This walk often takes longer than expected, such is the wealth of interest on the way, including the Tuscan-style old 'town hall', which dates from the late 18th century, and the interesting shops along Church Street selling Whitby jet or 'black amber' jewellery. Incidentally, tradition demands that you count the church steps; if you do not count 199, start again!

Dating from about 1110, the unique Parish Church of St Mary has a magnificent tiered pulpit with ear trumpets, box pews and a fine Norman chancel arch. Near by are the imposing ruins of Whitby Abbey, refounded in 1078 to replace the famous earlier foundation of St Hilda, dating from 657. It was St Hilda who gave her name to a local ammonite or 'snakestone'. These flat, coiled fossils are found in rocks below the abbey.

② From the cliff top the remains of a wreck can be seen, a reminder of the many maritime disasters which have occurred along this coastline.

③ The 93-mile Cleveland Way, the second long-distance footpath to be established by the Countryside Commission, was opened in 1969.

④ Whitby Harbour was the birthplace of the three ships, *Endeavour*, *Resolution* and *Adventure*, that carried Captain Cook around the world on his three great voyages of exploration.

WALK 4

COASTAL HERITAGE

This walk is generally easy with some steep parts. It follows the coast path from Staithes to Port Mulgrave before swinging inland to follow a pleasant wooded valley. As the walk does not return through Staithes it is a good idea to explore the attractive village at the start. Warning: part of the cliff path is poorly fenced, making the walk unsuitable for children unless carefully supervised by adults.

ROUTE DIRECTIONS

Approx. 4¼ miles. Allow 2½ to 3 hours
Start from Staithes car park (grid ref. NZ782184).

The car park stands on the site of the old coastal railway①.

Follow the road down into Staithes②.

From the harbourside follow steep Church Street from near the Cod and Lobster Inn, passing the Mission Church of St Peter the Fisherman on the right. Follow the Cleveland Way (signed) which continues at the top as a path and turn sharp left, past some farm buildings. Continue straight ahead for some distance, crossing two stiles, then go uphill steeply to the cliff edge. At this point children need to be kept close to adults as the cliff path is unfenced. Farther on the path is poorly fenced, although the cliff is less sheer③.

Follow the cliff path round to Port Mulgrave④.

Join the road bearing right through the village past the Ship Inn. Turn left at Hinderwell Church and cross the A174. Go down West End Close, turning right into Porrett Lane, which becomes a rough track. Follow this round towards the caravan site. Turn right and where the track turns sharp left continue ahead through a gate and cross two fields. Cross a stile and follow a signposted path to a footbridge over Dales Beck.

Cross the bridge and turn parallel to the beck. After 70yds start climbing through the wood and then follow a path down a ridge. Where three paths meet take the forward left which bears right (signed WW16) and after a short distance leave the wood. After climbing a stile cross scrubland and climb another stile before descending to a caravan site. Follow the access road to Dalehouse. Turn right up the steep road to reach the main road and turn right then left to reach Staithes car park.

POINTS OF INTEREST

① Looking across the valley you can still see the abutments of the railway viaduct which stood 152ft above Roxby Beck. Boulby Potash Mine is prominent, the only potash mine in the country. From nearly 4,000ft below the surface salts from ancient desert seas are mined to produce much-needed fertiliser.

② It is worth lingering in the village to explore the narrow lanes and alleys. Many of the waterfront buildings, including the attractive Cod and Lobster pub, have been knocked down by the sea several times over the last century or so and have been doggedly rebuilt. At least they served to protect the web of alleys that run between High Street and Church Street. Dog Loup, at 18inches wide, is reputed to be the narrowest street in the North of England.

The name 'Staithes', locally pronounced 'Steers', means a wharf or jetty.

③ Looking back from the top of the hill the great cliffs of Boulby can be seen, the highest cliffs on the east coast of England.

④ Looking down on the 'port' from the road a crumbling jetty can be seen marking one side of a small harbour. A steep path can be taken down to the beach for a closer look.

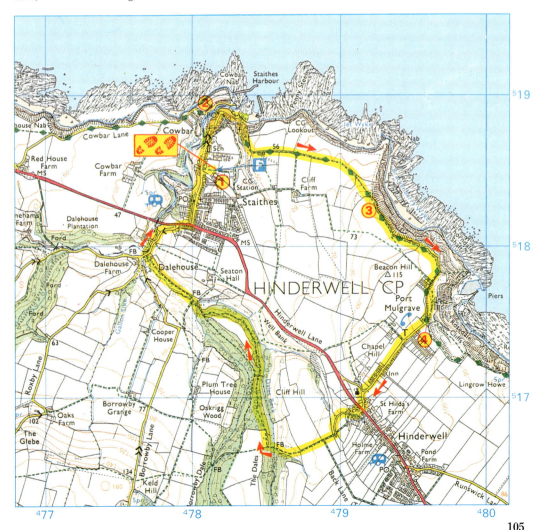

WALK 5

THE LITTLEBECK VALLEY

Waterfalls, woodland, stepping stones and open moor are all ingredients of this easy walk around the delightfully-named Littlebeck Valley.

ROUTE DIRECTIONS

Approx. 4½ miles. Allow 2½ to 3 hours
Start from a car park reached by turning off the B1416 at Redgates Corner and following the road signposted Falling Foss and Newton House (grid ref. NZ889035).

Walk down the track towards Falling Foss①.

At Midge Hall double back on the path leading alongside the gorge above the stream②.

Follow the path downstream to the Hermitage③.

Go down steeply towards the stream and pass an old alum quarry. Continue to join the road at Littlebeck④.

Turn right up the road, pass the village hall and follow the left fork for a short distance, then turn left off the road along a footpath (signposted). Bear right and cross the top edge of three fields with the hedge on the right. Cross the two stiles and drop down the side of Low Farm.

Go through the gate, pass below the farm and continue diagonally down to the right to the track and ford. Follow the track parallel to the stream. Avoiding the footbridge (unless the stream is in spate), cross the weir and then the stepping stones. Follow the path through the wood to a second set of stepping stones and continue downstream to a metal footbridge. Cross this and turn sharp right uphill, signposted Dean Hall⑤.

Turn right where the path joins a track which cuts up to the right between the buildings of Dean Hall and joins the road. Turn right on the road and very shortly veer forward left along the second (unsigned) bridleway towards the old quarry. Keep right at the fork and go up the side of the quarry on to the open moor, then keep right to go through the pine trees with the wall and fields on the right.

Emerging from the trees, continue ahead across the moor, still keeping the fields on the right. Gradually swing left to pass to the left of the new barn and keep forward on the track to the road.

Cross the road and follow the footpath (signposted) towards Thorn Hill, but shortly veer to the left of the buildings to follow a track over the moor to Newton House Lodge. Turn right down the road.

POINTS OF INTEREST

①The track towards Falling Foss is part of an old coach road from Whitby over the moors towards Hackness and Pickering. The Foss itself is a very attractive waterfall, plunging 40ft among woodlands that were once part of a large private estate.

②Midge Hall was the keeper's cottage. At one time it had a double-seater outdoor privy which was virtually suspended over the waterfall.

③Carved out of solid sandstone, the Hermitage was built about 200 years ago and will accommodate about 20 people. On its top are two stone armchairs, and in front is a small balcony from which the steep valley sides can be fully appreciated.

④The enchanting hamlet of Littlebeck grew up around a quiet pool in the stream from which the settlement takes its name. Its charming houses enjoy a seclusion rarely found nowadays, for it is reached only by tiny, steep, tortuous lanes.

⑤The path leading up out of the valley is a paved 'trod' or pannierway. There are many of these early routeways, slabs of sandstone laid in lines, in the Whitby area. Often running for many miles, they are probably medieval.

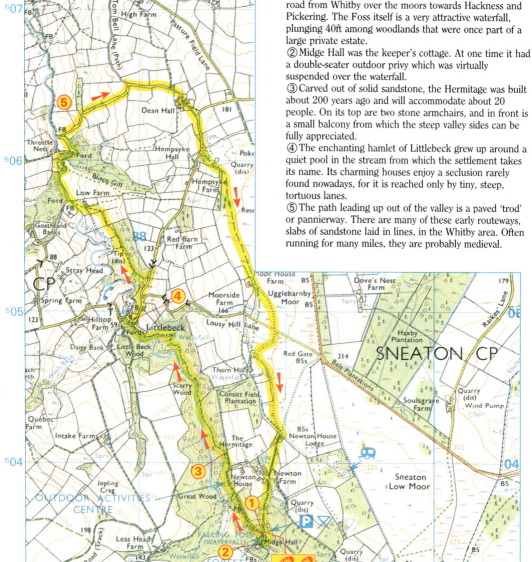

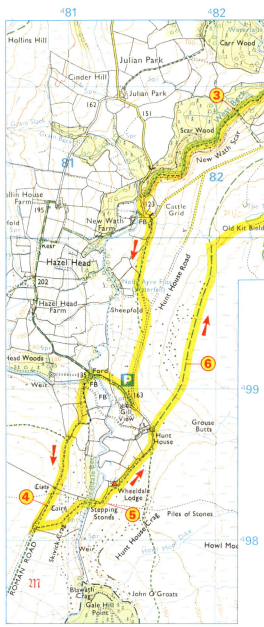

Reach the road and go straight ahead (left). At the second bend, just before the cattle grid, turn right past the house and follow the path over the moor towards Hunt House.

From the lay-by near Hunt House turn right down the track, cross the first footbridge and turn right along the stream bank. Go left uphill, signposted Roman Road.

Turn right over the stile at the top and bear left along the wall side to join the Roman road. Follow the road as it climbs to the moor④.

Cross the step stile and continue ahead for about 200yds before doubling back on a path (left) and dropping to the stepping stones over Wheeldale Beck. The route of the Lyke Wake Walk continues straight up the moor but take the more gentle route to the left⑤.

Follow the track past Wheeldale Lodge to Hunt House. A few yards along the road cut forward (right) up the moor. The track climbs gradually, in a straight line, to the rocky outcrop and then follows the edge of the hill towards Goathland⑥.

Bear gradually right and pass to the right of a small tarn before going downhill to Goathland.

POINTS OF INTEREST

① Goathland's late Victorian church is dedicated to St Mary, as was the 12th-century hermitage recorded at 'Godeland' that was one of its predecessors. The village itself has fine stone houses, broad grass verges grazed by sheep, and a station for the North York Moors Railway.

② With the lowest rainfall of Britain's National Parks, the North York Moors is not noted for its waterfalls. However, several falls can be reached from Goathland. Mallyan Spout, at 70ft, is the highest.

③ The West Beck is a delightful stream tumbling among huge boulders beneath tree-covered hillsides. Woodpeckers are common, and you may see the white-fronted dipper flitting low above the water.

④ Often called Wade's Causeway after the legendary giant who supposedly built it, this is one of the best-preserved sections of Roman road in the country. Built as a military project about AD80, it probably fell into disuse some 40 years later. The road has been traced from near Malton, a Roman town, to the lower slopes of the moors above Pickering. At Cawthorne, are the remains of four Roman military training camps and from here remains of the road become more visible until the route reaches this well-preserved section on Wheeldale Moor.

⑤ The Lyke Wake Walk takes its name from an old Cleveland folk song which describes a journey over the moors supposedly made by departed souls. The strenuous, 40-mile walk from Osmotherley to Ravenscar was established in 1955, and the traditional challenge is to complete it within 24 hours.

⑥ The rocky outcrops are inhabited by adders, but they usually disappear before you have a chance to see them. Britain's only poisonous snake, the adder has a characteristic zigzag line down its back and a V-shaped mark on the back of its head.

WALK 6
MALLYAN SPOUT

The steep-sided, wooded valley of West Beck is ideal for games or a picnic, and good for birdwatching too. The route later follows a Roman road before returning over open moorland. The walk is of moderate difficulty, and includes a scramble across boulders below Mallyan Spout. In poor weather it is advisable to return from Hunt House along the road.

ROUTE DIRECTIONS

Approx. 5 miles. Allow 2½ to 3 hours
Start in Goathland, opposite the church (grid ref. NZ828007)①.

Follow the footpath down the right-hand side of the Mallyan Hotel, signposted Mallyan Spout Waterfall. At the stream turn left, signposted Mallyan Spout.

On reaching the waterfall there is a scramble over boulders which can be very slippery②.

The path passes in front of the fall and continues to meander by the side of the stream. In places the path is very muddy, even on a hot day③.

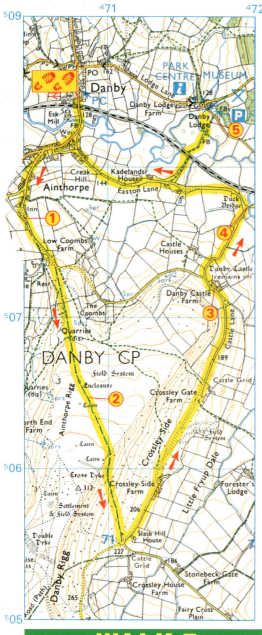

WALK 7
AINTHORPE RIGG

A breezy moorland walk followed by easy going along a country road. Broad views along the Esk Valley and Little Fryup Dale, a high-arched medieval packhorse bridge and a detour to the Moors Centre at Danby are some of the attractions of this moderately easy walk in the heart of the North York Moors National Park.

ROUTE DIRECTIONS

Approx. 5 miles. Allow 2½ to 3 hours
Start from the railway station in Danby (grid ref. NZ708084).

From the station, turn right to follow the road which crosses the railway and the River Esk. Follow the road into Ainthorpe and turn left up the road to Fryup①.

Just past the tennis court the road bends left. Take the bridleway (signed) to go straight forward up Ainthorpe Rigg and on to the moor. Pass through a gateway②.

Reach the edge of the hill, with views over Little Fryup Dale through a gap, into Great Fryup Dale. Where the path forks, take the left path down to the road junction and turn left along the road. Farther on, pass Danby Castle③.

Just beyond the castle, turn sharp right down the road to Duck Bridge④.

Do not cross Duck Bridge, but continue to follow the road as it bears left.

On the opposite side of the river stands Danby Lodge, now known as the Moors Centre. Cross a stile on the right to follow a public footpath to the centre, but take care crossing the railway and do not allow children to run on ahead⑤.

Retrace your steps to Easton Lane and turn right. Keep bearing right, over the railway, to return to the car park.

POINTS OF INTEREST

①Opposite the Fox and Hounds in Fryup is the village quoits pitch. The ancient game is becoming increasingly popular in villages throughout the length of the Esk Valley. A pitch 11yds long has a square bed of clay at each end in which is set an iron post or hob. Basically the game involves throwing a bevelled metal ring or quoit from post to post.

②At this point there are extensive views from the path, which farther on is clearly marked with a line of stone cairns. The North York Moors are rich in prehistoric remains, particularly from the Bronze Age, and hundreds of burial mounds can be found on the high moorland.

③William le Latimer built Danby Castle – a 14th-century palace-fortress. Tradition suggests that Henry VIII stayed here, but in fact there is no evidence that he ever travelled farther north than York. The building is not open to the public.

④Duck Bridge is a fine example of a medieval packhorse bridge and one of three remaining in the Esk Valley. The bridge was built in about 1386 and has low walls leaning out over the water.

⑤The Moors Centre was previously a shooting lodge on the estate of Lord Downe, but since 1976 it has been used as a visitor centre by the National Park Authority. A detour to view the exhibition, visit the grounds or enjoy the refreshments is well worthwhile.

▼ The Moors Centre and its terraced gardens, Danby, set within riverside and woodland grounds.

WALK 8

FROM ROSEDALE ABBEY

Less than a century ago, the peaceful landscape of rural Rosedale was the backdrop to a thriving ironstone industry. The slopes of this lovely valley are still peppered with the reminders of a past way of life.

ROUTE DIRECTIONS

Approx. 4 miles. Allow 2½ to 3 hours
Start at the village green in Rosedale Abbey (grid ref. SE724959).

Take the path between the school and church ①.

Cross the road and take the footpath ahead into the caravan site and turn right along the track through the site. Approaching the end of the site pass through a metal gate to continue the walk over fields.

About 15 minutes from the start of the walk the path descends to a footbridge over the River Seven ②.

Go across the field to steps over a stone wall and turn right along Daleside Road. Just before Thorgill turn right down a track and follow the signs through Low Thorgill Farm. Following the direction of a yellow arrow on a post, cross a field and continue over a footbridge across a stream. Proceed towards Hill Cottages ③.

Cross another footbridge and continue across two fields, then along a track which bears left. Pass through a gate and continue up the lane to the cottages.

Cross the road and follow the track up towards the white house. Turn sharp right before you get to the house, over a stile next to a small red-tiled outhouse and right again immediately, over a fence and on to a rough track.

Continue through a wooden gate and pass in front of the building. Cross a fence and bear left to a stile where a track leads up through the trees to a disused railway line ④.

Turn right and follow the track bed round the head of a steep-sided valley. After ½ mile cross a stile. In 200yds bear left up a track to a gate and follow the fence to a stile on to the road.

Cross the road and follow the signposted bridleway down to the left. At the gate turn right on to a footpath, passing a derelict farmhouse and pond on the left. At the end of the pond bear left and continue downhill into Northdale.

Pass through a gate in the field corner and cross to a step stile. Continue to a gateway on to the road. Turn left and in 15yds turn right on the path parallel to and above the stream, crossing the bottom of two fields. Just after leaving the second field, keep the stone wall on the left and continue down to a gate, crossing the footbridge.

Continue through a larger gate, crossing the corner of the field diagonally to a bridlegate. Go across the next field to reach a gate. In the next field drop down to reach a ladder over the stone wall in the corner of the field.

Continue, following a path parallel to the stream, through several more fields, to return to the village.

POINTS OF INTEREST

① Rosedale Abbey's Victorian church stands on the site of the 12th-century Cistercian nunnery from which the village takes its name. A few fragments of this earlier building, including part of a staircase, can still be seen.

② Here little more than a stream, the River Seven is one of several parallel rivers that drain the southern half of the North York Moors. All join the Derwent to flow out to the sea along the Humber Estuary.

③ The route climbs the hill on an old paved way. Sections of such tracks, known here as 'trods', can be found in many upland regions of Britain. In Rosedale, this would probably have served the early mining industry.

④ The railway track bed is a later legacy of the ironstone extraction industry. Ironstone from Rosedale was found to be very rich in ore, and the area was conveniently close to the Teesside blast-furnaces.

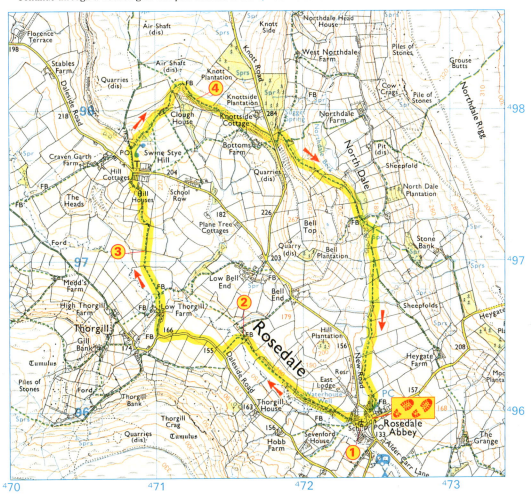

▲ The quiet village of Sinnington beside a fast-flowing stretch of the River Seven.

WALK 9

ALONG THE SEVEN

From the centre of Sinnington this walk goes through pleasant woodland often close to the River Seven. Above Appleton Mill the route climbs steadily to the top edge of the woods and then gradually descends towards the Hall and Sinnington church.

ROUTE DIRECTIONS

Approx. 2¾ miles. Allow 2 to 2½ hours
Start from the river bridge at Sinnington (grid ref. SE745858)①.

Follow the road from the bridge to the right past the school, on the east side of the river②.

Bear left down the no-through-road. Where the road ends, continue down the bridleway to the river bank. The bridleway is signposted left but continue straight ahead along the footpath into the woods, gradually climbing and then dropping to a field gate and through a meadow. About three-quarters of the way across the meadow cut up right to the corner of the wood and cross a stile to follow a path through the wood high above the river③.

Descend to the river bank but then follow the right-hand edge of a field, climbing steeply uphill after about 150yds. At a crossroads of paths turn right and continue to climb steadily to the top edge of the wood. Ignore the path to your left and follow the path to the right as it gradually descends. Leaving the wood, continue over an open area and bear left along a fieldside to a track. Turn right and after about 100yds turn sharp left towards Hall Farm. Join the road where it bends and continue between the buildings, past the church and downhill to return to Sinnington④.

POINTS OF INTEREST

① Many villages along the southern edge of the moors have names ending with -ton, a sure indication that they were established by invading Angles in the 6th and 7th centuries.

In the centre is a maypole, one of only a few remaining in this area. In 1708 the Quakers made several attempts to stop the fun and games around the maypole, but not, it seems, with much success.

Close by is a low hump-back bridge spanning a dry ditch which may have once been a flood channel or possibly an old water-course that conveyed water to a mill wheel. This bridge is medieval in origin but the bridge across the River Seven dates from 1767.

② Fed by moorland streams, the River Seven flows through the lengthy, pleasant valley of Rosedale which extends from the centre of the North York Moors National Park to its southern boundary.

③ These woodlands are a pleasure to visit at any time of year, but particularly so in the spring. Before the leaves are fully open on the trees the ground is a carpet early spring flowers including primroses, violets, wood sorrel and wood anemones. Later in the season bluebells, woodruff and wild garlic are found.

④ The Church of All Saints has many original features dating from Saxon and Norman times, although it was restored in 1904. The old Hall nearby dates from the 12th century, when it was built by the de Clere family.

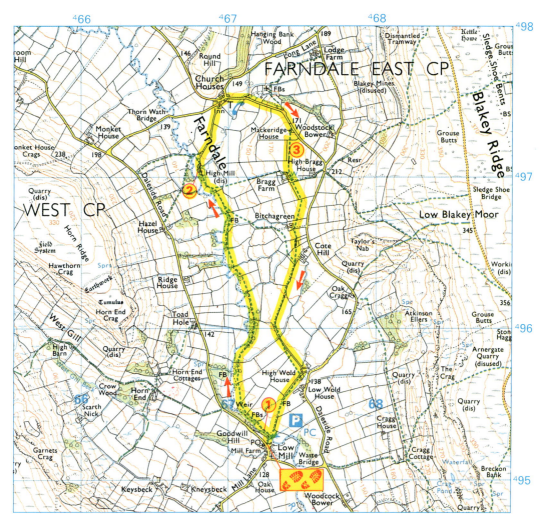

WALK 10

DALE OF THE DAFFODILS

This easy walk through Farndale is particularly popular in spring when thousands of wild daffodils line the path alongside the River Dove. It is however a stroll to be savoured at any season of the year. The return route along field paths down the flank of the valley has pleasant distant views of the dale.

ROUTE DIRECTIONS

Approx. 3¼ miles. Allow 2 to 2½ hours
Start the walk from Low Mill car park
(grid ref. SE673952).

Take the path beside the car park (signposted High Mill) which crosses the footbridge over the River Dove, then turn left and follow the path upstream parallel to the river ①.

Continue alongside the river for about 50 minutes, passing through several stiles before reaching the buildings at High Mill ②.

Pass between the buildings and follow the track up to Church Houses passing through a gateway. At the end of the track turn right twice (signed Hutton-le-Hole) on a tarmac road. Continue, passing the Church of St Mary on the left and gradually climb to pass Mackeridge House on the right. Just beyond the house turn right on the footpath (signed) by a stone wall. Keep the wall on your left to a step stile to cross the wall ③.

Keep the hedge on the right, then pass through a gate. Cross the field and pass through a second gate, then keep to the left of Bragg Farm. Go through a gateway and continue along the track. After about 200yds the path cuts down the field to the buildings of Bitchagreen Farm. Cross the stone wall and keep the farm on the right, passing through a gate. Cross the field to a stile and pass below a cottage. Then cross another stile towards Cote Hill. Keep the new barn on the left and descend to the right-hand field gate.

Follow the track, passing through a gate, then pass a gate opening on the left. Bear left at the end of the field through a gate and continue along the track to High Wold House (there may be ropes across the track). In the farmyard turn right through a gate and go down the field, over a stile, then cross the stream and follow the line of poles (paved track) down to the River Dove and back to Low Mill.

POINTS OF INTEREST

① Tens of thousands of people tramp this famous 'Daffodil Walk' in spring. It is not the only place in Farndale, or the North York Moors, where the wild daffodils grow, but it is one of the most spectacular. Nobody knows how the daffodils first came to be here though they have been here for many centuries.

For most of the year the Dove is a placid river but come the winter snows or autumn rains, and it is quickly transformed to a racing torrent and the river's waters once powered several mills along its course. It is shaded by alder trees and as the Gaelic word *ferna* means alder these may have given Farndale its name.

② High Mill was used to grind corn taking its power from the small Fish Beck. Some of the buildings are being restored.

③ From this viewpoint you can look up and across the dale to the moor-topped ridges. Up the valley is an area that has twice caused controversy when plans were announced by the local water authority to flood upper Farndale to form a reservoir.

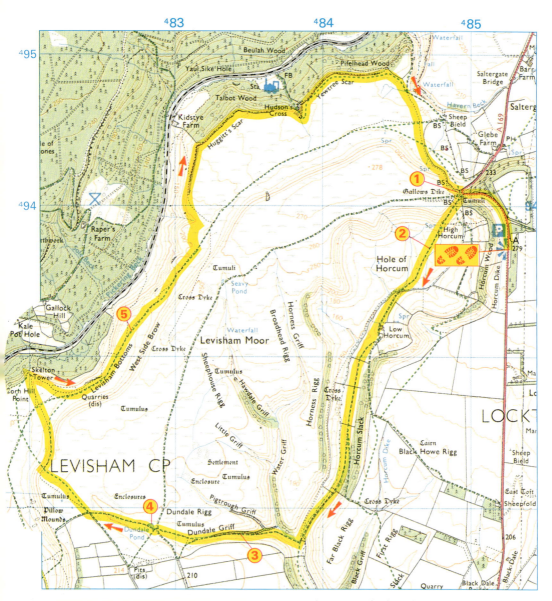

THE HOLE OF HORCUM

This long, exhilarating ramble on Levisham Moor sets out through the middle of the remarkable Hole of Horcum, returning along the edge of the steep gorge of Newton Dale. *Take care along the edge of Huggitt's Scar and Yewtree Scar.*

ROUTE DIRECTIONS

Approx. 6¾ miles. Allow 3½ to 4 hours
Start from the car park at Saltergate (grid ref. SE853937).

Follow the road to the hairpin bend on Saltergate Bank①.

Turn left over the step stile down into the Hole of Horcum②.

Continue down the valley, passing to the right of the old farm buildings. Carry on through the middle of the fields, avoiding any routes uphill.

Where the valley narrows keep the fence and wall on the left and continue down to the confluence of two streams. Cross and turn sharp right up Dundale Griff, signposted footpath③.

On reaching open moorland, bear right across the moors. Shortly pass Dundale Pond on your right④.

Continue up the dry valley, gradually bearing up to the left. At the corner of the walled field strike off on the path straight across the moor to reach the edge of the escarpment overlooking Newton Dale, then cut down to the right towards the ruins of Skelton Tower.

Continue along the path, bearing to the right and following the edge of the dale northwards to Yewtree Scar⑤.

Leave the broad track where it swings away from the edge of the valley and follow the path along the cliff top. **Take care if with children.**

At the north end of Yewtree Scar continue with the path as it bends right, away from Newton Dale. Go along the field side to the edge of a tributary valley and then almost immediately bear right again to cross the moor and climb towards the hairpin bend of Saltergate Bank.

Climb up to the road, keeping the fence line on the left, then turn right to the car park.

POINTS OF INTEREST

① From Saltergate Bank there is a good view northwards to Fylingdales Ballistic Missile Early Warning Station. In the foreground is the ancient Saltergate Inn, beside the old road from Robin Hood's Bay. Fish were brought here for salting before onward transit to inland towns.
② One of the geological curiosities of the North York Moors, the Hole of Horcum is a great steep-sided bowl in the moorland. Large enough to contain two complete farms, the hollow has been sculpted over the millennia by the action of springs. Needless to say, folklore has given it more colourful explanations: it was scooped out by the giant, Wade, to throw at his wife.

③The word 'griff' is used in this area to denote a very steep-sided little valley, often with cliffs along its flanks.

④Dundale Pond was probably constructed in medieval times as a watering place for livestock.

⑤Through the remote valley of Newton Dale, below the path, runs the popular North York Moors Railway, also known as 'Moorsrail'. The 18-mile privately owned line between Pickering and Grosmont is operated by both diesel and steam locomotives.

WALK 12

FORGE VALLEY WOODS

This is an easy walk along river-bank and woodland paths through the steep-sided Forge Valley, much of which is now designated a National Nature Reserve. Start this walk at daybreak on a fine June morning and an unforgettable dawn chorus will be ample recompense for a very early rise.

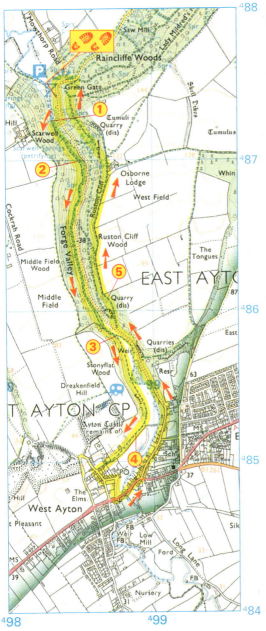

ROUTE DIRECTIONS

Approx. 4 miles. Allow 2 to 2½ hours
Start from one of the two small car parks on the road out of West Ayton towards the north end of Forge Valley (grid ref. SE983874).

Walk a short distance downstream to cross Jubilee Footbridge over the River Derwent①.

Follow the river-bank path downstream②.

Where the path enters a field continue straight ahead, keeping the fence on your right③.

The path merges into a rough track which bends gradually right uphill to pass close to the ruins of Ayton Castle④.

Continue ahead to join the road, turning left downhill then quickly left and right to the road bridge on the A170. Cross the bridge and turn left on the road to Hackness.

Follow the road as it drops back into Forge Valley and about 300yds beyond the weir (having passed one bridleway) cross the road to follow the signposted bridleway which cuts steeply uphill, bearing right of the road. Near the top of the wood where the path divides, take the left fork to follow the path along the top edge of the woods⑤.

Pass the back of Osborne Lodge Farm and within a short distance start dropping downhill. Continue on this path, which gradually swings round to join the road near Green Gate. Turn left to return to your car.

POINTS OF INTEREST

①Close to the bridge is the site of the old forge from which the valley takes its name. The forge dates back to medieval times and would have produced wrought or cast iron. With abundant wood for charcoal and an ample water supply, this was an ideal site.

②The woodlands here are among the best remaining examples of mixed woodland in north-east England. A wide variety of trees, including oak, lime, wych elm and birch, is complemented by a rich ground flora of wood anemone, primrose, bluebell, woodruff, ramsons, orchids and many other species. Look for the yellow globes of marsh marigold and yellow flag (iris) growing in the river.

③The small weir was built by the water authority to measure flow rates in the Derwent. A little downstream, although out of sight, are sink holes in the bed of the river through which some of the water percolates. After travelling underground for some miles the water is trapped in the limestone and is then tapped to supply Scarborough with its water.

④Dating from about 1400, Ayton Castle is a ruined pele-tower – a type of fortified building that is much more common nearer the Scottish border, for most of them were built as a defence against the marauding Scots. This one stands on the site of an earlier castle: Ayton is mentioned in *Domesday Book* and its name is derived from the Old English for 'settlement by the river'.

⑤The deciduous trees and shrubs along Forge Valley attract a tremendous variety of small birds including nuthatches, woodpeckers, several kinds of warbler and many common woodland species.

▼ The heavily-wooded slopes of the Forge valley.

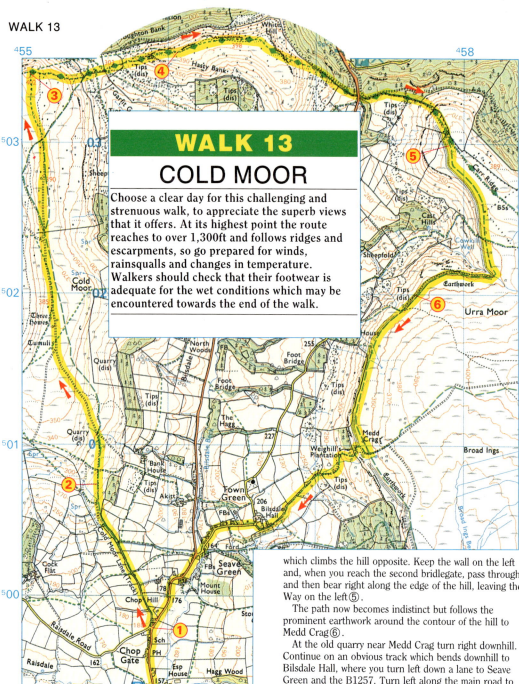

WALK 13
COLD MOOR

Choose a clear day for this challenging and strenuous walk, to appreciate the superb views that it offers. At its highest point the route reaches to over 1,300ft and follows ridges and escarpments, so go prepared for winds, rainsqualls and changes in temperature. Walkers should check that their footwear is adequate for the wet conditions which may be encountered towards the end of the walk.

ROUTE DIRECTIONS

Approx. 8 miles. Allow 4 to 5 hours
Start from the car park at Chop Gate (grid ref. SE559994).

Walk up the road into the village. Turn left to Carlton and almost immediately right up a track by the Wesleyan Chapel ①.

Follow the path up to the moor and, leaving the stone wall on your left, climb up the ridge. At the first cairn the path bends slightly to the right to follow the edge of the hill overlooking Bilsdale ②.

The path now joins a broad track. Follow this over Cold Moor to join the Cleveland Way at the escarpment overlooking Great Broughton ③.

Turn right along the Way, dropping down steeply then climbing up between the Wainstones on Hasty Bank ④.

Follow the track on the edge of the hill before dropping steeply down to the left towards the road. Towards the bottom of the hill climb the step stile and turn immediately right down the wall side.

Cross the B1257 and continue along the Cleveland Way,
which climbs the hill opposite. Keep the wall on the left and, when you reach the second bridlegate, pass through and then bear right along the edge of the hill, leaving the Way on the left ⑤.

The path now becomes indistinct but follows the prominent earthwork around the contour of the hill to Medd Crag ⑥.

At the old quarry near Medd Crag turn right downhill. Continue on an obvious track which bends downhill to Bilsdale Hall, where you turn left down a lane to Seave Green and the B1257. Turn left along the main road to return to Chop Gate.

POINTS OF INTEREST

① Chop Gate is one of only two tiny villages in Bilsdale, a peaceful, green valley whose farmlands were once cultivated by the Cistercian monks of Rievaulx Abbey. Pronounced locally as 'Chop Yat', the name of the village is thought to be derived from Chapman's Gate – 'chapman' being an old name for a pedlar.

② Impressive views open up as the walk climbs the ridge of Cold Moor. The head of Bilsdale unfolds on the right, while to the left the land falls gradually down into the remote upper reaches of Raisdale.

③ If the views on the way up Cold Moor are impressive, then those from the escarpment edge, which runs from east to west near the National Park's northern boundary, are quite stupendous.

④ Very popular with rock-climbers, the Wainstones are the largest group of rocks in the National Park. At the top of Hasty Bank, the path passes close to the edge of quarries, *so take care – especially with children.*

⑤ The Cleveland Way continues south-eastwards, soon reaching the highest point in the National Park, 1,490ft, on Urra Moor.

⑥ The long bank-and-ditch earthwork on the side of Urra Moor is one of hundreds to be found throughout the North York Moors. They may have been defensive works, boundaries or cattle enclosures.

WALK 14

ROSEBERRY TOPPING

Beginning at Gribdale Gate car park, this moderate walk follows the escarpment to a 'miniature Matterhorn' – perhaps the most prominent landmark in the North York Moors. The short but stiff climb to the summit of Roseberry Topping is optional, but those who do reach the top will be rewarded by fine views.

ROUTE DIRECTIONS

Approx. 4 miles. Allow 2½ to 3 hours
Start at Gribdale Gate, which can be reached on a narrow road from Great Ayton by following signs for the station. Approaching from Great Ayton, park in the first car park at the top of the hill (grid ref. NZ593110).

Cross the cattle grid and turn left up the hill, following the Cleveland Way. The path levels out at the top of the hill to follow the edge of the escarpment①.

Keep the stone wall (conifer plantation boundary) on the left and after 1¼ miles go through the bridlegate in the wall which crosses the path just above Little Roseberry②.

Drop downhill before climbing Roseberry Topping③.

(If you decide not to climb Roseberry Topping turn left through a field gate on the level ground before the hill and follow the track towards Airy Holme Farm.)

From the summit drop down the steep south-east slope, towards the Cook Monument high on distant Easby Moor④.

Pass through a bridlegate and down towards the old mines⑤.

Turn right along the track towards Airy Holme Farm, turning left to pass in front of the farm and join the tarmac road⑥.

Continue down to the crossroads at Dikes Lane and turn left up the road to reach Gribdale Terrace⑦.

The road bends sharp left here, but follow the track straight ahead with the Terrace on the left. Bear right to a stile, then continue straight up the fields to return to Gribdale Gate.

POINTS OF INTEREST

①On Great Ayton Moor, to the right, is an important archaeological site excavated during the 1950s and now known to be a complex burial site dating from the New Stone Age and Bronze Age. Prehistoric remains of this period are abundant on the North York Moors, and though there are few large or spectacular monuments, the number of barrows and cairns in the area runs to several thousand.

②This part of the walk follows the county boundary between North Yorkshire and Cleveland.

③Though only 1,057ft high, Roseberry Topping's craggy south-west face gives this charmingly named cone of rock something of the grandeur of a much higher mountain. Views from the top take in the sea, clearly visible to the east beyond Guisborough. Not surprisingly, Roseberry Topping has been used as a beacon station and, many centuries before the Spanish Armada, was occupied by prehistoric herdsmen and hunters.

④Erected in 1827 to commemorate Great Ayton's most famous son, Captain James Cook, the 50ft stone obelisk on Easby Moor is a landmark for many miles around.

⑤The lower slopes of Roseberry Topping have for centuries been worked for the alum and ironstone they contained. In fact it was early mining activity which led to the collapse of the hillside, giving the hill the dramatic rock face we admire today.

⑥As a boy in the 1730s Captain Cook lived with his family here at Airy Holme Farm, where his father worked. James went to school in Great Ayton. He later moved to Staithes and then Whitby before joining the Navy.

⑦The houses of Gribdale Terrace were built to accommodate the ironstone miners who worked the rich ores in the vicinity.

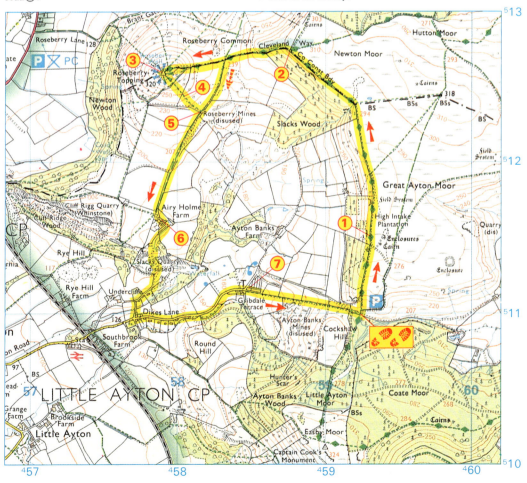

WALK 15
THE DROVERS' WALK

A gradual climb from Osmotherley reaches a high point with panoramas of the distant Pennines, then the path descends to Sheepwash, a favourite picnic place. The route of an ancient cattle-droving road is then followed before the path curls back to Osmotherley.

ROUTE DIRECTIONS

Approx. 5½ miles. Allow 3 to 3½ hours
Start from Osmotherley (grid ref. SE457973)①.

Leave the centre of Osmotherley and follow the Swainby road uphill, turning left into Ruebury Lane at the edge of the village. The route is now following the Cleveland Way②.

Follow the track, gradually bearing right. Pass to the right of Chapel Wood Farm and continue across the fields③.

Enter the conifer plantation and take the path forward right, gradually climbing to the top of the hill. Go through scrub woodland and past the TV station. Passing through two bridlegates on to the open moor, take the right-hand of the two paths, gradually veering away from the trees④.

Approaching Scarth Nick, leave the Cleveland Way and take the obvious path sharp right down to the road and follow this to Sheepwash. Cross the footbridge and follow the broad track uphill. This is the line of the old Hambleton Drove Road⑤.

Continue along the track, which becomes a tarmac road. Just before a junction turn right on to a path with a field

on the right and moorland on the left. Go through the right-hand of two facing field gates and continue through the field with the wall on the left. Turn left along the track, going downhill to rejoin the Cleveland Way at a good farm road. Turn sharp right, pass on the right of White House Farm and go downhill to cross the footbridge and follow the path uphill through the woods. Cross the field towards the church and return to Osmotherley.

POINTS OF INTEREST

①One of the first Methodist chapels in the Moors was built in a cobbled alley in Osmotherley; John Wesley himself preached his doctrines from the stone table in the market place.

②The Cleveland Way is a long-distance walk (93 miles) crossing both the Cleveland and the Hambleton Hills. It starts at Helmsley, reaches the coast at Saltburn, then heads south to Filey.

③Down on the left of the path are the ruins of Mount Grace Priory. Founded in 1398, this is one of only nine Carthusian priories left in England and is the best preserved. The monks lived in virtual isolation in individual cells, one of which has been reconstructed at Mount Grace.

④After leaving Arncliffe Wood there are distant views towards Live Moor and Carlton Moor, the onward route of the Cleveland Way.

⑤Hambleton Drove Road was used to drive cattle and sheep from Scotland and the northern counties to markets in London and the south. Drove roads were in use for several centuries before the development of a railway network in the early 19th century made them obsolete. This road followed closely the high ground of the moors to Sutton Bank, from where it dropped across the Vale of Pickering towards York.

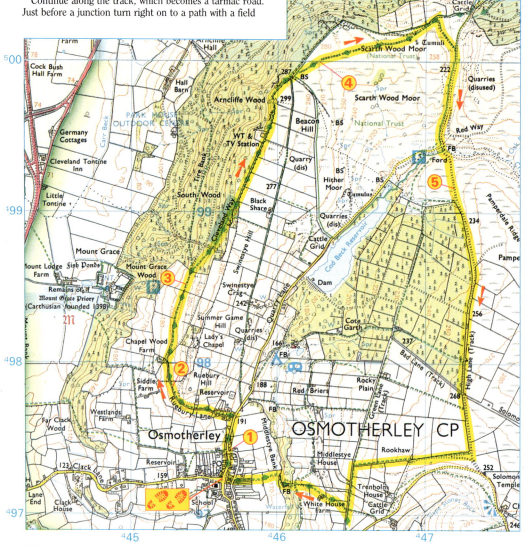

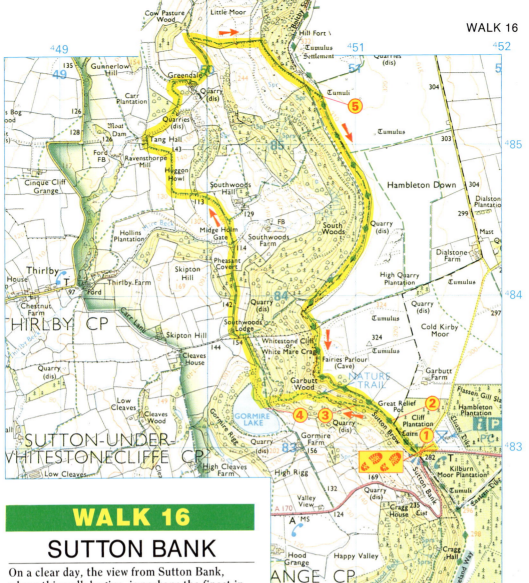

WALK 16
SUTTON BANK

On a clear day, the view from Sutton Bank, where this walk begins, is perhaps the finest in Yorkshire. The route down towards Gormire Lake is steep but not difficult and the path back along the top of the escarpment gives ever-changing views.

ROUTE DIRECTIONS

Approx. 5 miles. Allow 3 to 3½ hours
Start from the Information Centre at Sutton Bank (grid ref. SE515831)①.

Walk to the edge of the escarpment and turn right along the Cleveland Way②.

Follow the path of the Sutton Bank Nature Trail to where a narrow path (marked number 3) branches off to the left③.

Continue down to the edge of Gormire Lake④, forking left at point number 10.

Turn right along the lake side, and just beyond the end of the long boardwalk turn left to Southwoods Lodge and then right, through a gate and along a broad bridleway.

Approaching Southwoods Hall walk straight over the crossroads and continue up the tarmac to where it bears right towards the Hall. Continue through trees and a field gate, gradually turning left downhill, then go through a gateway and up a grassy track. At the top of the rise turn sharp right. Go through a field gate and then turn forward left to Tang Hall. Keep the farm on the left then turn sharp right at the electrified cattle grid up to Greendale.

Approaching Greendale Farm pass through a field gate on the left of the farm entrance and bear right to a gate, then left to a bridlegate on the edge of the wood. Turn left uphill and then right at the first junction of paths.

Pass through a young forestry plantation and then go over a stile into scrubland. Bear forward right to re-enter the forest and continue uphill.

Cross the broad forest track and, a little way uphill, bear right alongside an old wall. Follow this until you emerge on to the Cleveland Way⑤.

Continue along the edge of the escarpment back to Sutton Bank.

POINTS OF INTEREST

①As well as being justly famous for its views, Sutton Bank is notorious for its gradient. The A170 climbs the escarpment in a steady mile-long ascent with gradients up to 1 in 4.

②From the path there is a superb view down to Lake Gormire, one of the few lakes in Yorkshire and the only one in the North York Moors National Park. In the distance the Pennines can be seen, while to the south the cliffs of Roulston Scar provide a good take-off platform for gliders.

③The path descends the escarpment through pleasant woodland which provides cover for a wide range of birds, animals and insects. Garbutt Wood is a reserve of the Yorkshire Wildlife Trust.

④Formed by glacial action, Gormire Lake is rich in wildlife and is remarkable because no streams flow into or out of it. Local legends about the lake include the story that the devil leapt from Whitestone Cliff on a white horse and disappeared into a hole in the ground. This filled with water to form the supposedly bottomless lake.

⑤The 93-mile-long Cleveland Way, opened in 1969, runs from Helmsley right round the western, northern and eastern margins of the National Park to end at Filey. Part of the Way here in the Hambleton Hills follows the route of the old Hambleton Drove Road, which was used between the 17th and 19th centuries by Scottish drovers bringing their livestock to sell at southern markets and fairs.

ACKNOWLEDGEMENTS

The Automobile Association wishes to thank the following photographers, libraries and associations for their assistance in the preparation of this book.

R H Hayes 28 Incline Tragedy; *D A Idle* 27 Train, 28 Incline Cottage Beckhole, 29 Compton Tank No 5, Stripper Volunteer, 30 Engine; *International Photobank* Cover Blakey Ridge; *Mary Evans Picture Library* 12 Rievaulx Abbey, 24 Staithes, 26 Filey Lifeboat; *Nature Photographers Ltd* 16 Red Grouse (A J Davies), 19 Heron, 21 Bell Heather, Duke of Burgundy (P R Sterry), Grt Crested Grebe (C B Carver), 32 Whiskered Bat (S C Bisserott); *North Yorkshire Moors National Park* 9 Carlton Quarry; *North Yorkshire Moors Railway* 27 Map & Symbol, 28 George Stephenson; *W D Spence* 16 Shooting Butts, 25 W Sconesby Snr., Whalebone Scrapers

All remaining pictures are held in the Association's own library (AA PHOTO LIBRARY) with contributions from:
S Gregory, R Newton, V Patel, G Rowatt, H Williams, T Woodcock

Other Ordnance Survey Maps of the North York Moors

How to get there with Routemaster and Routeplanner Maps

Reach the North York Moors from Lancaster, Newcastle, Lincoln, Peterborough, Chester, Liverpool and Manchester using Ordnance Survey Routemaster map sheets 5 and 6. Alternatively, use the Ordnance Survey Great Britain Routeplanner Map which covers the whole country on one map sheet.

Exploring with Landranger, Tourist and Outdoor Leisure Maps

Landranger Series
1¼ inches to one mile or 1:50,000 scale
These maps cover the whole of Britain and are good for local motoring and walking. Each contains tourist information such as parking, picnic places, viewpoints and rights of way. Sheets covering the North York Moors are:
93 Middlesbrough and Darlington
94 Whitby
99 Northallerton and Ripon
100 Malton and Pickering
101 Scarborough and Bridlington

Tourist Map Series
1 inch to one mile or 1:63,360 scale
These maps cover popular holiday areas and are ideal for discovering the countryside. In addition to normal map detail ancient monuments, camping and caravan sites, parking facilities and viewpoints are marked. Lists of selected places of interest are included on some sheets and others include useful guides to the area.

Tourist Map Sheet 2 covers the North York Moors

Outdoor Leisure Map Series
2½ inches to one mile or 1:25,000 scale
These maps cover popular leisure and recreation areas of the country and include details of Youth Hostels, camping and caravanning sites, picnic areas, footpaths and viewpoints.

Outdoor Leisure Map Sheets 26 and 27 cover the North York Moors

Other titles available in this series are:
Brecon Beacons; Channel Islands; Cornwall; Cotswolds; Days Out from London; Devon and Exmoor; East Anglia; Forest of Dean and Wye Valley; Ireland; Isle of Wight; Lake District; New Forest; Northumbria; Peak District; Scottish Highlands; Snowdonia; South Downs; Wessex; Yorkshire Dales.

THE WORLD OF THE F...

STAR TRAVEL

TRANSPORT & TECHNOLOGY INTO THE 21st CENTURY

GW01158335

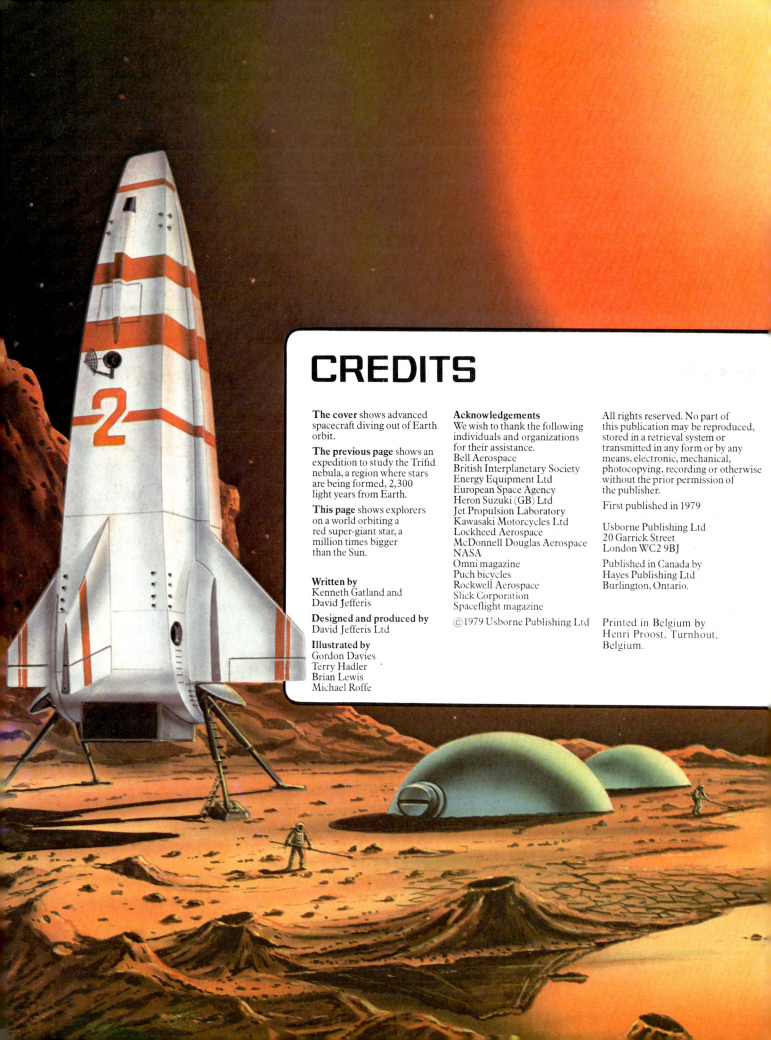

CREDITS

The cover shows advanced spacecraft diving out of Earth orbit.

The previous page shows an expedition to study the Trifid nebula, a region where stars are being formed, 2,300 light years from Earth.

This page shows explorers on a world orbiting a red super-giant star, a million times bigger than the Sun.

Written by
Kenneth Gatland and
David Jefferis

Designed and produced by
David Jefferis Ltd

Illustrated by
Gordon Davies
Terry Hadler
Brian Lewis
Michael Roffe

Acknowledgements
We wish to thank the following individuals and organizations for their assistance.
Bell Aerospace
British Interplanetary Society
Energy Equipment Ltd
European Space Agency
Heron Suzuki (GB) Ltd
Jet Propulsion Laboratory
Kawasaki Motorcycles Ltd
Lockheed Aerospace
McDonnell Douglas Aerospace
NASA
Omni magazine
Puch bicycles
Rockwell Aerospace
Slick Corporation
Spaceflight magazine

©1979 Usborne Publishing Ltd

First published in 1979

Usborne Publishing Ltd
20 Garrick Street
London WC2 9BJ

Published in Canada by
Hayes Publishing Ltd
Burlington, Ontario.

Printed in Belgium by
Henri Proost, Turnhout,
Belgium.

THE WORLD OF THE FUTURE
STAR TRAVEL
TRANSPORT & TECHNOLOGY INTO THE 21ST CENTURY

INTRODUCTION

In this book you can find out about star travel and some of the other amazing ways of getting around which could be developed in the future.

In the last hundred years, transportation has developed from horse and steam power to the jet age and space exploration.

Although star travel is not possible yet, you can see in this book some of the ways in which it might be accomplished – for new worlds and new horizons, of which there are none left on Earth, will be the objectives for the explorers of tomorrow.

CONTENTS

FROM FLOATING LOG TO SPACE SHUTTLE

For thousands of years, travelling from place to place was a slow affair. If you wanted speed on land, a horse was the fastest thing available. On the sea, a sailing vessel was the only alternative to rowing.

The steam-powered machines invented during the 1700s and 1800s made the world 'shrink' as journey times got shorter and shorter. Today you can fly around the world in a shorter time than a person of the Middle Ages would have taken to travel 200 kilometres.

In the future, there will be even quicker and, hopefully, very reliable ways of travelling as you can see in the rest of this book.

▲ The Stone-Age floating log was probably the first form of transport ever devised. The next stage in boat design was to hollow the log out to make a dug-out canoe, which could be sat in and which would not roll over as easily as a plain log.

▲ No one knows who made the first wheel, but the earliest record comes from Sumer in the Middle East. It is a sketch of a funeral wagon made about 3,500 BC.

The picture above shows an Assyrian war chariot of about 850 BC. The wheels of

▲ Richard Trevithick of Cornwall in England built the first steam locomotive in 1803. By the 1850s locomotives like the one above were opening up new frontiers in America, then the New World. In the USA alone, 50,000 locomotives were built between 1866 and 1900. The world speed record for steam trains is held by the *Mallard*. Its speed – 202 kph – has remained unchallenged for over 40 years. Today, almost all locomotives built are powered by oil or electricity.

▲ Steam power went to sea in the 1800s. The first Atlantic crossing without sail power was made by the British ship *Sirius* in 1838. The coal ran out while the ship was still at sea, so the Captain had the ship's furniture thrown into the furnace to keep

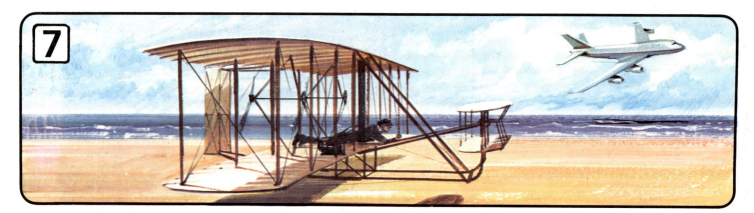

▲ In December 1903 Wilbur and Orville Wright, who ran a bicycle business, achieved their aim of flying a heavier-than-air flying machine (balloons had been in use for years). Orville made the first flight. After a run of 13 metres along a launching rail, the Wright Flyer rose into the air, covering 40 metres in 12 seconds. Since then, air progress has been swift and the Boeing 747 jet shown at the top right has a wingspan greater than the length of Orville's first flight. The 747 can carry up to 498 passengers with a cabin crew of 10 or more to look after them. It can cruise at nearly 1,000 kph, its wings carry 232,000 litres of fuel, and fully loaded it weighs over 350 tonnes. Even larger versions are on the way.

chariots like this were among the first to have metal 'tyres' around their rims to make them last longer. Carts, coaches and chariots pulled by horses remained the basic means of land transportation for the next thousand years.

▲ Sailing ships are nearly as old as the wheel. By the Christian era, Roman vessels were built up to 30 metres long and could carry up to 250 tonnes of passengers and cargo. The ship above is a carrack of the 15th century. Columbus's *Santa Maria* was

a carrack, about 25 metres long with three main masts. The fastest sailing ships ever made were the clippers of the 19th century. The most famous was the *Cutty Sark* which sailed from Australia to Britain in a record 67 days.

the engines going. The passenger liner *Queen Elizabeth*, shown above, was the largest (83,670 tonnes) of the ocean liners which raced across the Atlantic in this century. Now there are few passenger ships making the trip – practically everyone flies.

▲ In 1885, German engineer Karl Benz built the first car powered by a petrol engine. Early motoring was dirty, smelly and unreliable. Gradually the problems were sorted out and in 1908, the Ford Model T, the first car to be mass-produced,

was introduced. By the time production stopped in 1927, over 15 million had been made. Now there are so many cars that the congestion, pollution and accidents caused by their use are major problems world-wide.

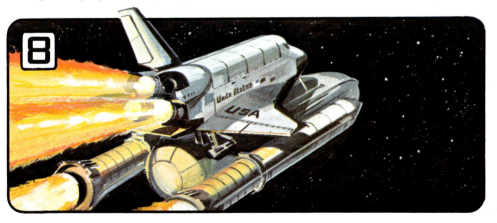

▲ The Space Age began in 1957 when the Russians launched the first artificial satellite, Sputnik I, into orbit. Four years later Yuri Gagarin became the first man in space, and on 20 July, 1969, Neil Armstrong became the first human to walk on another

world, the Moon. The Space Shuttle, shown above, is designed to make journeys into space an everyday affair – no less than 560 missions are planned between 1980 and 1992, more than one a week.

Now read on . . . into the fantastic world of the future . . .

But before taking off into space, the first part of the book gives you a look at some earthbound transport ideas. In the main, transport of the future will be a mixture of super-high technology and a return to simple ideas, like the cheap, efficient bicycle for moving around crowded cities.

PERSONAL TRANSPORT

Short-distance travel, especially in crowded cities, is one of the biggest problems of present-day life. In the future, fuel prices are going to be higher, making short car journeys more and more expensive.

In many cities, cars are (or will be) banned anyway as the pollution and congestion they cause are too severe. In London alone, car traffic has doubled since 1970.

The ideas shown here are designed for quick, cheap and easy travel about towns.

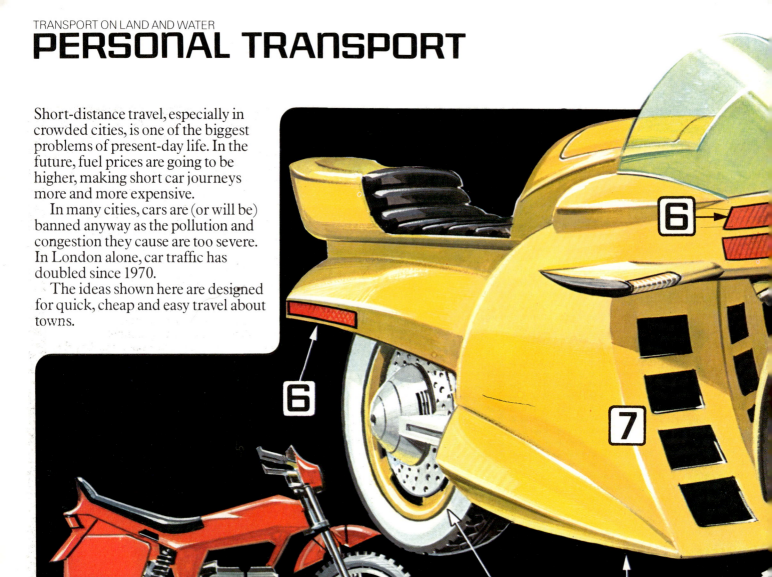

Commuting by rocketbelt

For anyone who has sat in a traffic jam or waited on a cold platform for a train, this idea, if made practical, would be a dream come true. The compressed-gas powered backpack shown was developed by Bell Aerosystems of the USA and flown in 1961. The problem was, and still is, that the fuel only lasts a few minutes. Developed versions could make traffic jams a thing of the past, though automatic radar equipment would be necessary to avoid other rocket-belt commuters!

In space, versions of the belt will be used on Space Shuttle flights, giving the astronauts perfect flight-control in the zero gravity of orbit.

Time — Road speed — 4500 Engine speed — Fuel in tank

9:36 — 136 — 13·

140 ← Speed limit

The Electronic superbike of the Future

Motorcycles cause little or no congestion, but their biggest drawback is their poor safety record. Collisions between cars and bikes are common, and in wet weather, skids are frequent. This design, whilst looking fast and sporty, has many practical features which should be included in tomorrow's superbike.

At the far left is a design from BMW for a modular motor bike. The different components can be mixed to make anything from a trail bike to a shopping bike like the one shown, equipped with big panniers to put the week's shopping in.

Both bikes have similar safety features.

1 Control panel is completely electronic, with glowing digital numbers giving all the information. This one, designed for the yellow superbike, shows the time, engine speed, road speed, the speed limit on the road the bike is on and the fuel remaining in the tank. If anything goes wrong with the unit, new components can be simply slotted in.

2 'White-wall' tyres are in fact covered in reflecting material showing the bike up at night.
3 Tyres are the run-flat type, they do not burst if punctured, allowing the motorcyclist to get home safely.
4 The disc brakes are 'cintered-steel', making them totally waterproof allowing safe braking in the wet. The brakes also have an anti-skid system.
5 Careful aerodynamic shaping of the bodywork. This protects the rider from the elements, keeps the bike firmly on the ground at speed, and improves fuel consumption, as less power is required for good speeds.
6 Large glow-lights front and rear help pick out the bike day and night.
7 The engine is a Wankel rotary. At present this type of engine is not perfected but it shows huge potential. The shopping bike could be electric – refuelled by plugging into the mains supply at night.
8 Wheels are made of injection-moulded foamed-nylon. Lighter than metal ones, they do not rust and are cheap to make.

And if you want to keep fit...

The bicycle is likely to be one of the major transport systems in tomorrow's towns. It is cheap, easy to park and provides healthy exercise. The important thing is to develop networks of cycle-ways to separate bikes from cars and trucks.

This Steyr-Puch design is a prototype for tomorrow's bicycle. It weighs just 8.61 kg, thanks to its sail-shaped frame which is made of aluminium and plastic. The bike has no separate tyre pump – its seat support can be moved up and down to do the pumping. The bar at the back includes a large rear lamp and indicator blinkers. Basic power for them is a standard battery, but it is recharged using a mini solar-cell on top of the unit.

Blinker unit →

CARS AND TRUCKS

Petrol is going to get more and more expensive as supplies dwindle in the future, so energy-saving design will be the theme for cars and trucks for the rest of this century.

By the 1990s, electric cars should be developed sufficiently to make them a good alternative to petrol-engined ones.

In the 21st century, many scientists think that liquid hydrogen (LH_2) will be used as the basic fuel for most vehicles including aircraft. Although LH_2 needs careful storing and requires big fuel tanks, it is clean and non-polluting.

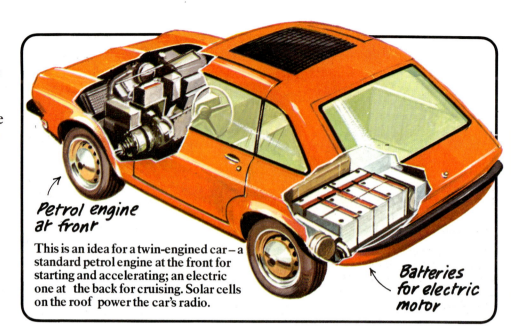

Petrol engine at front

Batteries for electric motor

This is an idea for a twin-engined car – a standard petrol engine at the front for starting and accelerating; an electric one at the back for cruising. Solar cells on the roof power the car's radio.

Small, sleek and silent truck of tomorrow

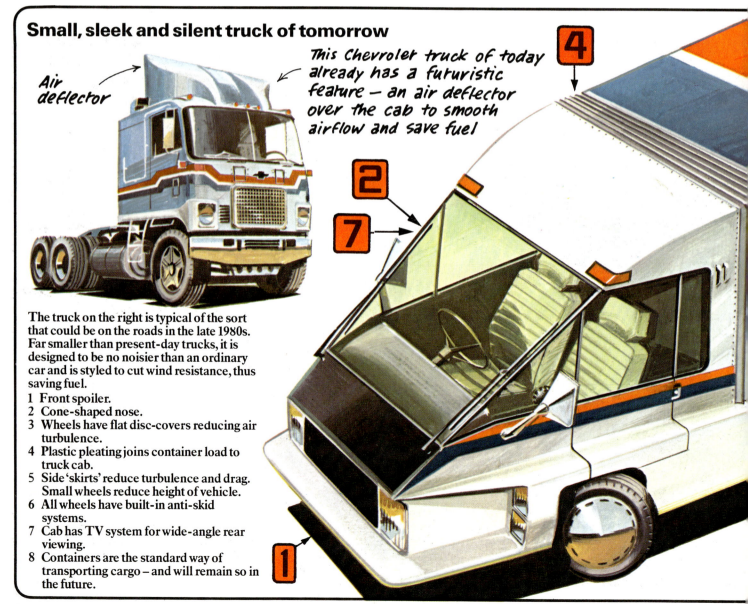

Air deflector

This Chevrolet truck of today already has a futuristic feature – an air deflector over the cab to smooth airflow and save fuel

The truck on the right is typical of the sort that could be on the roads in the late 1980s. Far smaller than present-day trucks, it is designed to be no noisier than an ordinary car and is styled to cut wind resistance, thus saving fuel.

1 Front spoiler.
2 Cone-shaped nose.
3 Wheels have flat disc-covers reducing air turbulence.
4 Plastic pleating joins container load to truck cab.
5 Side 'skirts' reduce turbulence and drag. Small wheels reduce height of vehicle.
6 All wheels have built-in anti-skid systems.
7 Cab has TV system for wide-angle rear viewing.
8 Containers are the standard way of transporting cargo – and will remain so in the future.

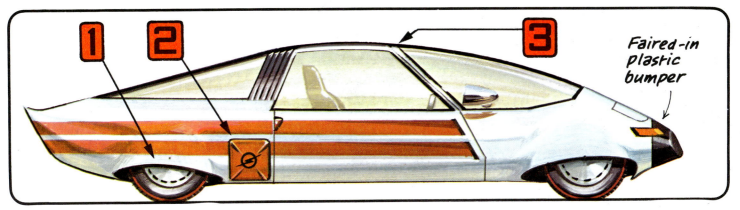

Faired-in plastic bumper

This streamlined electric car has lots of interesting features including covered-over wheels to cut down on air drag (1). It is powered by electric motors. The battery is in module form (2) being quickly replaced at any 'filling station'. For overnight stops, it could be recharged by plugging into the mains supply. The roof has solar cells (3) built-in to power small systems like radio, tape-player and the automatic navigation system. The car is largely made of aluminium and other lightweight materials.

Styling is done in the wind tunnel to cut drag and so improve fuel (in this case, electricity) consumption. Even petrol-engined cars should be fairly economical to run. Designers are even now working on cars which will run over 20 km on a litre of fuel.

7 Camera for rear-view TV system

Container has drop-down support legs

3 The driver is equipped with two-way CB radio. It gives information about road conditions ahead

This is a design from an American company, the Slick Corporation, for a 'minimum truck', the smallest vehicle able to carry a container. As you can see, the truck slides under the container, which has drop-down support legs. The driver sits in a low cabin at the front. His seat reclines like that of a racing car and he sits no higher than the driver of an ordinary saloon car.

TOMORROW'S TRAINS

Although most passenger train services in today's world lose money, they still have several advantages over other transport systems. They are very safe, and can take loads from city centre to city centre causing little pollution and no congestion.

Freight services, which already carry 70% of the world's inland freight, are likely to carry still more – few people wish to see the number of juggernaut trucks increasing in the future.

Most trains in the rest of this century will be electric powered. The train below is a futuristic solution to the problem of long-distance travel across the world.

An old-fashioned answer to a problem of tomorrow — coal power

The 'fluid-bed' furnace is one solution to the problem of powering tomorrow's trains. In a fluid-bed furnace, crushed coal (1) is fed into a sand-filled firebox (2), while jets of scorching hot air (3) vibrate and support the sand/coal mixture. Burning coal in this way is very efficient, giving off little or no pollution and generating great heat. Water contained in a boiler (4) is heated. The steam rushes along pipes to

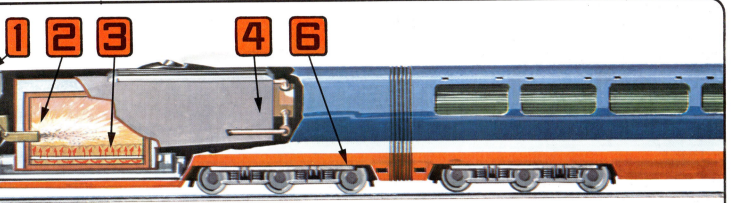

spin turbines (5). The spinning turbines power electric motors (6), one to each axle. The steam is condensed back into water after it has spun the turbines so there is no need to carry large quantities of water.

An alternative to carrying the furnace on the train is to have central fluid-bed power stations, each feeding electricity to an overhead pick-up line system like the one used on many of today's railways.

Whichever system is used, the outlook for coal as a power source is bright – experts estimate that the world's coal supplies will not run out for 1,000 years.

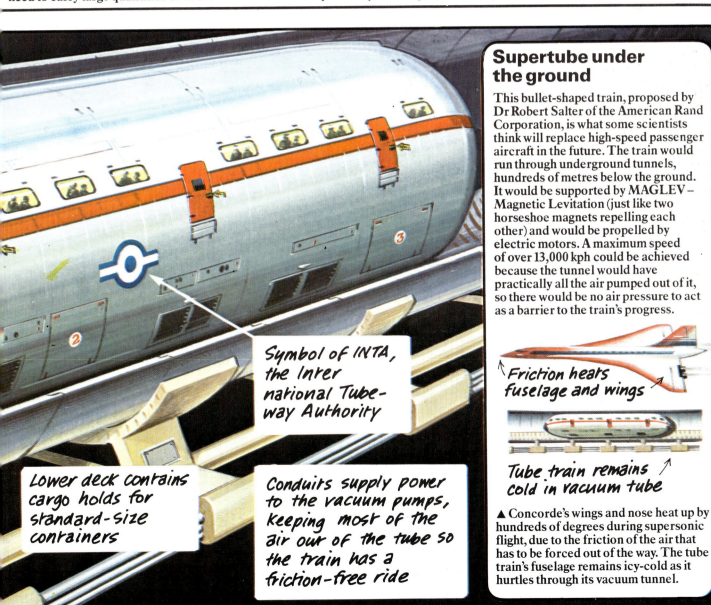

Symbol of INTA, the International Tubeway Authority

Lower deck contains cargo holds for standard-size containers

Conduits supply power to the vacuum pumps, keeping most of the air out of the tube so the train has a friction-free ride

Supertube under the ground

This bullet-shaped train, proposed by Dr Robert Salter of the American Rand Corporation, is what some scientists think will replace high-speed passenger aircraft in the future. The train would run through underground tunnels, hundreds of metres below the ground. It would be supported by MAGLEV – Magnetic Levitation (just like two horseshoe magnets repelling each other) and would be propelled by electric motors. A maximum speed of over 13,000 kph could be achieved because the tunnel would have practically all the air pumped out of it, so there would be no air pressure to act as a barrier to the train's progress.

Friction heats fuselage and wings

Tube train remains cold in vacuum tube

▲ Concorde's wings and nose heat up by hundreds of degrees during supersonic flight, due to the friction of the air that has to be forced out of the way. The tube train's fuselage remains icy-cold as it hurtles through its vacuum tunnel.

UNDER AND OVER THE WAVES

Transport on and in the water will be designed to help tap the almost untouched mineral riches under the seas and to provide world navies with more efficient defence systems.

Mining minerals underwater will be a big growth industry in the late 20th century. Already oil rigs operate in the North Sea. In the warmer waters of the Red Sea in the Middle East, mining operations are already underway to extract the rich veins of minerals under its sea bottom. In the future these operations will extend into deeper waters. Even the Antarctic will be an area of mining operations in the 21st century, as all Earth is plundered for minerals.

This Japanese-made underwater bulldozer is designed to operate either completely automatically or under remote control from a ship floating above. It can be used to clear harbours or dredge for minerals.

▲ In the crystal-clear waters of the Caribbean Sea, tourist submarines will operate giving holiday makers splendid views of fish and plant life under the waves. The submarine above is based on a German design of the 1970s. It can carry 14 passengers plus crew. Submarines like this could act as 'buses' to transport people to the underwater cities which may be built in shallow waters across the world.

▲ Submarines equipped with nuclear missiles could be out of date by the year 2000. Latest spy-satellite equipment shows that it may be possible to detect submarines underwater, so they will no longer be able to cruise in secrecy.

▲ This picture shows a robot loading dock of the year 2000. A cargo submarine is being loaded with containers by automatic machinery, ready for transporting across the world. One big advantage of travelling underwater is that there are no storms to battle through and no waves to slow the ship down. But many of the world's shipping lanes are very shallow: a big supertanker travelling through the English Channel, for instance, has only a few metres between the bottom of its hull and the sea bed. A submarine would not be able to submerge in waters like this – it would have to ride on the surface like all the other vessels.

▲ This picture shows an all-too-likely scene of the near future. A group of terrorists have successfully planted explosives in an oil rig. A fast patrol hydrofoil has fired an anti-shipping missile at the terrorists' boat – only to have it destroyed by an anti-missile missile fired by the terrorists. In the sky, two helium rig-patrol blimps cruise in – one to help fight the fire, one to try and sink the terrorists.

▲ Hydrofoil patrol boats are fast but small; they cannot carry much fuel so have quite a short range. Mid-ocean refuelling could be carried out by submarine using an aircraft-style probe and drogue system as shown above.

▲ This 200 kph craft could revolutionise naval warfare. It is an SES – a Surface Effect Ship. Its two sidewalls run in the water but flaps on bow and stern capture an air bubble to keep most of the hull out of the water. Water-jets would squirt the vessel along at high speed. The SES shown above is a mini aircraft carrier on top and a cargo carrier underneath. In this case the cargo consists of hovercraft troop carriers for amphibious beach assaults.

A commercial version of the SES could fill the speed gap between fast aircraft and slow ships. It could run fully loaded from Europe to the USA in about 30 hours, several times quicker than an ordinary cargo vessel.

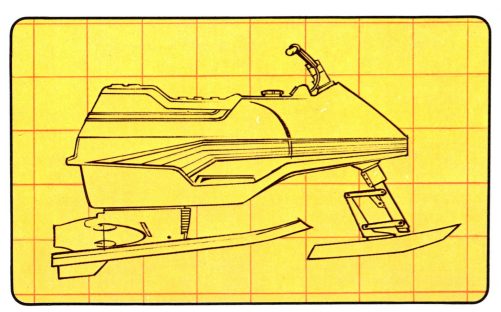

Aqua-ski marines

The Kawasaki Wet-Bike, already in production, skates along on twin skis. Powered by a motorbike engine, the Wet-Bike can whizz along at 40 kph. If the rider falls off, the Wet-Bike's engine stops and it floats nearby ready for reboarding.

Developed versions would be an ideal mount for marines to ride in amphibious attacks. They could be used in river patrol work too – the draught of the Wet-Bike is only a few inches and it causes little wash, so river banks and bottoms would remain undisturbed by its passing.

JUMBOS, SST'S AND AIRSHIPS

Air transport has hit a plateau in the 1970s – big improvements in speed, size and range are technically possible but too expensive in practice. The supersonic Concorde is a typical example of technical brilliance but bought at too high a price.

Aircraft now being developed for flight in the 1980s and '90s, such as the Boeing 757 and the Airbus A310, are designed to use less fuel than current types. They include detail improvements and new materials such as super-strong carbon-fibres, but look little different from jetliners which have been flying since the 1960s.

Really high-speed flight will probably be more easily achieved using spacecraft or tubetrains like the one on page 10 which, by 2050, could be competing successfully for some long-haul airliner business.

Fins and Sails

Longhorn business jet

Multiple wingtip sail

Marsh Harrier

▲ Curious fin-like wing extensions on aircraft wings provide more lift for slower landings and reduced drag for faster and more economical cruising. The multiple 'sail' immediately above is based on the feather structure of a bird, the Marsh Harrier. The first production aircraft with tip extensions, in this case simple fins, is the American Longhorn business jet. Detail improvements like this are going to be a feature of aircraft throughout the 1980s.

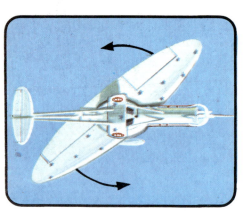

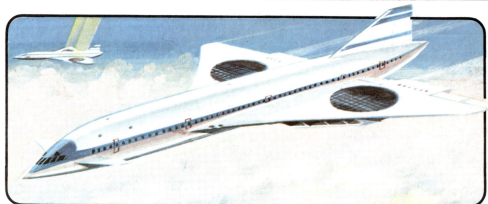

▲ This odd craft has a wing which sweeps from straight out for landing, to swept-back-and-forward for high speed flight. Experts think it will be a good system as it needs only one heavy pivot point for the oval-shaped wing.

▲ This airliner could use the power from satellite-borne laser beams to heat air in wing ducts. The superheated air would rush out of nozzles in the rear of the wing to propel the airliner forward. Computer systems on board the satellite would track the airliner, keeping the lasers aimed at the wing heater panels. The aircraft would only need to carry small reserve engines and sufficient fuel to make an emergency landing if the laser beams were cut off.

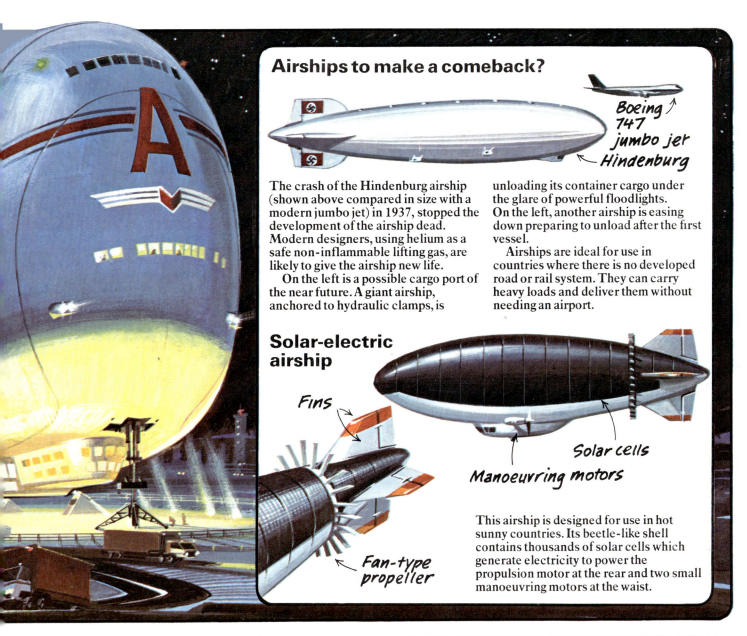

Airships to make a comeback?

Boeing 747 jumbo jet
Hindenburg

The crash of the Hindenburg airship (shown above compared in size with a modern jumbo jet) in 1937, stopped the development of the airship dead. Modern designers, using helium as a safe non-inflammable lifting gas, are likely to give the airship new life.

On the left is a possible cargo port of the near future. A giant airship, anchored to hydraulic clamps, is unloading its container cargo under the glare of powerful floodlights. On the left, another airship is easing down preparing to unload after the first vessel.

Airships are ideal for use in countries where there is no developed road or rail system. They can carry heavy loads and deliver them without needing an airport.

Solar-electric airship

Fins

Solar cells

Manoeuvring motors

Fan-type propeller

This airship is designed for use in hot sunny countries. Its beetle-like shell contains thousands of solar cells which generate electricity to power the propulsion motor at the rear and two small manoeuvring motors at the waist.

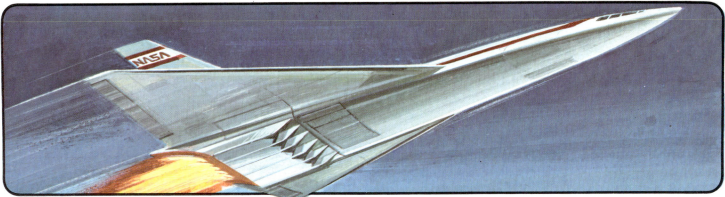

▲ Airliners powered by liquid hydrogen – LH_2 – could be common in the petroleum-short 21st century. This design, typical of the studies being made on future aircraft by major aircraft manufacturers, could fly 500 passengers at three times the speed of sound. It would fly so high that (in theory) its supersonic boom would have dissipated to little more than a mild thud by the time it got to ground level. LH_2 is a good substitute for petroleum-based fuel, but it takes up more fuel-tank space and needs very careful storage. It is plentiful, being obtained from water, which is not (yet!) in short supply. Current airliner designs could be converted to use LH_2 by hanging large fuel tanks from their wings or under their fuselage.

THE SPACE SHUTTLE

The Space Shuttle is the world's first re-usable spacecraft, designed to take off vertically like a rocket, manoeuvre in orbit like a spaceship, then fly home like a glider.

Because the orbiter section can be re-used up to 100 times, unlike ordinary rockets which crash to destruction with each space shot, the cost of flight into space will be greatly reduced. In everyday terms though, prices are high – customers will pay from $10,000 to more than $21 million for cargo space.

Its American designers believe that the Space Shuttle and craft like it will become as vital to our future as ships and aircraft are today, and that experiments undertaken in orbiting Shuttles will lead to advances that will affect every man, woman and child.

Spaceplane to orbit

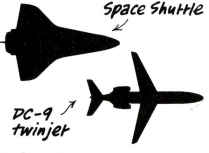

Space Shuttle

DC-9 twinjet

Shuttle orbiter to the same scale as a modern jetliner. It has an overall length of 37.1 m and a wing span of 23.8 m.

Spaceplane is covered with 34,000 heat resistant tiles to protect the craft from the fiery heat of re-entry

Delta wings enable the Shuttle orbiter to land back on a normal runway

The Shuttle can take heavy loads into space – a maximum of 29,484 kg. Its designers are already thinking about bigger versions.

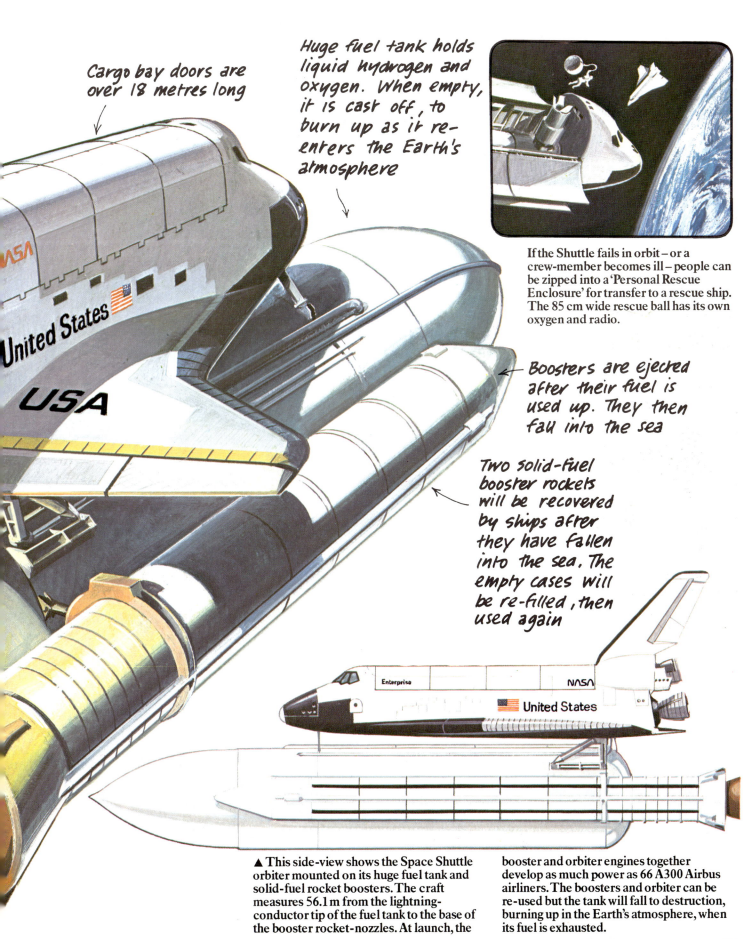

Cargo bay doors are over 18 metres long

Huge fuel tank holds liquid hydrogen and oxygen. When empty, it is cast off, to burn up as it re-enters the Earth's atmosphere

United States

USA

If the Shuttle fails in orbit – or a crew-member becomes ill – people can be zipped into a 'Personal Rescue Enclosure' for transfer to a rescue ship. The 85 cm wide rescue ball has its own oxygen and radio.

Boosters are ejected after their fuel is used up. They then fall into the sea

Two solid-fuel booster rockets will be recovered by ships after they have fallen into the sea. The empty cases will be re-filled, then used again

Enterprise   NASA

United States

▲ This side-view shows the Space Shuttle orbiter mounted on its huge fuel tank and solid-fuel rocket boosters. The craft measures 56.1 m from the lightning-conductor tip of the fuel tank to the base of the booster rocket-nozzles. At launch, the booster and orbiter engines together develop as much power as 66 A300 Airbus airliners. The boosters and orbiter can be re-used but the tank will fall to destruction, burning up in the Earth's atmosphere, when its fuel is exhausted.

17

JOURNEY INTO SPACE

By the mid 1980s, flights by Space Shuttle should be an everyday affair.

Loads for the huge cargo hold of the Shuttle, 18.3 metres long, will be many and varied. At present, planned cargoes include the ESA Spacelab for research work; the Grumman Aerospace beambuilder, a robot designed to manufacture girders for space stations; the Space Telescope, and dozens of different types of satellite.

Flights will leave from Kennedy Space Centre at Cape Canaveral in Florida or from Vandenberg Air Force Base in California; a typical mission will last anything from seven days to nearly a whole month.

▲ On the launch pad stands the complete Space Shuttle system, consisting of the winged orbiter connected to a huge fuel tank. Either side of the tank are two solid-fuel rocket boosters. The whole lot weighs over 2,000 tonnes. When countdown reaches zero, the two booster rockets and three motors of the orbiter all fire together. All five motors develop a thrust of over 3 million kg to push the Space Shuttle off the launch pad into space.

▲ The orbiter's two orbital manoeuvring engines thrust it into orbit at a speed of 28,300 kph and a height of 185 km. By using the orbital manoeuvring engines the orbital height can be varied between 161 and 966 km. The picture above shows the orbiter, cargo doors open, displaying a typical load – the ESA Spacelab. In this, four scientists can work in shirtsleeves on research experiments such as processing medicines or producing ultra-pure metals and glass.

The scientists aboard the orbiter will need to be healthy, but not superhuman – the Space Shuttle is designed to give a smooth take-off and landing. Maximum acceleration should be no more than 3G – three times the force of gravity. Early space flights subjected astronauts to 9G or more.

2

▲ As the speed builds up, the orbiter's wings generate lift just like those of an aircraft. The motors of the booster rockets have to swivel to offset this otherwise the craft would pull over into a loop and crash down to the ground.

3

▲ The craft accelerates skywards and when it is 46 km up the two booster rockets separate. Small thruster rockets push them away from the fuel tank. They will splash down into the ocean to be recovered by ships waiting for them.

4

▲ Still with its main engines on, the orbiter climbs, drawing its fuel from the huge tank. It casts off the tank just before it arrives in orbit. The tank will be destroyed as it falls back through the Earth's atmosphere.

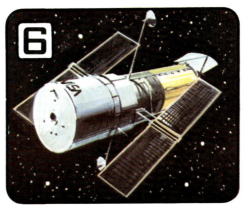

6

▲ The Space Telescope will be a typical Shuttle load. An orbiting telescope like this should make it possible to examine stars which are 100 times fainter than those seen by the most powerful telescopes on Earth.

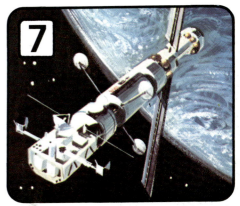

7

▲ Small space stations like this could be constructed by linking several Spacelabs together. Solar cell 'wings' would power the station. Plans are also being discussed to use the big fuel tank as the basis of a space station, perhaps the first of many.

8

During their stay in orbit, anything from a week to a month, crew and scientists (both men and women) will have many of the comforts of home, including a wide variety of food, washing facilities and a specially designed zero-g lavatory.

▲ After its mission is completed the orbiter glides back to Earth. During re-entry through the atmosphere, the nose and leading edges of the wings glow dull red with the frictional heat generated by smashing into the atmosphere at 26,765

kph. Almost as useful as the loads it can take up are the loads (up to 11,340 kg) it can return to Earth. A damaged satellite, for example, can be brought back for repair, then taken into orbit again.

EXPLORING THE SOLAR SYSTEM

Unmanned spacecraft will continue to explore the Solar System. Some, like the one on the right, are already in space. Others, like the comet-chaser shown opposite, could be launched by the Space Shuttle in the mid 1980s.

Eventually, manned spaceships will be launched from space cities orbiting the Earth. They will be pure 'Space' ships, not streamlined and unable to fly through the atmospheres of other worlds. Small shuttlecraft carried in cargo bays will carry astronauts from orbit to the surface of the planet they are exploring.

Craft like the one below might be plying the spaceways throughout most of the next century.

▲ This picture shows Voyager I as it passes through the 'flux tube of Io'. Io is a satellite of Jupiter, the flux tube a region of intense magnetic disturbance between satellite and planet. Future Shuttle-launched missions include the Solar-polar voyages. Two craft will fly above and below the Sun's north and south poles, regions which are unexplored. Scientists hope to learn more about cosmic rays, and solar conditions which cause weather changes back on Earth.

The mobile mini-planet

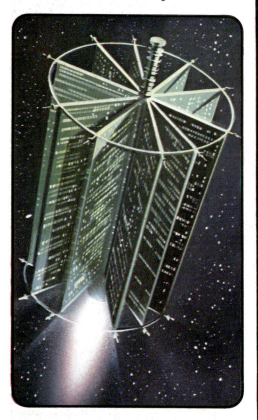

This curious-looking spaceship, based on the ideas of Dr Krafft Ehricke, is designed for long journeys through the Solar System. Its pencil-like spine contains nuclear-fusion powerplants to energise the propulsion system, laser drilling and communication equipment, life-support and other power needs. The 'wings' are like skyscraper blocks, containing living quarters. The craft spins, providing simulated 'gravity' in the wings by centrifugal force.

Dawn on Titan, moon of Saturn

In this picture you can see explorers, who have landed in a shuttlecraft from their orbiting 'mother ship', collecting samples of Titan's air, soil and rocks.

Titan, largest moon of Saturn (seen high in the sky in the picture), is about 5,800 km across – much bigger than Earth's Moon. Titan has an atmosphere of methane, hydrogen and other gases. Clouds of a strange orange colour have been observed, but their exact nature is, at present, unknown. Titan may have the conditions in which complex molecules may accumulate. On Earth, such molecules evolved into primitive lifeforms, so Titan is an extremely important place for scientists to study – there may be life on other worlds after all. If it exists on Titan, it will be very unfamiliar though – conditions are very different from those on Earth and evolution could create strange solutions to the problem of living on a world whose average temperature is about −150°C.

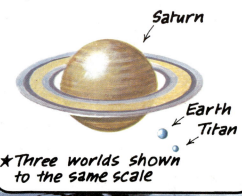

Saturn

Earth
Titan

★Three worlds shown to the same scale

▲ In 1986, Halley's comet will make its closest approach to Earth in 76 years. The ion-engined craft above has been proposed by the American Jet Propulsion Laboratory to fly by the comet. It would then zero in on the nucleus of another comet, named Tempel. Another possible target for the 1980s is comet Encke, which nears the Sun every 3.3 years. The wings of the craft contain solar-cells to power the ion-engines. Early versions of these power plants were placed in Earth-orbit in 1969 during the SERT (Space Electric Rocket Test) programme. Seven years later they were still in working order, a necessity for the long mission times planned for craft using them in the future.

STARPROBE 'DAEDALUS'

A journey to the stars, once thought to be fantasy, will be possible within a century according to a study called Project *Daedalus* carried out by the British Interplanetary Society.

The starprobe is named after the legendary Greek who made wax wings to escape from a Mediterranean island. His son, Icarus, flew too near the Sun. His wings melted and he crashed. Daedalus, shown in the 1493 woodcut above, was successful.

Starship Daedalus is designed to be powered by nuclear 'bomblets' which would accelerate it to a staggering 3,869 km per second. Its destination – Barnard's Star, six light years from the Sun.

▲ Construction of Daedalus is carried out in orbit around Callisto, a satellite of the planet Jupiter. Fuel for the ship, a chemical called Helium-3, could be mined from the atmosphere of Callisto or even that of Jupiter itself. Daedalus is huge and weighs as much as a small ocean liner. Building the star probe would take several years using mainly automated assembly machines under computer control. In the picture above, the two stages of the probe are ready to be joined together.

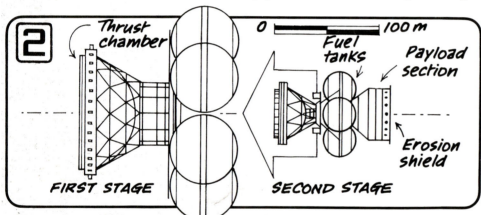

▲ This side-view shows some of the ship's design features. It is fuelled by nuclear pellets. These are injected, 250 per second into the thrust chamber. A ring of electron beams compresses each pellet to cause a nuclear fusion explosion. The reaction thrusts the ship on its way. When the second stage takes over, a similar but smaller system is used. At the front of the ship, ahead of the payload section, is a shield designed to protect the craft from erosion from interstellar gas and dust.

▲ Daedalus blasts off on its journey to Barnard's Star, nearly six light years from the Solar System. Astronomers think the star has at least one, and perhaps several planets orbiting it. The first stage accelerates the ship to 900 km per second.

▲ Daedalus is equipped with mobile robots called wardens to maintain and, if necessary, repair parts of the ship during the half-century journey. They can also repair each other if any damage or malfunctions occur.

▲ Contact with Daedalus is maintained using a vast three-km-wide radio telescope in orbit around the Earth. The array is made of hundreds of small telescopes, linked to a computer to form a super-powerful unit.

▲ As Daedalus approaches Barnard's Star, its collison protection system is deployed. This is nothing but a dust cloud ahead of the ship, but because of its high speed any object hitting it will be instantly vapourised.

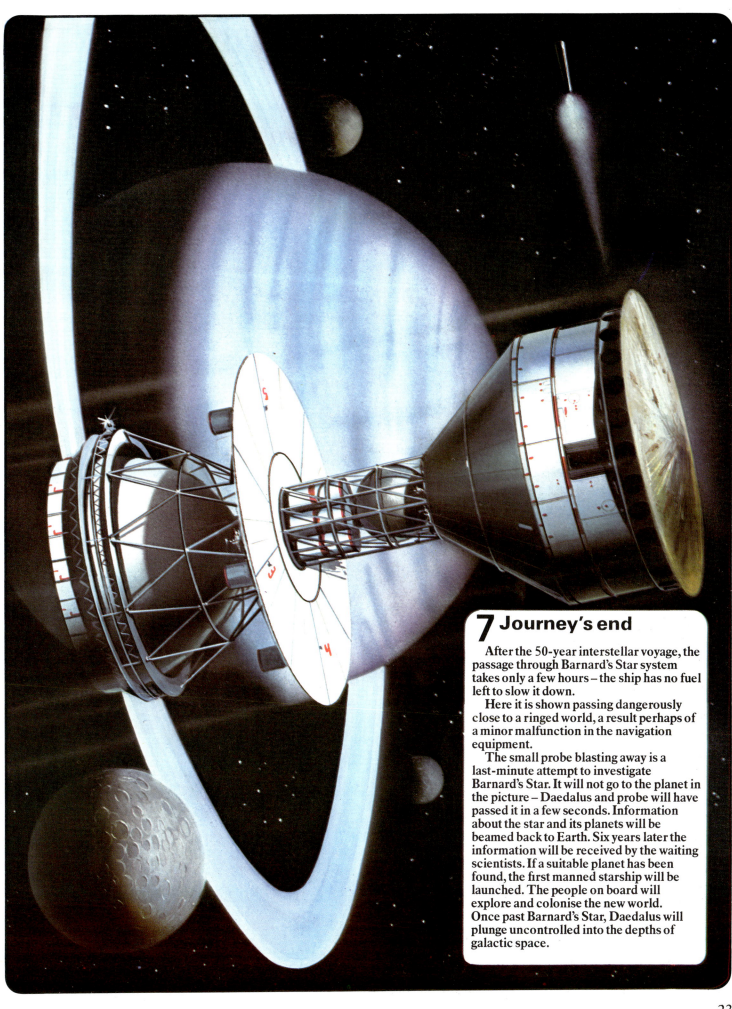

7 Journey's end

After the 50-year interstellar voyage, the passage through Barnard's Star system takes only a few hours – the ship has no fuel left to slow it down.

Here it is shown passing dangerously close to a ringed world, a result perhaps of a minor malfunction in the navigation equipment.

The small probe blasting away is a last-minute attempt to investigate Barnard's Star. It will not go to the planet in the picture – Daedalus and probe will have passed it in a few seconds. Information about the star and its planets will be beamed back to Earth. Six years later the information will be received by the waiting scientists. If a suitable planet has been found, the first manned starship will be launched. The people on board will explore and colonise the new world. Once past Barnard's Star, Daedalus will plunge uncontrolled into the depths of galactic space.

BY ASTEROID TO NEW WORLDS

If the Daedalus starprobe reports that a habitable world has been found, the next step could be the construction of a manned starship. The one shown here uses as its structure an asteroid, one of the millions of rocks orbiting between Mars and Jupiter.

Even though it uses ready-made material, its construction would be extremely complex and would take a long time.

The starship is an indication of the gradual expansion of the human race we might expect in the centuries to come. In the future, the 20th century will be seen as a major turning point in history – the point at which mankind took the first steps off Earth.

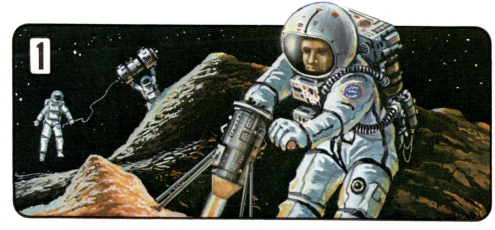

▲ This idea for hollowing out an asteroid is based on a method suggested by science fiction writer Larry Niven. Other science fiction ideas have come true – perhaps this one will too. Astronauts start by landing on a suitable roid (future slang for asteroid), drilling into its centre with super-powerful lasers. Water tanks are placed in the middle, the drill hole sealed up and the roid made to spin like a pig on a spit, using ion-drive engines mounted on its equator.

▲ A giant space mirror focusses intense solar heat onto the spinning roid, slowly melting it. When the water in the centre boils, the expanding steam blows up the roid like a giant balloon. Calculations will have to be precise for success!

▲ After the roid has cooled, robots and astronauts landscape the interior, in this case designed to resemble the countryside of 'Old Earth'. Spacelocks allow shuttles to enter and leave the roid, now christened 'Ark II'.

▲ Before Ark II starts its journey, ecological engineers like the one above check the internal environment. Ark II has been made to spin and the resulting centrifugal force plants the engineer's feet firmly on the 'ground' – which is the inside of the roid's skin. After testing, Ark II's environment will be shut down and darkened until it nears the target star system. The crew of Ark II is not human – the flight will be controlled by robots and computers.

5 The start of a fantastic voyage

Here you can see Ark II picking up speed under the power of its nuclear motors. The accompanying ships are making final external checks. If they do not keep clear, Ark II's exhaust beam will vapourise them. Ark II is aiming at Saturn to make a 'sling-shot' past it, using its gravity pull to boost the ship's speed out of the Solar System.

The humans on board Ark II are carried as 'seeds' – fertilised ova – in suspended animation. Animals, fish and birds are carried in the same way. When Ark II nears the target, robots will activate the seeds, raising them as 'test-tube babies', educating them on board the Ark for their life on the new world.

On the journey, passengers are protected from space radiation by the thick rocky crust of the Ark. Engines, observation posts, communications equipment and computer banks are all built into galleries surrounding the huge central living area.

STAR TRAVELLERS

Even the nearest star is so far from the Solar System that its light takes over four years – travelling at over 300,000 km per second – to get here.

Daedalus-type probes would take nearly half a century for the journey. According to Einstein's Theory of Relativity, it is impossible to travel as fast as light, which would be necessary to cut the journey to a reasonable time. So either people must be content to take centuries to reach their destinations or scientists must discover as-yet-unknown laws of nature to take a 'short-cut' across the Universe. Perhaps it could be a 'space-warp' in which a starship would disappear from one part of the Universe only to reappear in another.

One thing is fairly certain – if space-warps or something like them exist, scientists will discover and make use of them sooner or later.

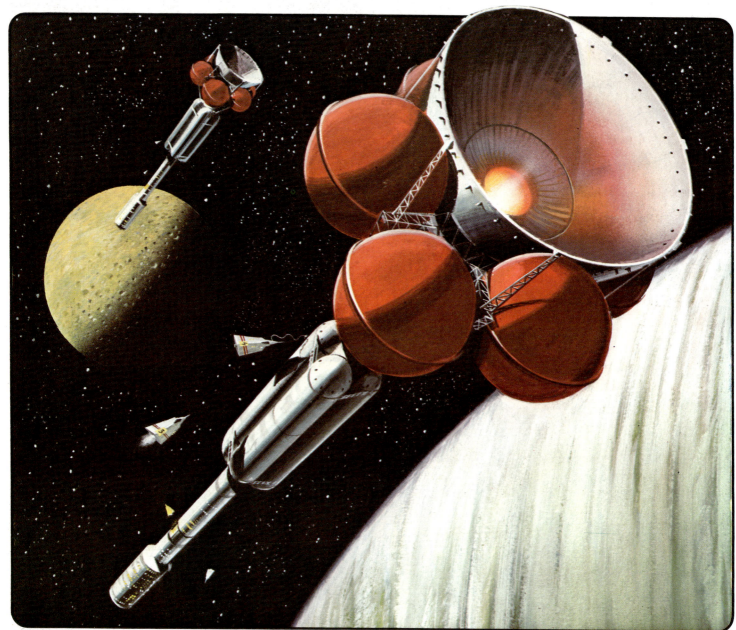

▲ These starships are shown parked in orbit round the Jupiter-type world of another star. The vessels are being refuelled by scoopships, which dip into the planet's atmosphere, gathering chemicals and gases suitable for the starships' engines.

The operation is monitored by an 'artificial intelligence', a super-computer aboard each starship. They have controlled the huge ships throughout their journey. The human crews have been in a deep sleep, induced by an artificial hibernation process, waiting to be woken from their centuries-long slumber by their robot captains.

Starships like this could slowly cross the galaxy, searching for habitable worlds and alien beings. The human crew could be woken at each stop, decide on the course of action to be taken, then go back into hibernation until the next target star is reached. The journey would be a one-way trip in time for them – if and when they returned to Earth, their families and friends would be long dead.

▲ Some scientists have suggested that 'black holes', tiny super-dense remnants of stars, may be gateways to other parts of the Universe. According to one theory, a starship entering a rotating black hole would reappear through a 'white hole' far away in space, defeating Einstein's law that nothing can travel faster than light. In the picture above, a starship, the *Galactica*, has made such a journey and is shown approaching a space terminal in a distant part of the galaxy. The ghostly lights hanging in space are 3-D laser-images designed, like runway lights of today, to guide the craft in to a safe landing. On the right, control officers in charge of approach and landing systems watch the *Galactica* from their pressurised pod.

▲ Future travellers check their arrival data with a robot clerk. Their journey has not been by starship, but by teleportation. They are, in fact, not 'real' people, but copies involved in a fantastic process, the reconstruction of living matter. Back on Earth, computers made detailed examinations of their atomic structure. This was put into code and the data transmitted across space using laser beams. At Starport Central, computers receiving the information used vats of the necessary chemicals to reconstruct the travellers in their original images.

Horrifying though this idea may sound, a laser-copying process already exists to make images of inanimate objects.

ACROSS THE UNIVERSE

If interstellar travel becomes commonplace – and that is a big 'if' – what sights could star travellers of the far future see? On these pages you can join a starcruise organised by ITC, the Interstellar Tour Company.

The design of the starship is totally fictitious: no one has designed such a craft yet. As shown here, its rear section contains engines for manoeuvring within planetary systems. The arrow-nose contains living quarters, navigation equipment and as-yet-unknown machinery to drive the ship from star to star at super-speeds – essential if the tourists wish to return to their homes within their lifetimes.

Witnessing starbirth . . .

Stars are formed within nebulae – vast clouds of gas and dust in the depths of space. As the gas and dust collects, it gradually heats up until eventually a star shines out, fuelled by the fusion energy of hydrogen.

First port of call for the ITC tour is such a nebula. This one is called M16, and it lies nearly 6,000 light years from the Solar System. Young, hot stars can be seen glowing through the misty veils of the nebula.

The square hatch in the kilometre-long starship contains shuttle craft to ferry passengers down to the surface of any strange world the ship comes near.

. . . and stardeath

Here, the starship is silhouetted against the glare of a giant star whose matter is being drawn out in a vast spiral by the titanic gravitational pull of its tiny partner star, a black hole.

A black hole is the ultimate death for a star. As a star runs out of its hydrogen 'fuel', it explodes, throwing its outer layers off into space. The remaining matter collapses in upon itself, getting smaller and smaller and denser and denser. Eventually it is so small and so dense that even light cannot escape its gravitational pull – it winks out of existence, becoming a black hole.

The glow you can see at the end of the spiral is not the hole, but X-rays given off by the giant star's matter as it is sucked in. The starship would need to keep well clear, otherwise it would be destroyed.

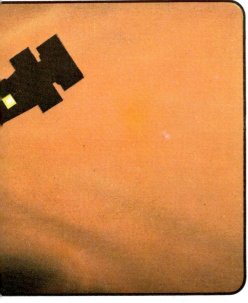

Outside the galaxy

A final, and spectacular, view before the ITC tourists return home – our own galaxy, the Milky Way, viewed from a point some 300,000 light years above its centre. The position of the Solar System is marked with an arrow, though from this distance it would be completely invisible except through a very powerful telescope.

You can see the Milky Way any clear night on Earth – it is the misty band extending across the sky. Its huge (100,000 light years across) spiral is formed of 100,000 million stars. The Milky Way is one of many galaxies – there are billions of others scattered like grains of sand across the Universe.

29

Early this century, spaceflight was regarded as just a dream.

As late as 1957, Britain's Astronomer Royal dismissed it as 'utter bilge'. Unfortunately for his reputation, the Russians launched Sputnik I a few months later and the Space Age began.

Star travel is at present as much a dream as the idea of satellites in orbit once was. But if it is possible at all, one day within the next century the first starship will travel through interstellar space.

USSR builds wheel-less hovertrain. It is powered by a linear electric motor. The train runs on a metal track, suspended just above it by a magnetic field, at speeds up to 800 kph. Train has the advantages of ordinary railways, such as all-weather and low-cost operation, together with the speed of an aircraft.

Research capsule from Galileo spacecraft enters the atmosphere of Jupiter in 1984.

Automatic navigator for cars in general use. Using a mini-computer aboard car and sensor equipment on the road, it gives the driver route instructions, computes fuel consumption, and so on.

Spacecraft using an ion-drive engine flies to intercept and photograph Halley's Comet, 1986.

Passenger aircraft fly powered by engines which use very little fuel.

Two spacecraft are launched to fly far above and below the Sun – a region so far totally unexplored.

Voyager spacecraft passes Uranus in 1986, Neptune in 1989. Eventually leaves the Solar System to pass into the depths of interstellar space.

1991-2000

Experimental civil airliners fly using liquid hydrogen as a fuel instead of petroleum-based kerosene.

Electric cars in general use. Batteries better than current types power them. They can be recharged from the mains supply overnight or exchanged at a 'filling station'.

High-speed hydrofoil gunboats in general use by world navies.

Helium-filled airships used for city-to-city transport. Quiet turbofan engines assist in take-off and landing.

2001-2050

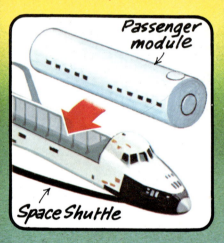

Passenger module

Space Shuttle

Passenger-carrying shuttle craft carry tourists into orbit.

Improved rockets, replacing the Space Shuttle, come into operation.

First human beings land on Mars.

Manned expeditions travel to most parts of the Solar System, including the asteroids and the moons of Saturn.

Experimental aircraft fly using satellite-based laser beams to power them.

Huge 'clipper ships' equipped with solar sails shuttle cargo between worlds. The ships are driven by the weak but continuous pressure of sunlight on the kilometres-wide sails.

1980-1990

USA launches NASA Space Shuttle into Earth orbit from Cape Canaveral, Florida.

USSR launches 'Kosmolyot' (spaceplane) which looks like a smaller Space Shuttle. It is designed to carry cosmonauts to and from Russian space stations.

Spacelab made in Europe flies into orbit in the cargo hold of the Space Shuttle. A mixture of astronauts and scientists are the crew for this and other missions.

First American woman astronaut flies aboard the Space Shuttle.

Safe airships using non-inflammable helium lifting gas are used for cargo and passenger transport in Brazil and Peru. Other designs are used in Africa and South-East Asia.

First high-speed underground vacuum-tunnel train developed. First route runs across the USA.

2051-2100

Scientists achieve the complete conversion of matter to energy – theoretically the most powerful source of power available.

Vacuum-tunnel trains replace aircraft on some long-distance routes across the world.

Mining of Helium-3 from the atmospheres of Callisto and Jupiter.

Helium 3 and deuterium processed into fuel pellets for use in Daedalus starprobe being built in orbit around Callisto.

Starprobe completed, using parts made in space factories orbiting Earth, Mars and Callisto.

Starprobe departs on its 50-year journey to Barnard's Star.

Last of petroleum fuel used up on Earth. Replacement fuels like liquid hydrogen, coal and solar energy now power the transport systems of the world.

2101-2150

Starprobe Daedalus arrives at target star. Information from the probe received by scientists in the Solar System about six years later (Barnard's Star is about six light years from the Sun).

Information received indicates that Daedalus has discovered a suitable planet for colonization.

Other starprobes launched at different target stars; first manned starship construction starts, using a small asteroid as a basis.

First manned asteroid-starship leaves the Solar System.

THE FAR FUTURE

Teleportation developed. A computer breaks down the atomic structure of an object into a code system which is transmitted at the speed of light to the target point. There another computer reconstructs the object.

'Space warp' achieved. Objects can be made to apparently vanish from one point, only to reappear in another. System developed to be used on board starships.

Explorers aboard early starships arrive at their target worlds, only to find people waiting to greet them. The reception committees have travelled virtually instantly by space-warp equipped starships.

Human civilization slowly spreads through the galaxy.

INDEX

GLOSSARY

CARBON FIBRE Very light, very strong material used at present in, for example, the fan blades of some jet engines.

CB SET Citizens' Band radio. Used, especially in the USA, by car and truck drivers to talk to each other from inside their vehicles, swapping information on road conditions.

DEUTERIUM Element required as a fuel by some types of nuclear power plant. On Earth, it can be extracted in large quantities from seawater.

HALLEY'S COMET Comets are balls of ice, dust and rock, drifting in huge orbits around the Sun. Halley's Comet will next near the Sun in 1986.

HELIUM Gas used in modern airships. It will not lift quite as much as hydrogen but it has the great advantage that, unlike hydrogen, it is non-inflammable.

HYDROFOIL Ship with underwater wings, called foils, which raise the hull out of the water at speed. There is little drag from the foils, so the hydrofoil can go much faster than an ordinary ship.

INTERSTELLAR The space between the stars. The word comes from the Latin 'inter' – between, and 'stellar' – star.

ION DRIVE System of powering spacecraft using electrically charged particles to provide thrust.

LASER Intense beam of light, used for a variety of purposes such as cutting, welding, and as a replacement for some types of radio communication.

LH₂ Liquid Hydrogen. The 2 indicates the number of atoms which make up a molecule of the substance. Normally a gas, but is a liquid when super-cooled and stored at $-252°C$.

MODULAR Device made up of various parts, modules, which fasten together. The different modules can be easily changed or rearranged.

SOLAR CELLS Flat panes of silicon material which convert the energy contained in light to electricity. Spacecraft often use fold-out 'wings' full of solar cells to generate power from sunlight.

WANKEL ROTARY ENGINE Type of engine in which, unlike an ordinary car engine where the pistons move up and down, the triangular piston spins round in a chamber.

PRINTED IN BELGIUM BY

proost
INTERNATIONAL BOOK PRODUCTION